# MEDIA AT WAR
## The Iraq Crisis

Howard Tumber and Jerry Palmer

SAGE Publications
London • Thousand Oaks • New Delhi

Researching and writing this book was a very intensive period for both of us and we owe apologies to our families for missing all the home schedules for the summer and early autumn of 2003.

To

Hila, Michal, and Judy (HT)

Stephanie and Christy (JP)

For always being there.

---

First published 2004

SAGE Publications Ltd
1 Oliver's Yard
55 City Road
London EC1Y 1SP

SAGE Publications Inc.
2455 Teller Road
Thousand Oaks, California 91320

SAGE Publications India Pvt Ltd
B-42, Panchsheel Enclave
Post Box 4109
New Delhi 100 017

**British Library Cataloguing in Publication data**

A catalogue record for this book is available from the British Library

ISBN 1 4129 0181 2
ISBN 1 4129 0182 0 (pbk)

**Library of Congress Control Number available**

Typeset by M Rules
Printed in Great Britain by Athenaeum Press, Gateshead

# CONTENTS

# ACKNOWLEDGEMENTS

This book could not have been written without the skilled and committed co-operation of a number of collaborators. The media coverage analysis that forms the second part of the book involved substantial data collection by our research assistants Giorgos Alimonos and Sigita Vergnes. We are grateful for the long hours and dedication that went into this data collection.

Special mention must be made of Dr Daniele Albertazzi's contribution to Chapter 7. He was jointly responsible with us for the design of the coding scheme that was used for this element of the data collection, carried out the data collection of the television coverage, and co-wrote the analysis of the media coverage in this chapter. He would like to acknowledge the contribution of Alex Choat and Louise Argile-Jackson, who assisted with collecting the data for this chapter and gave feedback on how to develop the coding sheet. He is grateful to Canterbury Christ's Church University College for financial support for his assistants.

Thanks also to Cathie Cremin at City University for downloading and filing numerous online articles. We would also like to thank colleagues at City University: Briony Fane, Oonagh Gormley, Steve Miller, Marina Prentoulis, Frank Webster and Tony Woodwiss.

We would also like to thank Julia Hall, our commissioning editor at Sage, who supported us throughout this project and never showed any doubts that we would deliver the manuscript to order. Thanks also to Jamilah Ahmed, Fabienne Pedroletti and Emily Lawrence at Sage, as well as Solveig Servian, the Copyeditor, and Audrey Scriven, the Proofreader, who also worked on this project. Thanks to Jan Taylor for her assistance with copyediting and proofing.

We would also like to acknowledge two inventions without which it would have been totally impossible to write this book: Hypertext Transfer Protocol and Google.

# INTRODUCTION

Twenty-four-hour news actually changes the reality of warfare . . . it is not just reporting on it.

Jack Straw, UK foreign secretary, quoted in the *Guardian*, 30.3.03)

The subject of this book is the media and their coverage of the second Gulf War. Other studies will concern themselves with the politics of that crisis and conflict, and public opinion and the conflict. Our spotlight is on the media. The media coverage is an integral part of both the crisis and the development of public opinion – that can be taken as axiomatic; however, this book's subject is exclusively the media themselves. It provides an analysis of the arrangements which allowed the media to have access to the theatre of war, and an analysis of the media coverage of the overall crisis as it developed. The primary focus is thus the news-gathering process and the thematic analysis of news output.

The chronological sequence of events with which our analysis is concerned begins with the coverage of the negotiations at the United Nations (UN) in late 2002, continues through the invasion of Iraq and into the post-invasion period. Since the motives, conduct and results of this crisis have been the subject of public contention, everything we say potentially enters the field of contention. For example, what is the appropriate label for the overall series of events involved? We use the term 'the Iraq crisis', on the grounds that it is relatively neutral; however, to many in the Arab world this neutrality would be unacceptable. Speaking on al-Jazeera television, Abdel Bari Atwan, the editor of the Arab language transnational daily *Al-Quds Al-Arabi*, referred to these events as the 'recolonisation' of Iraq (cited in Lamloum, 2003: 19). To refer to the 'military phase' of the crisis (20.3.03–1.5.03), this book uses the term 'invasion' on the grounds that it is the least evaluative term available for the process in question, given that calling it 'war', 'the military phase', or 'the combat phase' would not clearly distinguish it from what followed. President Bush's own phrase 'major combat operations' – which he declared were at an end in a speech on 1 May 2003 – is arguably even less evaluative, but is clumsy when repeated. Even the television news organisations did not agree on a title for their coverage: the BBC called it 'Iraq War'; CNN 'War In Iraq'; ITN 'War on Saddam'; Sky 'War on Iraq'; and Fox News 'Operation Iraqi Freedom'.

Gulf War II was the most media-covered war in recent times. More than 3000 journalists were assigned to the region; more than 500 of these were embedded with various military units and the others were scattered over the area, working for news organisations as staffers or freelancers.

The embedding of journalists with the military was one of the most significant aspects of the communications scenario of Gulf War II. Unlike the Falklands conflict in 1982, when journalists were 'embedded' with the British Task Force almost by accident, this time there was a deliberate plan set out by the US Department of Defense, in consultation with news organisations, for journalists to be 'situated' with various parts of the military.[1] The thinking behind this 'innovation' had been developing for some time. Ever since the Vietnam War, governments and military have experimented with different methods of 'controlling' and 'managing' the media.[2] Initial discussion was centred on the belief that television had somehow 'lost the war' in Vietnam and therefore stricter controls over the media were necessary in order to contain information and ultimately win the battle for the hearts and minds of the public. The information policy adopted by the British government and the military during the Falklands was poorly organised and lacked planning. There was an absence of agreed procedure or criteria, no centralised system of control and no co-ordination between departments (see Morrison and Tumber, 1988: 189–90). But whatever 'on the hoof' measures the British introduced were based on the myth of Vietnam.[3] During the Falklands conflict, the battle for public opinion was fought under the guise of 'operational security', an all-embracing term used as an excuse for delaying and censoring information and disseminating misinformation (see Morrison and Tumber, 1988: 189).[4] Military and defence officials in the US noted the experience of the Falklands. The use of both military and civilian minders, the stationing of reporters in military units and pooling arrangements were all adopted in various forms in future conflicts. In the 1980s, discussions took place between news organisations and the Pentagon in order to establish some ground rules for co-operation. Its first 'test' occurred in the invasion of Granada, known as Operation Urgent Fury. However, rather than setting a tone for harmonious relations between the military and the media, it provoked outcry from news organisations as more than 600 reporters were left stranded in Barbados, unable to report what was occurring in Grenada. It was to be two days (when all the 'action' was over) before journalists arrived on the island. The military had been logistically unresponsive to the needs of news organisations. The intense criticism that followed led to the setting up by the US Joint Chiefs of Staff of a commission, headed by General Winant Sidle, to look into future media operations.[5] One of the main recommendations proposed that a national media pool should be created to cover future operations where full media access was not available. These proposals were implemented during Operation Earnest Will (1988)[6] and then in Panama (1989) when US troops were engaged. This latter operation proved a disaster for the 'new' pooling system because Dick Cheney, then secretary of defence, obstructed the mobilisation of the pool and journalists were unable to cover the engagement.

By the time of Gulf War I in 1991 (known as Operation Desert Shield), reporters (if they did not opt for being based in Baghdad) covered military events via organised pools and formal briefings. Journalists were restricted in their travel movements and had to subject their copy to formal security review. The problem for the military became a logistical one of how to cope with hundreds of reporters flocking to the region. *Ad hoc* press pools were organised but many journalists decided to ignore them and move about independently. The outcome was frustration on the part of news organisations and continuing bewilderment on the part of the military about how journalists operate.[7] Whereas the military is all about order and co-operation, journalism is competitive, fragmented and often anarchic. When the two cultures clash, the result is often antipathy to and confusion about one another.[8] The experience and lessons of the Falklands should have been a blueprint for the military in future conflicts. Instead, a misinterpretation of how journalists operate meant that it was to be 20 years before an organised 'embedding' process was fully implemented. Embedding is not a new phenomenon, though. Versions of it were used in World War II, and in Vietnam. In more recent times, following the deeply unpopular pool system adopted in Gulf War I in 1991, variations were used in Haiti in 1994, Somalia in 1992–95 and Bosnia in 1995 (see Porch, 2002).[9] However, before the embedding in Gulf War II, military–media relations went through a further downturn during the Kosovo campaign (1999) to remove Yugoslavian troops from the region, a conflict where journalists had little access to the province and relied on the military for information about the bombing campaign. For the invasion in Afghanistan (2001), many editors, bureau chiefs and correspondents regarded the Pentagon's reporting rules as some of the toughest ever (see Hickey, 2002). The main grievances consisted of the lack of reasonable access to land and sea bases from which air attacks on Taliban positions were launched and the restrictions on access and information emanating from the Pentagon.[10] The grievances at one stage even received an apology from Victoria Clarke, assistant secretary of defence for public affairs and chief spokesperson at the Pentagon. On 6 December 2001 she wrote to bureau chiefs about media coverage issues:

> We owe you an apology. The last several days have revealed severe shortcomings in our preparedness to support news organisations in their efforts to cover US military operations in Afghanistan.
> We have a significant responsibility to provide your correspondents the opportunity to cover war. It is a responsibility that we take seriously. Our policy remains the same as it has always been keeping in mind our desire to protect operational security and the safety of men and women in uniform, we intend to provide maximum media coverage with minimal delay and hassle. That has not always been the case over the last few days, particularly with regard to the coverage of dead and wounded returning to the Forward Operating Base known as Rhino. (Clarke, 2001b)[11]

Clarke went on to list the actions that the Pentagon were taking to address its responsibilities and the media's concerns. In a bizarre twist to the problem of press–media relations during the Afghanistan conflict, Larry Flint – owner of *Hustler* magazine – filed a suit against Donald Rumsfeld and the Department of Defense for the right of *Hustler* correspondents to accompany US troops in Afghanistan.[12]

Throughout all these conflicts the technology used by news organisations changed considerably. The comparative ease with which individual journalists are able to transmit material and the ability of media companies to provide live transmissions from virtually anywhere on the globe, now means that military media relations are in constant reassessment. It is these technological developments, together with the increased competitive nature of the news industry, that led to a change in strategy by the Pentagon towards the accommodation of journalists during Gulf War II.

Previous analyses of the media coverage of wars have tended to concentrate on the actual wartime period. In some instances, such as the Vietnam War, the duration of wartime makes any other procedure impossible: even if the history is restricted to the period of direct US involvement in Vietnam, the duration is about 15 years. The media coverage of the first Gulf War – which could easily have been set in a wider context – is largely analysed in terms of the combat period only, despite some analyses of the media coverage of policy debates in the period preceding fighting (for example, Bennett and Manheim, 1993; Lang and Lang, 1994; Dorman and Livingston, 1994; Entman and Page, 1994). However, clearly the motives for going to war and the willingness of public opinion to accept military operations with their normal infliction of death and suffering, are integral parts of the politics of war. Moreover, if the distinction between 'optional' wars and wars of 'national survival' is accepted, then we may reasonably expect that the role of public opinion will be very different in the two cases: the motives for war are utterly dissimilar, and the role of opposition to the war should be differently evaluated according to this distinction.[13] For these reasons, this book deals not only with the reporting of the invasion phase of the crisis (20 March to 1 May, the day President Bush declared that 'major combat operations' had finished), but also with the periods that preceded and followed the actual invasion.

In the aftermath of Gulf War I, there was general agreement that the UK and US media treatment of the conflict had been favourable to the US-led coalition policy, even though evaluations of the media profile of the war varied. For example, in introductory remarks to the collection of essays *Taken by Storm* (Bennett and Paletz, 1994), the journalism critic Marvin Kalb and the US General Thomas Kelly agreed on the profile, albeit from entirely different perspectives and with diametrically opposed evaluations. The authors in this collection concur that news about Gulf War I was dominated by official sources and the policy options they had pre-selected (Bennett, 1994: 21–4). Similarly, the French broadcasting regulatory body le Conseil

Supérieur de l'Audiovisuel (CSA) had complained about the 'naivety' of broadcast coverage of Gulf War I (Valo, 2003). Keeble argues that the media served policy purposes in two ways in this war: first, by excluding the historical context of events from their accounts; and second, by excluding any but military options from accounts of policy debates (Keeble, 1997: 81–96, 93–107). O'Heffernan analyses some of the ways in which US media managers were able to arrange coverage that was favourable to administration policy and the war effort:

- thwarting national media from examining the basis for a policy – or the lack of it, as in the early stages of the Gulf War – by configuring its public relations to appeal to local stations and newspapers that are more subject to public demands for local human-interest, while intimidating the deeper-digging network news teams with phone calls to network business offices questioning the patriotism of skeptical reporters;
- releasing powerful visuals which co-opt television news agendas, such as the smart-bomb video tapes and the images of Patriot missiles appearing to knock out incoming SCUDS;
- providing a daily mountain of insignificant details in press releases and background reports that overwhelm hard-pressed reporters; this technique also worked well in the Joint Information Bureau's daily briefing;
- policing agency employees to control information flows and to stop leaks, as was done both in the Joint Information Bureau and in the field during the war;
- stonewalling – refusing to provide information through normal press-distribution channels, knowing that only a small percentage of the reporters have the time, expertise, or funds, to dig out a story while it is relevant. (1994: 242–2)

Even ten years later, on the anniversary of Gulf War I, the US press overwhelmingly concentrated on official or ex-official sources, and on the already-emerging policy option of regime change in Iraq; a small minority of material considered any alternative approaches.

The media coverage of the second Gulf War in the UK and the US has already been scrutinised, both by interested participants and by academics. Even before the invasion had started, Fairness and Accuracy in Reporting showed that US network news about Iraq policy was sourced primarily to officials or ex-officials, that only 6% of sources were sceptical about the need for war and that less than 1% were associated with anti-war activism (FAIR, 2003). The Dean of the Journalism School at Berkeley commented on the narrowness of the political debate in US media (cited in Mitchell, 2003a). On the other hand, conservative websites have complained about systematic 'liberal bias' in US network news.[14] During the first half of the war, John Reid, then Chairman of the Labour Party, accused the BBC of being 'the friend of Baghdad' (Brown and Elliott, 2003: 6). In a linked statement, 'sources close to the Prime Minister' complained that broadcasters were acting as if there was a 'moral equivalence' between the Saddam regime and the UK, a phrase that appears to have been taken from a speech by Home Secretary David Blunkett.[15] This claim was dismissed by broadcasting executives (Hinsliff, 2003); indeed, the BBC news presenter George Alagiah had already said in a public lecture before the war that the BBC did not accept any moral equivalence between the two.[16] During the row between the BBC and the government over the latter's 'dossier' on weapons of mass destruction (WMDs), the BBC complained that the government had put pressure on it over the tone of its coverage of the conflict (see Chapter 9). Peter Arnett, who had reported for CNN from Baghdad during Gulf War I and covered the second one for NBC and *National Geographic*; he was fired for saying on Iraqi television that he thought the US army had underestimated the fighting capacity of the Iraqi military, and because his reports 'help those who oppose war'; he was promptly re-hired by the *Daily Mirror*.[17] After the war, the CNN reporter Christiane Amanpour complained that pressure from the Bush administration and the stridency of Fox News coverage of the war had led to self-censorship on the part of CNN journalists; however, the president of CNN denied that there had been any 'undue influence' on his news.[18] Amanpour's comments echo earlier remarks by Greg Dyke, director general of the BBC, that he was shocked by 'how unquestioning' the US media were (Timms, 2003b). In the UK, there were complaints about the treatment of the war on Fox News (available on satellite in the UK); however, these complaints were rejected by the regulators.[19]

During and after the combat phase, complaints were made about the media 'getting it wrong'. President Bush was reportedly frustrated with the US media's querying of military progress and their focus on civilian casualties.[20] During the second week of the war, both US and UK media had suggested that all was not going according to plan (see Chapter 2).[21] On the other hand, journalists criticised each other for swallowing unconfirmed military reports and passing them on as fact: the fall of both Umm Qasr and Basra was multiply reported in advance; unconfirmed claims on the first night of the war that Saddam was probably dead were reproduced; and false reports that a large Iraqi armoured column was moving south were given media space as if they were fact.[22]

More systematic analysis has come from the German-based media consultancy *MediaTenor*, commissioned by the *Frankfurter Algemeine Zeitung* to do a comparative, international analysis of television coverage of the conflict.[23] British television coverage has also been analysed by a team from Cardiff University.[24] Both of these studies consist of quantitative content analysis, and make inter-channel comparisons of the levels of attention given to the various actors involved in the war, as well as to other indicators of objectivity of coverage. The Belgian francophone academic journal *Médiatiques* published a special issue on the 'Iraq–American Crisis', which compares media coverage of US policy and related matters across a number of countries; these studies are largely qualitative (Lits, 2003a). *Transnational Broadcasting Studies* devoted an issue to studies of Arab-language media, published shortly after the conflict (2003).

As a leading participant in the Iraq crisis, the UK position was subject to continuous and intense scrutiny in domestic media, especially since opinion polls made it clear from a relatively early stage in the development of the crisis (winter 2002–03) that there was substantial public opposition to a war that was not conducted under the auspices of the UN.[25] The media themselves were the object of intense scrutiny from politicians and pressure groups. Moreover, journalists themselves constantly examined their own and other journalists' efforts, and commented on the communications strategies of other actors. Both the *American Journalism Review* (May, 2003) and the *Columbia Journalism Review* (2003(3): May/June) published special reports on the war coverage. Lits (2003b) argues that the level of self-reflexivity on the part of media practitioners was unprecedented. The same point is made in *Transnational Broadcasting Studies* issue no.10: 'Media on Media' (2003). The new phenomenon of web logs ('blogs'), especially the many set up by journalists themselves (see Chapter 2), is part of the process of self-reflexivity, as much of their content is given over to the journalistic process.

This book is divided into three parts. In Part I the focus is on the institutional arrangements made to 'facilitate' the reporting of Gulf War II. In particular, the 'embedding' of journalists in combat units and the arrangements for facilitation at the command headquarters in Qatar are considered.

The embedding process was carefully planned by the Pentagon in consultation with news organisations. No-one, least of all the journalists and their news organisations, relished the idea of a return to the pool system or the sole reliance on official briefings employed in previous wars. Many journalists expressed apprehension about the embedding process, particularly about their ability to maintain impartiality. Others embraced the opportunity to go to the front line, whilst the news organisations looked forward to continuous live broadcasting. A second concern to emerge in the days following the invasion was that the embedded journalists were only providing a snapshot of the war. Both US and UK governments complained that the public was receiving a distorted picture of the conflict. The initial enthusiasm for the process was also tempered (in reality) for some journalists because they hardly saw any interesting combat. Some estimates suggest that only 50 to 60 of those embedded saw a lot of action, whilst others were stationed with units that were never deployed or saw very little action (Shafer, 2003b). Others complained about their reliance on military communications for sending their copy back. A third major issue to arise was the safety of journalists. Those embedded with the troops could rely on the protection of their units with the risk, like their military protectors, of injury or death. But there was also the potential problem of capture, and if that happened whether they would be regarded as prisoners of war under the protection of the Geneva convention, or treated as spies and therefore not entitled to the same protection. For those operating independently of the military ('unilaterals', as they came to be called), the dangers were all too obvious. Not only did the military often treat them as second-class citizens compared with the 'embeds' by refusing access, transport and communications, but also many of them were killed or injured in the conflict. One of the most sinister aspects of the 'information' war was the warnings issued by US officals before the start of the invasion about the dangers of reporting outside of the embedded process. For those journalists based at the communications centre in Qatar, the military's information management was an all too familiar catalogue of obfuscation and delay. The military command in Qatar were unable to match the speed of communications going from the embedded journalists to their news organisations, leaving the journalists based there facing long delays over confirmation of reported military activity.

In Chapters 1 to 5, we attempt to understand how journalists worked and to gain an insight into the news-gathering process in time of war. By providing accounts of the differing perceptions of events from the perspective of journalists, military and government officals who we quote at length, we provide a context for understanding how these individuals operated in gathering and providing the news.

The analysis of media coverage in Part II of this book is concerned primarily with UK media, making occasional reference to coverage in other media systems. It is not an 'agenda-setting' study, since it contains no analysis of public opinion despite references to it; it is not even a 'framing' study, although it contains analysis of patterns of media coverage that may amount to a frame – but the frame is not very consistent. It analyses the patterns of media attention to the various elements of the unfolding crisis, seeking to determine which elements of the crisis were seen as relevant for news purposes, and which were excluded or marginalised.

Analysis of the media coverage is divided into three chapters. These are arranged chronologically to follow the development of the crisis: the pre-invasion, invasion and post-invasion phases. In the first of these, Chapter 6, the main focus is on the extent to which UK media gave a favourable or hostile reception to the policy initiatives adopted by the US government (and largely followed by the UK government). In Chapter 7, the focus is on the reporting of the actual invasion itself, and in particular, on the extent to which the war was reported in a positive or a negative light in various titles and broadcast channels – this was an issue which aroused complaints from coalition political leaders at the time of the invasion itself. Chapter 8 is concerned with the selection of themes linked to the post-invasion scenario that have been the focus of media attention and which have been relatively marginalised.

The final part of the book is devoted to the controversy about the existence or non-existence of Iraq's WMDs and the subsequent row that developed between the British government and the BBC over the reporting of this. The issue over whether the government had exaggerated the threat of Saddam's weapons assumed enormous importance because it struck at the heart of the government's rationale for going to war. The issue became one of a government fighting to maintain its legitimacy (post invasion) in the minds of the public. The subsequent setting up of the Hutton Inquiry to investigate the circumstances surrounding the death of David Kelly, the UK government's chief weapons expert, has opened for public debate two issues most often confined to journalism scholars. The first is the nature of the relationship between journalists and their sources, and the second is the concept of objectivity in journalism.

## Notes

1  For an account of how journalists were assigned to the British Task Force during the Falklands conflict see Morrison and Tumber, 1988: Ch. 1.

2  For historical accounts of military–media relations and information policy battles see, for example, Carruthers, 2000; Stewart and Carruthers, 1996; Young and Jesser, 1997; Taylor, 1997; Thrall, 2000. See also Ethiel, 1998; Aukofer and Lawrence, 1995.

3  For one of the best accounts of the media and Vietnam, see Hallin, 1986.

4  Following the end of the conflict, Parliament conducted an enquiry into information policy; see the House of Commons First Report from the Defence Committee, Session 1982–83 (HMSO, Dec.1982, Vol.1); the Ministry of Defence also set up a study group under the leadership of General Sir Hugh Beach to look at censorship and information in light of the Falklands experience.

5  For details see the Sidle Report (1984).

6  During the Spring of 1988, the US Navy was engaged in Operation Earnest Will, which had as an objective to maintain freedom of navigation in the Persian Gulf as Iraq and Iran continued to fight a seemingly endless war.

7  For varying accounts of the media coverage of the Gulf War see, for example, Bennett and Paletz, 1994; Kellner, 1992; Mowlana et al., 1992; and for an Australian perspective, see Goot and Titten, 1992.

8  For examples of the competitive nature of journalists whilst stationed with the military, see Morrison and Tumber (1988), Ch. 4.

9  For studies on the media and Yugoslavia, see Allen and Seaton, 1999; Gow et al., 1996; Sadkovich, 1998.

10  For details of news organisations' complaints and the response from Secretary of Defence Donald Rumsfeld, see Hickey, 2002. Interestingly Victoria Clarke, assistant secretary of defence for public affairs and chief spokesperson at the Pentagon, received praise from journalists during both the Afghanistan conflict and Gulf War II for her approach to information policy.

11  Neil Hickey conducted a Q&A with Victoria Clarke about the reporting in Afghanistan. In it, she discusses the apology and also elaborates on reporting restrictions and the quality of reporting (see Hickey, 2002). For an insight into the dialogue between Clarke and Bureau Chiefs see Clarke (Nov. 2001, Dec. 2001).

12  Flynt lost the suit. For the opinion see www.dcd.uscourts.gov/ Opinions/2003/ Friedman/01–2399a.pdf. See also Q &A Larry Flynt's War (2002) www.cjr.org, January/February.

13  In a critique of American liberals, the conservative columnist George Will wrote: 'In a process without precedent, America has been, for more than a year,

walking slowly – never mind nonsensical headlines about the 'rush to war' – toward an optional war. Optional, that is, in the sense that although it is a defensible choice, it is a choice. War has not been unambiguously thrust upon us, as in 1861 by secession, or in 1917 by unrestricted submarine warfare, or in 1941 by surprise attack, or by aggression across international borders as in June 1950 or August 1990' (Will, 2003).

14  e.g. 'profiles in bias' at www.mediaresearch.org.

15  http://archives.econ.utah.edu/archives/a-list/2003w13/msg00139.htm.

16  Both London Metropolitan University, 6.3.03

17  http://edition.cnn.com/2003/world/meast/03/31/sprj.irq.arnett/; *Daily Mirror*, 1.4.03.

18  Both quoted in Plunkett (2003).

19  Reported in Wells (2003).

20  CNN 28.3.03, quoted www.globalissues.org/Geopolitics/MiddleEast/Iraq/Attack.asp.

21  There is a detailed analysis of the abrupt shifts in the tone of US media coverage in Smolkin, 2003.

22  See Mitchell (2003c) for a list of stories that were not true.

23  We have accessed this in the form of a CD-ROM PowerPoint presentation, also in a brief outline commentary in *MediaTenor*, 2003, 2: pp. 1, 39–43. The full report is obtainable from the company, and will be more fully reported in a future edition of *MediaTenor*.

24  Presented in outline in the Lewis (2003a).

25  See the regular polls conducted by ICM for the *Guardian* at www.icmresearch.co.uk.

# PART I

The Media go to War

# 1

## JOURNALISTS GO TO WAR

In the arrangements for media facilitation in Gulf War II, the most important innovation was the large-scale presence of journalists on the battlefield, embedded in military units.

The process of embedding journalists with the military was an organised strategy planned well in advance of the conflict. Speaking at a symposium held at the Brookings Institute in June 2003, Victoria Clarke, assistant secretary of defence for public affairs and chief spokesperson at the Pentagon, outlined some of the reasons for developing the embedded process:

> It was actually an extraordinary evolution of a concept that already existed. If you've followed the Pentagon for some time, you know we've tried and Secretary Rumsfeld has tried since the very beginning to be very transparent in our business, to provide as much access as possible. If you put two or three of his predecessors together or my predecessors together, you would not have seen them do as many briefings, as many interviews, as many public events. They take communications very seriously. In previous conflicts, including Afghanistan, we made the best effort possible to provide access to the media. Iraq was different for a lot of reasons, and so there was an extraordinary evolution of what we were already doing, and it had to do with the fact that we knew if we went to war, we'd have a lot more people out there, a lot more soldiers, sailors, airmen, and marines. It had to do with the fact that we knew the more people saw the US military, the more they would understand the mission and how they were going about their jobs. I've used this story several times, but I knew with great certainty if we went to war, the Iraqi regime would be doing some terrible things and would be incredibly masterful with the lies and the deception. And I could stand up there at that podium and Secretary Rumsfeld could stand up there and say very truthfully the Iraqi regime is putting its soldiers in civilian clothing so they can ambush our soldiers. Some people would believe us and some people wouldn't. But we had hundreds and hundreds of credible, independent journalists saying the Iraqi regime is putting their soldiers in civilian clothing. (Clarke, 2003d)

Another Pentagon spokesman, Lt Cmdr Jeff Davis, said the embedding programme would play a crucial role in the pending war to remove Hussein from power:

> We recognize the value of having independent journalists say in an unbiased way what the truth is. It's an important programme, and we stand by it. I think it is something that the American public will benefit from by having a true understanding of what is going on. (Cited in McClintock, 2003)

The process of organising the embedding of journalists with the military involved an ongoing dialogue between the US Department of Defense (DOD) and news organisation bureau chiefs. A number of briefings took place in the months leading up to the start of the war in March 2003.

At a Foreign Press Centre briefing held by the DOD at the end of January 2003, Bryan Whitman, deputy assistance secretary of defense for public affairs at the Pentagon, talked about the DOD's plans for media support should war occur (or 'something happens in the future', as the DOD put it).

Speaking about the plans for how the Pentagon would support the media should anything come about, Whitman stated:

> One of the principal means of coverage that the United States government is pursuing for any potential conflict with Iraq is this embedded nature, of having journalists that are alongside our forces in the field and on ships, at departure airfields, and for extended periods of time so they can develop the relationships, so that they can provide the very deep and rich coverage that you get by being with a unit.
>
> The press pay for that, of course, because it is very deep, rich coverage, but it's not very broad . . . So if you're with a rifle company, you may get some very good reporting of what the unit is doing, but you may not have good situational awareness of what's happening to your right, to your left, behind you – that type of thing.
>
> . . . there's a need for all the types of coverage that are going to be available out there . . . we are going to try to use embeds to the maximum extent possible. We're doing it because that's what news organizations tell us they want to do . . . They want their reporters to be able to cover any potential conflicts on the front line.
>
> . . . We think that there are a lot of benefits to getting reporters out there with our units. Besides facilitating the type of access that they want to, we know that any time a reporter can spend an extended period of time with a particular unit, he or she gets to understand what that unit's mission is about; they can report more accurately on their activities . . . given our potential adversary and his propensity to use disinformation, this will allow for objective reporting from the field on what the actual situation is.
>
> So there's a lot of good reasons to embed. It's a challenge to the Defense Department . . . It's developing not only confidence in reporters, and their abilities to go out there and spend with the unit on the ground for extended period of times, but also instilling in commanders the confidence that reporters are going to be able to be out there and not compromise the operations that they're involved in or jeopardize the personnel that are conducting those operations. (Whitman, 2003a)

The organisation of the embedded process was based on a plan of allocating places to news organisations, not individual reporters. This made it difficult for freelancers to gain accreditation unless contracted to a news organisation. It also enabled the DOD to 'control' the process more easily through possible sanctions on news organisation for 'misbehaviour' on the part of their correspondents.

As Whitman commented:

We looked at television, radio, print, news wires, still photography, and we said it would be to our benefit, to the value of the American people and our international audience out there, if we had all forms of medium.

. . . we made a key decision that we were going to deal with news organizations and not individual reporters . . . And we're doing that for a couple of reasons. One is that we believe that there is nobody that's in a better position to determine how they want to cover any potential conflict and what the strengths and weaknesses are of their individual reporters than the bureau chiefs that assign reporters to their assignment. We made that decision . . . to allocate embed opportunities to news organizations, and that news organizations be partners with us in determining, then, who would go on that type of embed. (Whitman, 2003a)

Outlining the process of control, Whitman added:

We view an embed as an opportunity to stay with a unit for an extended period of time. So we're not talking about a couple-day jaunt out to the field and returning back to a media centre somewhere. We're talking about a long-term commitment on the part of the news organization as well as the reporter to be able to go out with the unit and stay with it for weeks, months, however long it might be out there. (Whitman, 2003a)

But with the caveat:

. . . the reporter is not going to be held hostage. If a reporter wants to leave a unit after a certain amount of time, they are certainly going to be welcome to do that. And to the extent that we can get them back to a place where they can obtain civilian commercial transportation out of the theatre, we will do that. (Whitman, 2003a)

At a later DOD briefing held at the end of February 2003, this point was reiterated by Whitman. In response to a hypothetical 'what if my reporter goes off and does independent reporting from his unit?', Whitman described the procedure:

First of all he won't be permitted to do that. An embed is precisely an embed. You stay with that unit and you stay with that unit for as long as you want to stay with that unit. If you want to leave that unit the military commanders out there have been instructed to provide you with the means to get back to the first point of disembarkation or the first point in which you can get commercial transportation to get you out of the theatre. Or back to one of the media centres where your reporter, you may assign your reporter to cover from there or you may be sending them there because you want to try to get another embed opportunity somewhere else.

Again, it's a very hypothetical situation but I would disabuse anybody of the idea that you can go out in embed status and then when you get tired just do some independent coverage out there and then perhaps link up with another unit or accidentally even run into another unit. You would in all likelihood either be, like I said, treated just like another civilian found on the battlefield, or evacuated back to the first point in which you could get commercially available transportation out of the theatre or to one of our media centres. (Whitman, 2003b)

The journalists embedded with the troops were given special rules for how they could operate. The guidance, policies and procedures on embedding news media during possible future operations and deployments were detailed in a document released in February 2003 (see US Department of Defense, 2003).

Policy was laid out explicitly in the document:

2.a. The Department of Defense (DOD) policy on media coverage of future military operations is that media will have long-term, minimally restrictive access to US air, ground and naval forces through embedding. Media coverage of any future operation will, to a large extent, shape public perception of the national security environment now and in the years ahead. This holds true for the US public; the public in allied countries whose opinion can affect the durability of our coalition; and publics in countries where we conduct operations, whose perceptions of us can affect the cost and duration of our involvement. Our ultimate strategic success in bringing peace and security to this region will come in our long-term commitment to supporting our democratic ideals. We need to tell the factual story – good or bad – before others seed the media with disinformation and distortions, as they most certainly will continue to do. Our people in the field need to tell our story – only commanders can ensure the media get to the story alongside the troops. We must organize for and facilitate access of national and international media to our forces, including those forces engaged in ground operations, with the goal of doing so right from the start. To accomplish this, we will embed media with our units. These embedded media will live, work and travel as part of the units with which they are embedded to facilitate maximum, in-depth coverage of US forces in combat and related operations. Commanders and public affairs officers must work together to balance the need for media access with the need for operational security. (US Department of Defense, 2003)

Journalists and news organisations were required to sign documents[1] complying with the rules set out at the beginning about what they could or could not report, for example, no details of future operations, no private satellite telephones or cell phones, no travelling in their own vehicles whilst in an embedded status, no photography showing level of security or an enemy prisoner of war or detainee's face, nametag or other identifying feature.[2] Reporters also had to agree to honour news embargos that could be imposed to protect operational security.

After meeting journalists who were due to embed with their units, Major

General Buford Blount III, commander of the US army's 3rd Infantry Division, said:

> This is going to be new for us and I think new for you too. The embedding process has got top priority of the army to make it work. The embedding process is an attempt to get reporters to tell the army story more actively by allowing them to share the experience and rank of past soldiers in the field . . . you are not happy with coverage in the past and we were not happy either. Over the years, I guess stemming from Vietnam, there has been a gradual mistrust that had developed between the media and the army and we are trying to stamp that out. We have got a younger generation of officers who don't have the stigma with them and so we are going to try to embed and open up and we are going to make it work you know, we'll have some bumps but we will work through it. (Cited in Synovitz, 2003)

According to Michael Getler, the ombudsman for the *Washington Post*, the long-term strategy of having so many journalists embedded with the troops had a further result.

> The embedding concept has meant that hundreds of reporters have already spent weeks and may wind up spending months with military units. This means that many news organizations will now have a cadre of journalists who have some real knowledge and understanding of the military. Since the draft ended in 1973, the number of reporters who cover the military and have served in it has diminished substantially. (Getler, 2003)

The US Department of Defense did not entirely trust the embedded journalists not to reveal tactical military ploys, particularly on board ship. As a precaution, they introduced 'arbitrary and capricious' reporting windows. Rear Admiral Steve Pietropaoli, US navy chief of information, outlined the process:

> The challenge we have here is that we would like to afford you guys the opportunity that you've had for the last several weeks to be out there at sea reporting about the things that are going on day in and day out. But at some point, and we've had this in the past with every military operation, if you're on the ship at sea, preparations for a significant military action become relatively apparent to any good reporter out there on an aircraft carrier. The pace picks up, the adrenalin starts to flow, more ordinance on deck. What happens is the commanders invariably shut down the reporting window in order to maintain some level of tactical surprise, and then the 24-hour news channels or wire bureaus or whatnot are unable to get hold of their correspondents for four hours, six hours, eight hours, and you start getting stories about something must be happening because I can't talk to my reporter on board the *USS Neversail*. And this is basically an intractable problem for us to maintain some level of tactical surprise and yet let you be out there in real time.
>
> So what we've hit upon, and if anybody has a better idea I'm happy to hear it, but for years we've thought of this and not come up with any better way to do it. So starting next week we're going to just roll the dice and you'll be able

to hear from your reporter and then you won't be able to hear from him for two hours or 24 hours or 12 hours or whatever it is. And that way you back here at the bureau or your assignment editors and whatnot shouldn't and won't read anything in particular into not being able to contact your woman or man for eight hours.

It is clearly an artifice and we're not crazy about it, but quite frankly, the alternative is to send them out there at some point and just shut down reporting until some military action kicks off and I don't think that benefits anybody. So this is the way we're going to try and do it. This should go into effect for the first time. I think we've actually done this wholesale. It will be that way across the Mediterranean and ships in the CENTCOM area of responsibility. Although they haven't decided yet whether or not they'll let individual ships decide the windows. Frankly, I think that's what it will come down to. The individual ship will decide how many dice to roll. (Pietropaoli, 2003)

The initial enthusiasm for embedded reporters was very marked. The editor and publisher interviewed a number of other editors to elicit their views on the first few days of the war. For example, John Walcott, the Washington bureau chief for San Jose, California-based Knight Ridder, said that nearly all of his 32 embedded reporters were able to file in virtually real time with no censorship from the military, although sandstorms and rapid troop movements had caused a few delays (Berman, 2003). Susan Stephenson, deputy managing editor of the *Atlanta Journal – Constitution*, said she was surprised at the embeds' ability to file under the circumstance but was pleased with the result:

The sense of immediacy and humanity made our stories very real today. From what a blinding sandstorm feels like to reporting how one of our embeds broke his unit's coffee pot, we're giving readers a better sense of the field. (Cited in Berman, 2003)

The sentiment was echoed by Colin McMahon, foreign editor of the *Chicago Tribune*, who reported that his journalists were able to file stories quickly without blackout restrictions from the military. McMahon, commenting on the mood among his five embedded journalists, said:

Some folks are nervous about going into combat but they are ready to be involved. (Cited in Berman, 2003)

## Local Heroes

The Pentagon's agreement to allow large numbers of journalists to be embedded with the troops enabled news organisations and outlets not normally on the Pentagon's top priority list to gain access to the war. It gave them a prestige – 'we were there' – with their audiences, something which was rare in previous conflicts. The Pentagon planners:

. . . reached out to diverse outlets where public opinion is shaped by including reporters from MTV, *Rolling Stone*, *People Magazine* and *Men's Health* and foreign journalists running the gamut from al-Jazeera to Russia's Tas. (Perdum and Rutenberg, 2003)

For example, Dave Sirulnick, executive in charge of MTV News, thought that it helped the military with its image:

I do know that by allowing their soldiers to speak openly and freely to us they are coming off a lot more credibly. Instead of thinking of these guys as GI Joe's and Robocops you get to meet them and see that they are young guys and girls just like the folks who are watching. (Cited in Perdum and Rutenberg, 2003)

With so many hundreds of places available for embedded reporters, smaller locally-based newspapers were able to have a presence in the conflict. For example, *The Leaf – Chronicle*, based in Clarksville, Tennessee, has a readership of approximately 20,000. They had a woman reporter, Chantal Escoto, embedded with the troops. Her brief, according to the editor of her paper, was to provide families with glimpses of the daily lives of some of the almost 20,000 troops in the US army's 101st Airborne Division (Bartholomew, 2003a).

Local paper briefs were very different from those of the main network and cable news organisations or agencies such as Reuters or AP. Many of these local newspapers have a very close link (back home) with the military. For example, Columbus, Georgia where the *Ledger-Enquirer* is based is also home to the 3rd Infantry's Fort Benning and Savannah is next to Fort Stewart, an army base with more 3rd Infantry soldiers. As Managing Editor Dan Suwyn of the *Morning News*, based in Savannah, said:

What we can do is to make the local connection with a war half way across the world. (Cited in Bartholomew, 2003a)

The *Ledger–Enquirer* and the *Leaf Chronicle* printed personal messages from the troops to their families and friends back home. A 'Hi honey' feature ran twice on the *Ledger-Enquirer*'s front page and a similar department in the *Leaf Chronicle* called 'From the troops' became one of the paper's most popular features.

Even for large organisations such as Knight Ridder, the local angle was very important. Talking about military families amongst his readers, John Walcott, Knight Ridder's Washington bureau chief, said:

Here in Washington, I think we tend to talk about war as if it's another policy issue. And that's not the way it looks if you live in Columbus, Georgia, or you live outside Fort Campbell, Kentucky . . . War is what your Dad or your Mom or your son or your daughter or your brother or your sister is off doing and why they're not home. And one of the reasons we had so many embeds was to perform that function which other papers don't necessarily have, and that is, being the hometown paper, telling the folks back in Columbus what the 3rd Brigade or the 3rd Infantry Division is doing. We had a young reporter from the little newspaper we own in Biloxi, Mississippi, with a marine amphibian assault unit, and he became a local celebrity because he became the main line of communication between those reservists – most of whom seem to work at Wal-Mart. Every story that came through mentioned – Lance Corporal So-and-so from the Wal-Mart. The Wal-Mart must have been empty in Biloxi . . . that was a function that we took very, very seriously, that I think, you know, other papers may not have because of where they circulate. (Walcott, 2003)

Although Chapter 3 deals with the issue of safety, it is worth noting here that the local papers often provide more of an insight into, or at least their editors give more of an insight into, the degree of experience and safety of the reporters. Leonore Devore, the managing editor of *The Ledger* based in Lakeland, Florida, remarked that their reporter Diane Lacy Allen had found the experience harder than expected.

Her American online screen name is Disaster Di. It surprised me to hear her admit she's scared. (Cited in Bartholomew, 2003).

Some of the editors of the smaller papers instructed their embedded reporters not to accompany marine reserves on potentially dangerous convoy missions. Dennis Sodomka, the executive editor of the *Augusta Chronicle*, said he wanted their reporter, Johnny Edwards, to:

. . . write about the local soldiers, not be a wartime correspondent. (Cited in Bartholomew, 2003a)

Chantal Escoto from the *Leaf Chronicle* was one of the women journalists who covered military action previously in both Kosovo and Afghanistan. Before becoming a reporter she was a soldier. As her editor said:

She understands the military and the lifestyle. She is certainly not a babe in the woods. (Cited in Bartholomew, 2003a)

In the Falklands and other previous conflicts, knowledge of the military helped reporters to gain the trust of the troops and, in some cases, enabled them to get their copy back. Max Hastings, for example, knew how the military worked more than others and was more successful in getting his stories home (see Morrison and Tumber, 1988).

Other female journalists embedded with troops commented on how some of the male journalists seemed to have an easier entrée. Lisa Rose Weaver of CNN stated:

The thing is you've got to schmooze . . . I was concerned initially. I thought that it might be hard to talk to the military people. It's very much a man's world, but there are women everywhere – there are women in this unit. (Cited in Huff, 2003)

Weaver worked for CBS during Gulf War I, but couldn't get an assignment covering the battles. She volunteered to go to the Gulf for the current conflict:

> When I learned what the assignment would accomplish, I thought this would be hell . . . it's been daunting to say the least. (Cited in Huff, 2003)

Tamala Edwards of ABC was embedded with the 33rd Second Air Expeditionary Wing, an air base in which fighter pilots make bombing runs around the clock. Commenting on the uncertainty about a woman's presence, she said:

> . . . people weren't sure how it would work because of the customs in the region. (Cited in Huff, 2003)

Edwards didn't feel that being a woman in the war zone presented a disadvantage, either in terms of physical danger, or in access to sources:

> I see women just at the front as I see men – they are all there just smelling bad together. (Cited in Huff, 2003)

Whilst the process of embedding started off with a wave of enthusiasm from the both the military and the news organisations, it was not long before tensions began to emerge. In the following chapter, we explore these problems and look briefly at the technology used by the journalist to send their copy back to their news organisations.

## Notes

1 The release indemnification that all embedded media and their news organisations were required to sign can be viewed at http://www.defenselink.mil/news/feb2003/D20030210embed.pdf.
2 All the procedures, ground rules, immunisations and personal protective gear, security and miscellaneous/coordinating instructions can be viewed at: http://www.defenselink.mil/news/Feb2003/d20030228pag.pdf.

# 2

## EMBEDDING DOWN

One of the key aspects of journalism, particularly for war correspondents, is the ability to send copy back to news organisations. Whatever the degree of access to the military, failing to get your piece back (as many journalists found to their cost during the Falklands conflict) can lead to big problems. The recent advances in technology have limited this problem for journalists considerably.

In a report in the *New York Times*, Fred Frances, an NBC correspondent based in northern Iraq, explained how the compact satellite dish that he was using weighed about 140 lbs compared with the one 800 lbs heavier that he lugged into Panama during the 1989 US invasion, and spent five hours setting up as the fighting went on half a mile away (Harmon, 2003).

Technology also blurred the lines between professional journalists and the wide range of observers and participants who were recording and publishing their impressions on the web. This included some members of the military and journalists who, as well as filing copy for their news organisations, also contributed to their news organisation's web log. In some instances, journalists also set up their own websites producing a diary or web log to record their experiences.[1]

One of the most innovative of new technologies in broadcasters' kit enables them to send back reports that are not live and where journalists don't have access even to miniature satellite dishes. News operators provided their journalists with a small kit enabling them to capture, edit, compress and send video with a small digital camera, laptop computer and a satellite phone. For example, Don Dahler and Joe White of ABC News had the ability to travel anywhere with the 101st Airborne Division, in which they were embedded. They produced a profile of a day in the life of a sniper.

> The technology is turning reporters and camera operators into producers and editors making often painful judgements about what to include. Their two and a half minute piece took four hours to compress and send but the video quality from such set ups is good and the reporting can get quickly out to the world. (Harmon, 2003: 2)

Don Dahler of ABC said:

> The fact that we can file stories at all without a dish or having access to a dish is stunning to me. We have made a quantum leap in our ability to conduct journalism. (Cited in Harmon, 2003)

Sherry Berg, the vice president of news operations for Fox Television, said:

> It was a good thing that so much of the equipment the network's correspondents are using are souped-up consumer products, not much different to the video cameras commonly used to shoot weddings. That means that they can be replaced without too much expense, although reporters do not have too much room for back-ups. We're sending them with plenty of plastic bags and Q-tips. It's amazing what a couple of granules of sand can do. (Cited in Harmon, 2003)

Other reporters commented on the way that they reported the conflict and how they were able to send their reports back. Preston Menden-Hall was equipped with US$15,000 in satellite phones and computers. Menden-Hall called himself a one-man band who writes stories, snaps photographs and shoots video in combat zones:

> 'You get a connection, set up the camera, point it at yourself and just do it. You're live. But if there's any weapons of mass destruction I'm outa here,' Menden-Hall said from a satellite phone. (cited in AP, 2003)

Menden-Hall, the international editor for MSNBC.com, was labelled one of the new breed of reporters known as 'backpack journalists' who are able to offer greater mobility and flexibility than a camera crew.

> They fire real-time reports with equipment that is a fraction of the cost and size of conventional shoulder-mounted cameras and other gear. They file primarily for the web, with images they've edited themselves at the scene and occasionally contributed to television. (AP, 2003)

And the technology has made the job of journalists much more instantaneous and immediate:

> They are people who can shoot video, write stories, do radio on the side, basically do it all. These are the journalists of the future. (Schidlovski cited in AP, 2003)

These backpackers are also known as solo journalists or 'sojos' for short. These solo journalists, though, come with a health warning:

> Backpack journalists have to know the difference between when you are a lone wolf and when you are part of the greater whole and they have to file with that in mind. (Stephens cited in Konrad, 2003)

Some media organisations, though, have eschewed the use of backpacker technology because the quality of the images is not very good. Associated Press Television News (APTN), for example, relies on Sony's £70,000 pack that includes a shoulder-mounted camera, tripod, lens, batteries, lights and microphones, and APTN usually dispatch a camera person who lugs a 30 lb camera, as well as an on-camera journalist.

An experienced reporter, Jack Lawrence of *Esquire Magazine* and National Public Radio's 'Morning Edition', suggested that there are a lot of similarities to covering the Vietnam War. One of the problems for him was the instant technology, which had made the reporting more difficult because of the responsibility to withhold some information and avoid giving away military secrets.

> The challenge of knowing so much and being able to say only in general terms what you do know in a live or nearly live broadcast is extraordinarily difficult. I am holding in my head all the information at the same time as I am centering myself, ad libbing to the host in Washington who is asking questions that I could easily answer and give away information that would break the ground rules. For the television people doing it from the frontlines it must be even more challenging. (Cited in Jensen, 2003)

## Tensions and Doubts Begin to Emerge

It was not long, though, before some reporters were getting into difficulties with the military for broadcasting information perceived to be classified. News organisations were also beginning to receive flak in Washington and London for questioning the military strategy and for not providing a comprehensive picture of the invasion.

Although the embedding process was a Pentagon proposal agreed in conjunction with news organisations, criticisms began to emerge from sections of the military and from politicians only a few days after the start of the war.

Geoff Hoon, the British defence secretary, was critical, although careful not to blame journalists directly, by saying that:

> . . . while viewers might be seeing more of the war than ever before, they may actually be learning less, albeit in a more spectacular way. (Hoon, 2003a)

Hoon went on to suggest that people who saw the 'hectic pictures of a night-time infantry assault on an Iraqi held position during the battle for Umm Qasr will not easily forget them.' What they may not have understood, however, is that the picture hid a more complex story:

> With our air superiority we could have blown that building and other targets to pieces, but that would have run counter to our strategy of leaving the infrastructure intact for the Iraqi people, with whom we have no argument, to use after the regime falls. (Hoon, 2003a)

Journalists could not be expected to know this unless the military or the government said that this was their policy. However, UK correspondents in Iraq were shown the battle plan and the *Daily Telegraph* reporter at the taking of Basra makes exactly the point Hoon makes here (see Chapter 7). It was the military and the government that agreed to the embedding of journalists and a few days following when the coverage was not going exactly how they wanted or intended, the media organisations were accused of not providing explanations about the bigger picture. Hoon went on to add:

> I believe the public's understanding of what our troops are achieving is increased by the access we've given the media. The professionalism, courage, dedication, restraint of the British and coalition forces shone through. The Ministry of Defence sanctioned the 'embedding' of 128 British journalists and technicians within our units. Almost every type of British military unit has at least one journalist attached to it. The imagery they broadcast is at least partially responsible for the public's change in mood with the majority of people now saying they back the coalition . . . yet, on a wider scale, as the military and media find their feet in this new arrangement, we are both learning that free media access does not always equate to a balanced picture reaching the viewer or the reader. (Hoon, 2003a)

A few days into the war Victoria Clarke, assistant secretary of defence for public affairs and chief spokesperson at the Pentagon, warned editors, in a conference call, that some reports had already provided too much specific information about troop locations and movements, and that even if commanders on the scene divulge such information, it was up to news organisations to withhold it under the detailed guidelines to which each agreed in exchange for their reporting berths (Perdum and Rutenberg, 2003).

In fact, US Secretary of Defense Donald Rumsfeld delivered his first briefing on the war in front of an image of a little girl in pigtails and gave a warning echoing sentiment from World War II about helping the enemy:

> Don't kill her daddy with careless words. (Perdum and Rutenberg, 2003)

Terence Smith, media correspondent of 'NewsHour', with Jim Lehrer drew a distinction between television and print in presenting the 'big' picture:

> It was immensely compelling to watch Kerry Sanders going up with units as they approached a berm and engaged the enemy. And it was almost addictive television to watch because it was close – it was either real time or close to real time. And yet what did you actually learn from that? You could see some puffs of artillery landing at the target three-quarters of a mile or a mile or two away. And yet what was the strategic significance of that target? That often got lost. What was the larger significance of the whole move in that direction, down that highway, circling that city? What was the picture? That's what your rewrite man did. Many of the papers had somebody who would sit either in Kuwait City or one location or another and pull it all together. And I thought you got that in print. I thought you could see the big picture. But you had to search for it in some of the television coverage because it was so immediate and understandably focused on the most dramatic. (Smith, 2003)

And commenting on the complaint by Rumsfeld concerning the rapid mood swings in the media coverage from positive to negative, critical to adoring, Smith commented:

> I mean, remember those first two weeks. Remember the sense of inevitable and immediate victory that permeated the first 48 to 72 hours of reporting. There was an assumption that the Iraqis were going to roll up like a cheap carpet and this parade would proceed to Baghdad uninterrupted. Well, that was unrealistic to begin with, I would argue, and then when, of course, it didn't go that smoothly and, of course, there were problems and the plan was not perfect in every regard and the weather intervened, the horrendous sandstorms, all these things, in my opinion, news organizations should have anticipated better and worked into the coverage and kept it in some kind of perspective so that – I mean, you had stories, Johnny Apple in the *Times* and others writing about a quagmire within a week or ten days. I mean, that is a simply unreasonable parallel to make. And as a result, news organizations then, I think, began to see the glass half-empty. And they were somewhat surprised when the sandstorm cleared, supplies caught up with the front units, the march to Baghdad resumed. And so, yes, I think news organizations should learn from this that these things are not set piece affairs and stand back a little and temper this assessment. (Smith, 2003)

Air Marshall Burridge, commander of British forces in the Gulf, admitted that he felt ambiguous about the decision to attach journalists to the troops:

> Embedded journalists see very localised action and it's a pinprick . . . what has gone wrong is that the television news programmes don't have the ability to lay a strategic overview. (Cited in Sylvester, 2003)

Knight Ridder Newspapers had more embedded journalists than any other publication. John Walcott, Knight Ridder's Washington bureau chief, explained how they synthesised and distilled all these reports and turned them into the larger picture:

> Well, the simplest part of that is that we brought up from the *Miami Herald* the guy I think is the best rewrite man in American journalism, a guy named Marty Merzer, to integrate all of those soda-straw views so that what you got was not so much isolated views but a fly's-eye view looked at through a lot of different lenses, looking in different directions, and trying as best we could on a daily basis to put that together into some kind of a coherent picture along with the reporting we were getting from reporters who were not embedded. So we would do one main story every day that incorporated all of that and then take the best of the soda-straw views because . . . the highest value here was actually being at the point of the spear. And so, for example, when we had moments like . . . the release of the POWs, Peter Baker from the *Washington Post* and Juan Tamayo from the *Miami Herald* were able to get onto the airplane that flew them out, and that was a terrific story. It wasn't the whole story that day. So we did a story that mentioned that fact, and then we did a separate story on that flight out that the POWs made. (Walcott, 2003)

It was often from the reporters' own notebooks, diaries and web logs that the strains of the relationship between the military and journalists were glimpsed. In his notebook, Ron Claiborne, an ABC news reporter, suggested that there were problems even from an early stage aboard the *USS Abraham Lincoln*, the aircraft carrier deployed to the Gulf region. Some of the journalists on board were unhappy that they had to be accompanied by escorts and that interviews with the ship's personnel were monitored. Claiborne reports an incident when two photographers accidentally wandered into the hangar bay and were castigated by the Admiral. In another incident, Claiborne reveals a story about another journalist who was going to do a piece on the ship's personnel but it was cancelled because the Admiral didn't like the subject matter (Claiborne, 2003). Other journalists commented on the co-operation of the military and their curiosity into the way that journalists behave. It was very alien to them. Jason Bellini, a CNN correspondent, explained:

> Many of them (the military) had been very intrigued by what we were doing, by our presence and why we even want to be living in the dirt and the sand. They warmed up to us. The people who want to talk to us talk to us and the people who aren't happy with our presence pretty much stay away. (Cited in Bauder, 2003a)

Bellini's comments echo the experiences of other journalists in other conflicts working close to the military (see, for example, Morrison and Tumber, 1988).

A number of incidents occurred due to misunderstandings and ambiguities regarding the nature of the embedded rules that journalists were supposed to adhere to. Indeed, some well-known journalists like Geraldo Rivera, the former daytime television presenter turned war reporter, were ordered to leave their unit because they had broken the prescribed rules. Rivera was kicked out of Iraq after allegedly compromising army operations.

According to Bryan Whitman, deputy assistance secretary for defense for public affairs and Pentagon spokesperson:

> He was with a US military unit in the field and the commander felt that he had compromised operational information by reporting the position and movement of troops. The commander thought it best to get the reporter out of his battle space and we understand he has been removed out of his battle space. (Cited in Deans, 2003b)

Another example concerned Brett Lieberman, a journalist for *The Patriot News* in Harrisburg, Pennsylvania. Lieberman was ordered to exit his assignment with the 2nd Battalion, 25th Marines when they were in Nasiriyah, because one of his stories allegedly included too much military detail. Lieberman was accused of endangering the lives of the troops with his story, which described the unit's mission to remain in Nasiriyah to secure the city after other units left.

Major Brad Bartlett, spokesperson for central command in the Middle East, said:

> The commander on the ground made the decision that (the reporter) put servicemen in danger and violated the grounds that were agreed upon. (Cited in Bartholomew, 2003b)

The executive editor of *The Patriot-News*, David Newhouse, received a letter from the military listing three reasons for Lieberman's expulsion:

> reporting on the specific number of troops below the corps level, providing information on future operations, and providing information on false protection measures. (Bartholomew, 2003b)

Newhouse defended his reporter, suggesting that the story didn't compromise military operations or endanger soldiers and that many other stories had included similar details. He maintained that this was a strict interpretation of the guidelines which, if enforced elsewhere, would have led to hundreds of reporters being asked to leave. Newhouse argued that the current rules left too much room for interpretation and that the problem was that his reporter did not know what level of detail would be acceptable. The looseness of the guidelines gives military commanders who are less sympathetic to journalists the discretion to remove unwanted reporters. Official guidelines for the embedded journalists indicated that reporters would have the opportunity to contest their removal. It is not known though, in this case, whether Lieberman's appeal had received this treatment (Bartholomew, 2003b).

There were other incidents when unilaterals joined up with units but were then kicked out of the unit for apparently inadvertently breaking the rules. One correspondent was Philip Smucker of the *Christian Science Monitor*. He had not been officially embedded but managed to join up with a US marine unit south of Baghdad. He joined the division along with a colleague, *Monitor* photographer Andy Nelson. Problems began when Smucker was interviewed by CNN and apparently revealed more information about the unit's location than the unit commander would have liked (Strupp, 2003d).

Bryan Whitman, deputy assistance secretary of defense for public affairs and Pentagon spokesperson, said:

> My understanding of the facts at this point from the commander on the ground is that this reporter was reporting, in real time, positions, locations, and activities of units engaged in combat. The commander felt it was necessary and very appropriate to remove Smucker from his immediate battle space in order not to compromise his mission or endanger personnel of his unit. (Cited in Strupp, 2003d)

In his defence, Smucker's employees argued that he was not embedded and had not undergone the same preparations that the other embedded reporters had gone through (Strupp, 2003d).

Reporters' diaries also provided an insight into the reporters' states of mind and to some extent into war correspondent culture. Some experienced journalists described the living conditions as awful. Jim Axelrod, CBS news correspondent, assigned to live with the 1st Brigade Combat Team of the 3rd Infantry Division in Kuwait, described his living conditions after just 24 hours of the embedding process:

> The living conditions are a bit, shall we say, rugged. I'm not going to complain about tent life: the freezing nights, the broiling days, crude toilets, no showers and a cot you wouldn't even find at San Quentin. I bravely told the private spooning out eggs this morning, 'Hey, they don't look so bad.' (I was lying.) 'Let's see if you ask for them again tomorrow,' was the answer. (He knew it.) Now, I come from a long line of people for whom 'roughing it' means the Holiday Inn instead of the Marriott. But I think I can handle this for a while. Especially if it's the price of admission for a show where we get the kind of front-row seat never offered before. Front row? Actually, we'll be sitting on the stage. (Axelrod, 2003a)

And *Minneapolis Star Tribune* reporter Sharon Schmickle, aged 60, said:

> We haven't showered for two weeks, we sleep in dirt because it is impossible to keep it out of our tents. We have made several quick dives into bunkers because of missile attacks, we have spent long hours in gas masks, flak jackets, and Kevlar helmets when security at our camp was breached. That's where the story is and it's a big story . . .
>
> The greatest advantage is that living with the story you see the nuances and thus are in position to deliver a better informed report . . . what keeps me going is the access to stories. It couldn't be much better than this. (Cited in Astor, 2003)

In a diary piece in *Media Guardian*, Jason Burke described his experiences whilst on the Turkish border waiting to cross into the Kurdish enclave of northern Iraq:

> . . . around us, 150 or more journalists unpacked bags, ordered drinks, bitched about the journey, worked out where they had last seen each other (Kabul usually), and speculated on the likelihood of the Turks actually fulfilling their promise to allow us into northern Iraq. (Burke, 2003)

Burke described the strains and stresses that emerged in the situation:

> We booked into our fleet hotels and checked out, we got on our buses and got off them again, we signed up on lists and then found that a new list was being drawn up which we were not on. The strains began to tell . . . lending a shred of dignity to the proceedings was Don McCullin, the great British war photographer. McCullin's gritty black and white pictures, full of held-back death and burned-in darkness, had inspired me on my first trip to Kurdistan, as a student in 1991. Then I had wanted to be a 'combat photographer' and, as I stumbled about with the Peshmerga guerrillas through that summer,

Kalashnikov over one shoulder, cannon A1 over the other, it was visions of McCullin in the rubble of Hue city that kept me going. Now I was on a job with him. This was genuinely incredible. I felt like the pigeon-chested youth team trainee who finds himself pulling on a first team shirt alongside players he had pretended to be during lunch break kickabouts. It took me three days to pluck up the courage to introduce myself. McCullin was friendly, gracious and modest. Few others were. I made my own contribution to the general idiocy when a Frenchman with a black polo neck and a pipe began berating the governor in language that was ingenious in its obscenity. Fearing that some random freelancer was about to irredeemably anger a man who could send us all back to Ankara, I told him to shut up. When he didn't I hit him quite hard. He turned out to be the foreign editor of *Libération*, the great leftist Paris-based newspaper that I have always admired and enjoyed. This did not make me feel any better about the episode. (Burke, 2003)

Burke's comments about his fellow journalists are not uncommon, particularly amongst war correspondents where the myths and legends of experienced journalists are rife within their culture. What is common are the references to both heroes and fictional characters within journalism who are often mentioned in dispatches. Ernie Pyle is one name often quoted. Here is a small excerpt from the diary of M.L. Like, a reporter for the *Seattle Post Intelligencer* who was based aboard the *USS Abraham Lincoln*, posted on Thursday, 20 March at 6.44 a.m.:

Restless sleep with clanking, scraping of cattle bolts and pounding of slingshot jet launches directly overhead. The war call came at 4 a.m. Fell out of bed, wishing I hadn't stayed till 2 a.m. reading *Scoop*, Evelyn Waugh's wicked send up of war correspondents inclined to make up news in the dearth of it. But as the day proceeded, the book seemed all too appropriate. People talk about the 'fog of war'. We are in the thick of it knowing precious little. Were the Tomahawk strikes this a.m. the beginning of the war? Were they a taste for Saddam of what's to come? (Like, 2003)

In an earlier posting on 17 March she wrote:

It's day 11 of the embed program for journalists, who've railed against unreasonable restrictions in this experimental (improbable?) collaboration between the media and the military. The squeaky wheel turns. Today public affairs officers tell us we no longer need escorts. That means no one sitting in on interviews, taking notes on what is said, reporting to public affairs. (Though we're supposed to file reports on who we interview and what we write/film ourselves,) we can also eat with the enlisted crewmen in the mess – we had been confined to officers' wardrooms. The Captain says the crew is getting a little more comfortable with the two dozen journalists crawling the decks. All those cameras and notebooks can be intimidating. 'We're adapting,' he said. (Like, 2003)

By the end of March 2003 a number of the embedded journalists had left their assigned slots with the military units in Iraq. The reasons varied from safety concerns, battlefield weariness and concerns that they were not getting enough good stories from the units to which they were assigned. Many more had wanted to leave but because of the 'no substitution' rule for news organisations,[2] remained with their assigned units.

In one case the *Los Angeles Times* fired a photographer, Brian Walski, for altering a front-page photograph of a British soldier and a group of Iraqi civilians. Walski had used a computer to combine elements of two photos to improve the composition. The two photographs, taken moments apart, showed a British soldier directing Iraqi civilians to protect themselves from possible Iraqi fire on the outskirts of Basra. Only after the altered photo appeared did editors notice that some civilians in the background appeared twice.[3]

The most famous sacking of the war was that of Peter Arnett. His employers, NBC News and *National Geographic Explorer*, dismissed Arnett at the end of March 2003 for remarks he made in an interview with Iraqi television. Arnett, the veteran reporter famous for his Baghdad dispatches for CNN during the last Gulf War, was vilified across the US for suggesting that the first war plan had failed because of Iraqi resistance; that a new plan was being written; that there was growing domestic opposition to Bush's war. At first NBC News defended Arnett, saying:

> His impromptu interview with Iraqi television was done as a professional courtesy and was similar to other interviews he has done with media outlets from around the world. His remarks were analytical in nature and were not intended to be anything more. His outstanding reporting on the war speaks for itself. (Cited in Shafer, 2003d)

Twelve hours later, NBC decided that his comments constituted a sacking offence:

> It was wrong for Mr Arnett to grant an interview to state-controlled Iraqi television, especially at a time of war...And it was wrong for him to discuss his personal observations and opinions in that interview. (Cited in Shafer, 2003d).

The consensus was that his employers were exercising damage control to their reputations because of the enormous flak that arose following his interview. There were plenty of defenders of Arnett's right to talk to Iraqi television and some support for his right to state his opinions. Other criticism centered on Arnett's supposed stupidity in making comments without any firm basis to support them (see Shafer, 2003d).

Problems came from many different directions for the journalists based in Baghdad. Political pressure emanated from politicians complaining about aspects of the reporting. For example, David Blunkett, the British home secretary, commented that western news media were treating the supervised reports as the:

... moral equivalent of those from coalition sources. We have broadcast media behind what we describe as enemy lines reporting blow by blow what is happening. Those of an aggressive or liberal bent, in my view, are egged on into believing that this is the right way to get to the true facts. (Cited in Rutenberg, 2003)

Operating conditions were also a problem in Baghdad. For example, Richard Engel from ABC News was concerned about becoming a mouthpiece:

There is a community pressure to follow the government line. No one will give you the truth on the street. You can get a sense that you are wasting your time if you are talking to people and they start singing the government's praises and pretending like they're on a pro-Saddam video. (Cited in Rutenberg, 2003)

And Nic Robertson, from CNN, confirmed the difficulties:

When minders are around you can see people have a hard problem opening out and being honest. A lump will rise in people's throats because they know they have to give the right answer. (Cited in Rutenberg, 2003)

Some reporters though, whilst admitting the problems, still maintained that they could paint an accurate picture of events in Baghdad. Rageh Omar of the BBC felt confident:

... that people are expressing their genuine feelings when they say, well, I'm Iraqi, my country's being attacked. They'll ask: what kind of government am I going to have? Is it going to be run out of Washington and London? That's been interesting reporting, and it's important to get out. (Cited in Rutenberg, 2003)

Some of the news organisations decided to pull their journalists out of Baghdad once the conflict started and others such as CNN were expelled by the Iraqi government. On 21 March the Iraqi authorities ordered four CNN journalists to leave Baghdad, accusing them of being a propaganda tool for the US army. CNN was the last US team to remain in Baghdad in this conflict. Fox News were expelled from Baghdad a month before the conflict and CBS, ABC and NBC decided to pull their journalists out of the region just before the conflict started. BBC, ITV and the British press stayed in Baghdad.

The problems and debates about journalistic integrity continued after the war. Following a BBC documentary alleging that a war dispatch, showing the firing of a cruise missile, was filmed from a docked sub rather than one at sea, Sky News suspended reporter James Furlong and producer Lucy Chator. Furlong later quit after Sky admitted that some of the scenes were reconstructions or taken from library footage.[4]

## The Unilaterals

In contrast to the journalists embedded with various military units, the ability of the unilaterals (those journalists not officially embedded to report on the war) was often hampered by obstruction from the military and concerns over safety.

Geoffrey York of the Canadian *Globe and Mail* commented on the way that even the military accreditation badge announced that he was a unilateral:

> It's a reminder of my lowly status designed to make certain that no gatekeeper accidentally allows me any privileged access to the American forces. Unilateral is the Pentagon's bureaucratic term for the distrusted rabble of independent minded journalists in Kuwait, those who are unable or unwilling to 'embed' with American military units. We are outsiders, powerless and marginal, lacking any propaganda value in Washington's media strategy. (York, 2003)

York likened himself and his colleagues to rats scurrying around breathlessly searching for a way past checkpoints and across the border into Iraq:

> Life outside the charmed circle of American media insiders is an exercise in frustration. Borders and checkpoints while normally manned by Kuwaiti soldiers are essentially controlled by the US military. Roads are tightly sealed. It is virtually impossible to visit the US military base or get anywhere into the northern half of Kuwait without American escort. In fact it is almost impossible for a unilateral even to obtain a face-to-face meeting with a US military spokesman . . . For correspondents who prefer to be Independent and mobile it is a humiliating situation. It began to hit home to me when my editors learned that the embedded spot the *Globe* was being offered was in Texas. We turned down the invitation to join the 1st Cavalry in Fort Hood, a unit that was not assured to participate in the Iraq war except perhaps as a post-war peacekeeper. So did our colleagues from CTV, who were offered an equally peripheral place at an air defence battery that would remain in Kuwait for the whole war. The ultimate indignity is the Pentagon's plan for the post-invasion period. The US forces will take small selective groups of unilaterals by bus or helicopter from Kuwait to carefully chosen 'liberated' sites in Iraq where the battlefield will have been tidied up, the collateral damage will have been removed, and cheering crowds of pro-American civilians will presumably be provided. In desperation some unilaterals tried to camp at isolated farms in northern Kuwait, near the Iraqi border, several days before the war, in hopes of sneaking across the border. But the Americans vowed to clean out the farms and send any occupants back down the road to Kuwait city. (York, 2003)

York believed that in the end he and his colleagues may have been glad of this outsider status in contrast to the embedded journalists who would only have seen a war from a narrow military viewpoint.

In any war, the bigger picture is the story of civilians, refugees, reprisals, religious conflicts, political struggles, reconstruction problems, and all of the broader issues that illuminate the truth of the conflict. (York, 2003)[5]

Roy Goering of the *Chicago Tribune* was a unilateral based in Kuwait for several weeks who managed to get into southern Iraq:

It now appears that unilateral reporters cannot operate in Iraq with the current security situation without being sort of unofficially embedded with troops, or at least being able to camp at night near them. Unilaterals have had mortars and RPGs fired at them by Iraqi troops. Lack of supplies is an enormous problem. Unilaterals who are up closer to Baghdad are having to abandon their vehicles as they cannot get gasoline to keep them running, even with the military help. I hear a small group of unilaterals up there are actually siphoning the last of their gas into one vehicle, getting in together and trying to make it to Baghdad in that vehicle. (Cited in Mitchell, 2003b)

Jeremy Thompson of Sky News was not an embedded journalist, though he attached himself to various military units. According to reports, Thompson became a thorn in the side of the forward transmission unit 'the hub' which was, before the war, the frontline for journalists embedded with the troops. Thompson apparently caused some parts of the military to be almost obsessive about his 'roaming maverick operation'. Officers at the joint headquarters in Northwood, Middlesex were exasperated by his reports and his was the only journalist's name to crop up in conversation at Northwood on an almost daily basis. Those high up seemed determined to remove him from Iraq, repatriate him to Kuwait and then tell him to apply to be an embed (Byrne, 2003e).

Thomson apparently blamed rival journalists at the hub for the Ministry of Defence's determination to eject him from Iraq. Echoing parallels with the Falklands, some of the journalists frustrated at not being at the heart of the action had complained to a high-ranking officer who in turn felt he had to take action against Thompson (Byrne, 2003a).

One of the problems for the embeds, as Thompson pointed out:

. . . was that whilst they may have had very good access, they may be stuck with a unit and command centre in which they weren't seeing much action. One of the problems appeared to be that the embed system had bad sides to it . . . the bit that was the most frustrating of all, was the bit that was supposed to be the command centre and was supposed to move up with the battle lines and see everything that went on. That's where the frustration arose and that's the bit that needs rethinking. (Cited in Byrne, 2003a)

Issues of safety compounded the problems for journalists and it is this area that is examined in the next chapter.

## Notes

1 Kevin Sites, CNN correspondent, started his own web log on his own personal website (www.kevinsites.net) not affiliated with, or endorsed by, or funded by CNN. Four days after 21 March, Sites told his readers on the website that he had been asked to suspend his war logging for a while and was negotiating with CNN to make them available, that he was carrying on with his chronicle, his war experiences and was negotiating with CNN to make them available in some shape or form at a future date. Many of the news organisations provided their own reporters' logs. BBC News online, for example, logged the impression and personal experiences as their correspondents watched the events unfold (see news.bbc.co.uk/1/hi/world/2866547.stm). For details of other news organisation web logs see www.cyberjournalist.net/features/iraqcoverage.html. The number of individual web logs mushroomed during the war, the most famous was that of Salam Pax, a pseudonym for an individual blogging from inside Baghdad. The authenticity of his reports, initially doubted, was later confirmed by several other bloggers offering confirmation of his descriptions emanating from the Iraqi capital. For details and discussion of what was on offer, see Weblog Central www.msnbc.com/news/809307.asp?0ql=ckp&cp1=1.

2 If a journalist left an assigned unit, their news organisations could not replace them. Instead they were put back on the list along with everyone else.

3 An editor's note appeared in the *Los Angeles Times* on 31 March 2003 explaining Walski's dismissal and showed the actual photos and the altered one; see www.latimes.com/news/custom/showcase/la-ednote_blurb.blurb.

4 The use of reconstructions is nothing new to news organisations; the apparent 'seriousness' in this case was that Furlong had told viewers that he was beneath the waters of the Persian Gulf. For more details of the episode, see Wells, 2003a; Deans, 2003e; O'Farrell, 2003; Wells and O'Carroll, 2003.

5 The results of the coverage of reporters' location are visible in the content analysis in Chapter 7.

# 3
# THE SAFETY OF JOURNALISTS

Gulf War II was a critical one for the safety of journalists. According to the Committee to Protect Journalists (CPJ), 17 journalists were killed or died covering the war in Iraq. Media personnel have also been amongst the casualties during the post-invasion phase and as of October 2003 the number killed has reached 20. The high death toll has led to concerns that Gulf War II could spell the end of the independent witnessing of war. 'The unexplained killings of seven journalists by coalition forces in four separate incidents in Basra and Baghdad provoked unprecedented outrage among journalists around the world' (IFJ, 2003b: 1). The International Federation of Journalists (IFJ) was very critical of a military and political culture that led to astonishing complacency and neglect over the safety of journalists. 'The impulse to monitor, control, and manipulate the information process had led to a casual disregard of journalists, rights to work safely and to report independently' (IFJ, 2003b: 1).

Figures from the IFJ show that the levels of killing of journalists in Gulf War II were unprecedented. Over the 21 years of war in Vietnam between 1954 and 1975, some 63 journalists were killed. In the Iraq conflict 17 journalists or media staff died in just six weeks. The casualty rate among media staff was higher than in any other conflict and, in proportion to the numbers present, even higher than among soldiers of the coalition (IFJ, 2003b).

Similarly, the conditions of coverage during Gulf War I defined the role of the journalist during the conflict. The sense of risk that was felt by journalists (for their lives as well as that of the troops) was exploited by the military when they warned that the satellite telephones used by journalists could 'radiate signals to the Iraqis' (Taylor, 1992: 58). Those journalists who rejected the pool system (unilaterals) faced even more outrageous conditions. Their safety was seriously compromised as a result of their refusal to comply – 'sneaking through military roadblocks, living off their wits and disguising themselves as soldiers' – they faced the possibility of capture by the enemy and subsequent prosecution for spying (Taylor, 1992: 59, 61). During the mass departure of western journalists from Iraq in 1991, Reuters photographer Patrick de Noirmont and two European colleagues were accused of spying, and 'were beaten up with rifle butts' as they tried to leave for Jordan. Another group of reporters were arrested and accused of helping the allies to target the bombing (Taylor, 1992:99). The working conditions for reporters in Baghdad during Gulf War I also deteriorated due to the allies' bombing. Selected journalists, permitted by the Iraqis to remain in Baghdad, described scenes of chaos and panic. Explosions buffeted their hotel. The lights went off and in an atmosphere of chaos everybody rushed to the hotel bomb shelter in the basement. Another group of journalists (John Simpson and his crew) had to return to the hotel despite their desire to watch the action (Taylor, 1992: 92).

IFJ reports show that 1100 journalists and media staff were killed in the line of duty over the last 12 years (IFJ, 2003c). These deaths do not just occur under hostile regimes and in war zones. The majority of journalists killed are local, targeted because of their reporting of organised crime, drugs and arms deals. Casualties are not confined to one or two areas in the world. IFJ reports identify killings in 38 countries. The numbers indicate that the physical safety of media workers is under increasing threat and consequently the pressure on media organisations to create a safety framework that will safeguard the lives of their employees is intensifying (see Tumber, 2002a).

The need for safety measures is becoming a major issue in war reporting. The deaths of two journalists in Sierra Leone in May 2000 led many news organisations (Reuters, Associated Press, CNN, BBC, ITV, and the big American networks) to sign a code of practice on safety (Owen, 2001). The International Code of Practice for the safe conduct of journalists, formally introduced at the News World conference in Barcelona in 2000, requires media organisations to provide risk-awareness training, social protection (that is, life insurance), free medical treatment and protection for freelance or part-time employees, coupled with the public authorities' respect for the rights and physical integrity of journalists and media staff (IFJ, 2000). Although this Code of Practice was accepted by some leading media organisations (such as CNN, the BBC, Reuters and Associated Press), an industry-wide response that would enable all media workers to benefit from risk-awareness training has not yet been established. Broadcasters and agencies have kept their pledge to extend training to all of their local stringers and 'fixers', but newspapers have not made a similar commitment so far.[1] Furthermore, the killings of journalists in Iraq is leading to more urgent demands for a better understanding of the reasons behind those deaths.[2]

Apart from the killings in Gulf War II, journalists received threats, expulsions, detentions and confiscation of equipment.[3] The attacks on reporters were not confined to Iraq and surrounding countries. Reports from Madrid, Spain and Cairo told of journalists being attacked while covering anti-war protests (IFJ, 2003b).

Philip Knightley described the Iraq War as the one 'when journalists seemed to become a target' (Knightly, 2003) and John Simpson, the BBC world affairs editor, who was injured in a 'friendly fire' incident, blamed the deaths of many of the journalists on the 'ultimate act of censorship'. He believes that the system of embedding meant that journalists operating independently of the US and British troops became potential targets:

In this war, the Americans were more than twice as dangerous to the proper exercise of journalism, the freedom of reporters to see for themselves what was happening, as the Iraqis were. (Cited in Byrne, 2003c)

Andrew Caine, the managing director of the AKA Group, which provides safety training to journalists, thought that Gulf War II was probably the fastest moving conflict in history, posing bigger problems for journalists because by definition their work requires them to move quickly:

By the very nature of the conflict the very best it could be is organized chaos. If you think of the number of friendly fire incidents there have been – bearing in mind that everything that can be done is being done to reduce friendly fire – the fact that innocent people get caught up in it is not unexpected. Our advice to media organizations would be to think about where the journalists are positioning themselves in the chaotic centre of the conflict and try to think about how they could be perceived by those on the other side. The important thing for the media to do is to dissect and analyse each incident to determine if it could have been a genuine accident – was there any malicious intent, are there lessons to be learned? To walk away from it is not the answer. This is probably the fault of politicians in previous conflicts. Before the Kosovo campaign they almost encouraged the view that you can have a bloodless war. The military have gone to extraordinary lengths to minimize civilian casualties, probably to the detriment of military operations, yet there are still civilian casualties. Because of the idea of a bloodless war people are raging against it. However, in reality the number of civilian casualties is miniscule compared with previous conflicts. (Cited in Byrne, 2003c)

## The Pentagon View

The US Department of Defense organised training courses for journalists as early as November 2002 in anticipation of a conflict.

Bryan Whitman, deputy assistance secretary of defense for public affairs at the Pentagon, in discussing preparations for the embedded process, stated in January 2003:

If we're going to ask news organizations to make this commitment and reporters to go out in the field with us and to put themselves in dangerous situations, we ought to also give them some of the basic training that will help them survive on the battlefield. And we've been doing that. We haven't been able to fulfill all the requests that we've had for training. We have another training session that starts next week at Quantico. But it's basic skills training. It's designed to make sure that a reporter that's out there with a unit knows how to don basic nuclear-biological-chemical protective gear, to respond to any given situations, how to respond to indirect or direct fire, that they know basic survival land navigation . . . a certain amount of first aid, that they know how to get on and get off a helicopter in a safe manner, since that is a common means of moving around the battlefield.

. . . we want to give reporters confidence that they can operate alongside our forces for those extended periods of time. We want to give our commanders confidence that these reporters are coming to them having received some training that will assist in them not compromising their operations or jeopardizing their personnel. And we wanted it to also act as some self-selection criteria for those people that go to do some self-assessment of themselves. Am I up to this? Am I the right person to be going out with an infantry unit for two months or three months or whatever it might be? So that's why we did it.

We're going to provide rations. So we're going to provide all the food – the wonderful, lovely food that you eat in the field when you're with a US unit. And I'm sure many of you have been out there. Some days it's better than others. Most of the time it comes out of plastic bags. (Whitman, 2003a)

For some areas like transport, safety involves an element of control and provides points of tension between the military and news organisations. Whitman outlined the procedure:

. . . we're going to provide you transportation because we don't think it's in your interest or our interest for you to be out there driving around the battlefield in whatever kind of vehicle you might be able to procure. So we're going to provide you your transportation if you're embedded (Whitman, 2003d)

A further source of potential conflict in the embedding process involved the question of clothing. If journalists are physically similar to the military, there is always a danger that in the event of enemy capture they could be regarded as prisoners of war. Whitman in his January briefing stated:

What do we expect you to show up with? We expect you to show up with whatever other personal protective equipment that you or your news organization feels is appropriate for you. That's everything from protective vests to headgear, helmets if they want you in helmets, if you want to be in a helmet. And the only thing that we require is that, of course, it be conducive to the tactical environment. Bright orange vests with 'press' on it probably aren't good for us and probably aren't good for you either. It just makes you a more visible target if somebody was looking for something to shoot at.

So there is some concern that if we provide you with all of that equipment, when you're suited up you don't look any different than an American fighting soldier or Marine on the ground, and that's a concern, maybe not for some of you, but to some of your news organizations, some of your management, that is. So we want you to be camouflaged to the extent that you're not going to stick out, that you're not going to compromise your unit. We want you to be attentive to light and noise discipline.

But at the same time, we expect you to come with that personal protection equipment and that personal gear to be able to survive. And we are continuing to provide advice and suggestions and help for those people that might be less experienced in the ways of the world. (Whitman, 2003a)

Embeds were also provided with anthrax and smallpox innoculations by the Department of Defense, but at the cost of their own news organisation.

Journalists due to be embedded with the military were the main focus of attention in all these briefings. Independents or unilaterals were viewed as dangerous and uncontrollable.

At the February 2003 US Department of Defense briefing with bureau chiefs, there was very little ambiguity in the comments made by Bryan Whitman about the potential dangers for journalists working in the 'field' outside of the embedded process. Talking about reporter safety, he stated:

> We've talked about this with you before but I don't think we can emphasize it enough. The battlefield's a dangerous place and it's going to be a dangerous place even embedded with our forces. It will be even a more dangerous place, though, for reporters that are out there not in an embedded status, that are moving around the battlefield, as I call it, running to the sounds of the guns. And I guess we can't caution you enough as to the dangers that that presents to a US military force in combat, moving across the ground, coming across reporters that may or may not have armed guards for their own security out there. So I think it's important at any time we meet that we would stress how dangerous we believe that it is not only to forces that are out there engaged, but to the reporters that are out there that could find themselves in that situation.
>
> The other issue I think is reporters, that are in Iraq right now, particularly reporters that are in Baghdad . . . We cannot tell you that Baghdad is a safe place to have reporters right now. We cannot give you any assurance that there will be a point in time when we can tell you, pull your reporters now. We don't know what Saddam Hussein may do or when he may do it. So we would be irresponsible I think if we didn't give you that very clear warning today that we don't believe that Baghdad is a safe place to have reporters.
>
> We know that you have to make those decisions and we know that they're your decisions to make. But don't look towards us – I'm telling you that you can't look towards us for any sort of guaranteed safety or any sort of specific warnings when it comes to your reporters that are in Baghdad or any other Iraqi city should it come to conflict. (Whitman, 2003b)

This was a very clear warning to the news organisations and was reiterated in very stark terms by Victoria Clarke, assistant secretary of defence for public affairs and chief spokesperson at the Pentagon:

> . . . journalists operating independently of an embedding status. We cannot guarantee their safety and I think most of them recognize that and most of you all recognize that but it's worth putting up on the table.
>
> And Baghdad specifically. It's not a good place to be now, it will not be a good place to be if there is indeed military action. Remember, we preface all these conversations with no decision has been made.
>
> This will not be anything like 1991. In 1991 the purpose was to get them out of Kuwait, limited targets in Baghdad, and not to go into any great detail, but this will not be like 1991. For instance, communications targets in Baghdad are very obviously something we would like to take out. (Clarke, 2003e)

And just to emphasise, in case the message had not got through, Captain T. MacCreary, joint chiefs of staff public affairs, followed Clarke's comments with his own:

I guess we've struggled with this from two perspectives because I know, and I'll be frank, I've heard some expression from some different media outlets that is this just a ploy somewhat for us to not have anybody there. And I've got to tell you from a pure military perspective, it's a great benefit for us to have cameras behind what could potentially be enemy lines and I'll just lay that to you flat out because we can pick up stuff off of just your normal, every day broadcasts that would help us.

But there's a trade-off here as you deal with the moral conundrum that we always deal with in targeting about the potential of killing innocent civilians who are not engaged on one side or the other as combatants. I've got to tell you, I know you hear a lot of things like this war will be different, and all these things. But I've got to tell you, the difference in the kinetics will be extreme if this would ever come to pass. I think Torie [Victoria Clarke] mentioned communication facilities, whether they be military or the way he [Saddam Hussein] can communicate and control his populace are always of interest to a military operation. You can pull that out of any military doctrine you want or any open source you want, so I'm not giving away the farm on the types of things you would look at. But I think that makes it very very dangerous for people who are either operating in the region or forced to operate out of certain areas, that you may become tools of a regime that really doesn't give a damn about your safety. (McCreary, 2003)

Implications for the safety of non-embedded journalists, an issue we have already discussed at length, were made very clear.

The problems for journalists reporting from Baghdad started before the invasion when in February 2003 Iraq decided to expel 69 journalists. On 17 March there were 450 journalists present in Baghdad according to NBC estimates, but by 20 March, through a combination of expulsions and withdrawals by news organisations, only 150 remained (IFJ, 2003b).

A number of news organisations pulled their Baghdad correspondents and photographers out of Baghdad because they were concerned that their reporters would be targets of Iraqi reprisals and would be used as human shields. Charles Moore, editor of the *Daily Telegraph*, thought the risks too great:

We felt that the combination of a serious threat to the lives of our people and the political advantage to Saddam Hussein of taking hostages was too serious to ignore. (Cited in Leonard and Born, 2003)

Some editors left the decision on whether to stay to the reporters. The editor of the *Daily Mirror*, Piers Morgan, put his faith in his experienced journalists:

You can only put your most experienced people in there. You need people who have done enough of these things not to be remotely gung-ho – otherwise you risk an Yvonne Ridley scenario.[4] The most dangerous thing in terms of how history records this war would be for every journalist to be pulled out. (Cited in Leonard and Born, 2003)

Charles Moore, though, disagreed with Morgan's view to leave the decision to individuals, believing that it was the editor's job to decide and that leaving journalists to make the decision would be based on courage rather than judgement. Using the experience of Gulf War I, Stuart Purvis, ITN's chief executive, took the Morgan line, believing that it was better to let people on the ground make the decision.

Safety considerations for journalists based in hostile environments, though, can lead to compromises by news organisations over editorial integrity. Two examples of this arose subsequent to the war. The first concerned CNN, one of the few organisations to remain in Baghdad during Gulf War I. The chief news executive of CNN, Eason Jordan, wrote an opinion piece in the *New York Times* in April 2003 stating that over the past 12 years CNN had buried a series of deeply damaging stories about the brutality of Saddam Hussein's regime. The reason for burying the stories was ostensibly to protect the lives of Iraqis, particularly those who were working for CNN. According to Jordan, during 13 trips to Baghdad to lobby the government to allow the news network's bureau to remain open and to arrange interviews with Iraqi leaders, he had become increasingly disturbed about what he heard and saw, but could not report because it might jeopardise staff.

According to reports, in the mid 1990s for instance, an Iraqi CNN cameraman was abducted and tortured by the secret police because they believed Jordan worked for the CIA. CNN said Jordan had been in Baghdad long enough to know that telling the world about the torture of one of its employees would almost certainly have led to his death and would have put his family and co-journalists at serious risk. Jordan also stated that at other times stories went unreported because of the risk to non-CNN Iraqis.

Jordan recounted that in 1995 Saddam's eldest son, Uday, had informed him that he was going to assassinate two of his brothers-in-law who had defected. Jordan stated that he was aware that he couldn't report it because he was unsure whether Uday would have responded by killing the Iraqi translator. Jordan also related how Iraqi officials told other disturbing stories that could not be reported and it was only now, at last, that these stories could be told.

Jordan's 'confessions' were regarded with outrage by sections of the American media. He was accused of compromising CNN's journalistic mission in order that the network could continue to report from Iraq. According to Richard Noyes of the Conservative Media Research Centre:

If accurate reporting from Iraq was impossible, why was access to this dictatorship so important in the first place? (Cited in Fletcher, 2003)

Other commentators started querying whether other unpleasant regimes were receiving the same treatment from CNN and other news organisations.

In defence of his position, Jordan said to his staff that Saddam Hussein's brutality was already well documented and his decision to tell all only after the downfall of the regime had saved innocent lives. CNN had reported on Iraq's human rights record from outside the country instead. He pointed out that CNN was expelled from Iraq six times, most recently just three days into the war when reporters such as Christiane Amanpour and Brent Saddler were thrown out (Fletcher, 2003).

Further damning criticism of Jordan and CNN came from Peter Collins. He wrote a piece in the *Washington Times*, recalling his time as a junior CNN reporter in Baghdad in 1993 and accusing CNN's president and others of eventually grovelling to the Hussein regime in order to maintain interviews (Fletcher, 2003).

Another case involved Rageh Omar, the BBC correspondent based in Baghdad. Documents discovered in the Information Ministry in Baghdad after the downfall of Saddam Hussein by Richard Beeston, the diplomatic editor of *The Times*, showed that Omar had written to the director of the ministry, Uday al-Taie, saying:

After promising and promising to have dinner with you for such a long time – we finally did it. Alhamdullilah!!!! For me, this was the main achievement of my visit. (Cited in *Media Guardian*, 2003)

In his defence Omar stated:

Reporting closed and fascist societies is extremely difficult journalistically. I've lost count how many times I have told bare-faced lies on borders. You have to have a sense of cunning about you, it's true of any journalist. But there was nothing unprofessional or untoward [in the letter] and nothing that in any way, shape or form affected my journalism. (Cited in *Media Guardian*, 2003)

More generally Omar also defended the compromises that news organisations have to make in a hostile environment:

If you stood up on the rooftop of the Palestine Hotel, whether you were BBC, CNN, Fox News or Sky and said 'Saddam Hussein, a sociopath who's murdered tens of thousands of people, tonight went on television . . .' you would be chucked out of Iraq. But that would be the least of it. All the Iraqis that work for you as drivers, guides and translators would have been in much greater awful danger. I don't think that by being in Baghdad you are saying that the Iraqi government is morally equivalent. (Cited in *Media Guardian*, 2003)

One of the most widely-covered incidents involving the deaths of journalists occurred at the Palestine Hotel in Baghdad.

On 8 April 2003, a Spanish television cameraman and a Reuters cameraman were killed and four others wounded when US troops fired on the Palestine Hotel, the base for most of the western media in Baghdad. On the same day, an al-Jazeera cameraman died when a bomb hit the television station's office in the city. Abu-Dhabi television was also hit, which in effect meant that the US military had attacked – whether by design or accident – all the main western and Arab media headquarters in the space of just one day.

Chris Cramer, the president of CNN international networks and the honorary president of the International News Safety Institute, stated:

> As we all feared this conflict has become the worst ever for our profession. Each and every day, journalists and media professionals are being killed and injured at an alarming rate. Unlike the military they are all there voluntarily and I hope the public appreciate the risks they're taking to cover the crisis. (Cited in Byrne, 2003d)

Cramer has long been a champion of journalist safety and recently attacked the old culture of news gathering, in which a display of emotion or psychological anguish was a potential threat to one's career. Cramer argued that employers should allow a display of emotion, especially when back from a war zone: 'people should be allowed to do their laundry . . . and their head laundry too' (Hodgson, 2001; see also Tumber, 2002a).

The initial explanation by US military officials for the attack at the Palestine Hotel was that one of the tanks had fired on the building in response to sniper and rocket fire. General Buford Blount III, commander of the US 3rd Infantry Division in Baghdad, told Reuters:

> The tank was receiving small arms fire . . . from the hotel and engaged the target with one tank round. In addition US military officials said that the al-Jazeera office that was hit was a mistake. (IFJ, 2003b: 27)

Following the attacks on the Palestine Hotel representatives of editors in 115 countries wrote to Donald Rumsfeld to condemn the 'inexcusable' and 'reckless' American attack, and leaders of unions representing thousands of US journalists also wrote to the defence secretary (see IFJ, 2003b). Johann Fritz, director of the Vienna-based International Press Institute, and Vice Chairman Richard Tate, a former ITN editor-in-chief, told Rumsfeld that the IPI believed that the US could have been in breach of the Geneva Convention when one of its tanks opened fire on the Palestine Hotel.

> Although the US military have expressed regret at the loss of life and reiterated the fact that it is not their policy to target journalists, IPI's been left with the overwhelming impression that the attack was carried out recklessly and without regard to the potential for civilian casualties. Throughout the war

it has been common knowledge to both sides in this conflict that international journalists were using the Palestine Hotel as their base – and the failure of the US military to act upon this information is inexcusable, even in what has been termed the fog of war. The consequence is the United States may be in breach of international law, particularly the Geneva conventions. Under the Geneva conventions and the precedence of customary international law, journalists enjoy protection from the dangers arising from military operations and the US military forces are bound not to conduct indiscriminate attacks. In shelling a civilian hotel known to be occupied by international journalists, it is the strong belief of IPI that US military may have conducted just such an indiscriminate attack; a possibility supported by the use of a means of combat – namely tank shells and combat sniper fire – that cannot be solely directed at a specific military target and is of a nature to strike military objectives and civilians without distinction. Therefore, on the basis of international law, irrespective of whether there was sniper fire or not, IPI finds that the actions of the US military to be indiscriminate and taken with complete disregard for the lives of the journalists living and working in the Palestine Hotel. (Cited in Byrne, 2003e)

The attack on the hotel was fully investigated by the Committee to Protect Journalists. Their report detailed the incident and provides statements from witnesses, finding that 'there is simply no evidence to support the official US position that US forces were returning hostile fire from the Palestine Hotel. It conflicts with the eyewitness testimony of numerous journalists in the hotel' (CPJ, 2003a). The report ended by demanding a full inquiry:

These and other questions can only be answered by the Pentagon, which should provide a full, public accounting of the events as they took place on April 8. Although US Secretary of State Colin Powell remarked in April that the incident was still under investigation, there have been few indications that a full, thorough, and public inquiry is forthcoming. (CPJ, 2003a)

The Pentagon inquiry into the affair, released in a two-page summary at the end of August 2003, exonerated the US military of any responsibility and claimed that the soldiers responsible had determined that an Iraqi 'hunter-killer' team was using a spotter in the hotel to fire at them and were well within the rules of military engagement in responding. The summary was widely condemned by the IFJ as a 'cynical whitewash' for glossing over false claims by US officials and press staff immediately after the attack that troops were fired on from the hotel (IFJ, 2003b. 28).

The realisation among journalists that they are a serious target post-September 11 was encapsulated in an e-mail from Leroy Sievers and the CBS Nightline staff to list-serve members following the murder of Daniel Pearl[5] and the shooting at journalists by Israeli forces in the West Bank:

Covering wars has always been dangerous, but it used to be different. In Vietnam . . . reporters were pretty free to travel with American units. When I was covering the wars in Latin America in the late 1980s, we all put 'TV' in big letters on our cars. That was supposed to provide safe passage. It did, until the death squads started putting TV on their cars too. But I think no-one but us actually believed that we were the neutral observers that we thought we were. Now I know some will want to take this in a political direction, and the old accusation of political bias. But that is not what I mean by neutral. In a war setting, neutral means the ability to cover both sides, if possible, and to cover the war as objectively as possible. But at best we were seen as agents of our government. John Donvan . . . remembers that in his days in the Middle East, anyone who was obviously American was always assumed to be CIA. In those same years, in Latin America you were assumed to be DEA [Drug Enforcement Agency]. But the result was the same. But journalists will still flock to wars for their own reasons. It just seems that in recent years, our ability to cover these conflicts has been steadily eroded. And the Pearl case shows that terrorists see journalists as simply American targets, and handy ones at that. All of this adds up to less reporting, and less information for all of you. And some journalists face even more dangers in their own countries. All over the world, repressive regimes are arresting, jailing, and killing journalists for trying to shine a light on what is happening. I think that the bottom line, and it's all fairly simple, is that in all these cases, people do not want the rest of the world to see what is happening. And the easiest way to stop that is to go after the journalists. (Sievers, 2002)

One way forward for the protection of journalists was set out at the launch of the International News Safety Institute in May 2003 when three new laws were proposed that would enhance respect for media independence in war reporting and deliver transparent and extensive investigation whenever journalists are the victim of violence:

1  To establish an international framework for the independent investigation of killings of journalists and media staff. This must include the capacity to call witnesses and to obtain information from all relevant sources of information.
2  To make the deliberate targeting of journalists and media staff an explicit crime punishable under international law.
3  To make the failure to provide adequate protection to journalists or to act in any way that recklessly endangers the lives of media staff or leads to the death of journalists or media staff an explicit crime under international law. (IFJ, 2003b: 36)

Apart from the terrible human tragedy of the deaths and injuries of journalists, the wider implication of these incidents is very serious for the reporting of future conflicts. If armies, terrorists and assassins target journalists in order to prevent independent reporting and witnessing of events, the public will undoubtedly suffer from the absence of reliable information. Journalists are becoming increasingly vulnerable to physical and verbal attack. If the embedding process is widely repeated, journalists run the risk of becoming identified with the military units they accompany, leading to possible attack and/or capture by enemy armies. Should reporters retain the status of 'unilaterals', they run the risk of attack or lack of protection by both sides. Both groups run the risk of accusations of spying. Freelancers are the most vulnerable because in addition to the dangers experienced by 'embeds' and 'unilaterals', they do not enjoy the same protection (e.g., equipment, training and insurance) from news organisations as do the staffers.[6]

This chapter examines safety issues surrounding reporting of the war for both the embedded and independent journalists and implications for coverage. Chapter 4 looks at the relationship between journalists and the military and whether access gained through the embedding process led to a loss of independence.

## Notes

1  For details of risks, training, protection, insurance, see CPJ (2003b).
2  For a discussion on the physical and emotional safety of journalists, see Tumber (2002a).
3  For details of many of the casualty incidents, see the IFJ report on the safety of journalists and killing of media staff during the Iraq War (IFJ, 20003b).
4  The issue of journalists' motivation became a major story during the Afghan War, when *Sunday Express* reporter Yvonne Ridley was captured in Taliban-ruled Afghanistan. Ridley, who fuelled a heated discussion between newspaper personnel after her return home, said her illegal entrance into Afghanistan was a 'calculated risk' that she had been prepared to take in order to get at the truth. It was reported that her decision to enter Afghanistan divided editors and news editors on her newspaper. Those in favor saw the operation as 'plausible', while after her captivity and release they praised her courage and professionalism. Those against the escapade viewed her enterprise as 'sheer folly'. After her return, reporters from other newspapers criticized her not only because of the 'foolishness' of her decision, but also because she endangered her still imprisoned guides who could face execution (Morgan, 2001). According to Ridley, her decision was based on a desire to find and report the 'truth'; see Tumber (2002a).
5  Daniel Pearl, the *Wall Street Journal* reporter, was kidnapped and then murdered in Pakistan in March 2002.
6  The cost of insurance has escalated. The IFJ reported that in January 2003 it cost US$5000 per week for death or disability coverage of US$1 million; by the beginning of March 2003 the cost was US$10,000 a week and by 20 March US$20,000 per week for a journalist working in Kuwait, Iraq or Turkey (IFJ, 2003a).

> The cost of sending each reporter, crew member or photographer on assignment to a war zone may include at least $2,500 for a training course, up to $1,600 for a satellite phone, up to $1,900 for basic protective clothing and more for chemical warfare suits, respirators, decontamination kits and various medications. (Cowell, 2003)

# 4

# EMBEDDING AND IDENTIFICATION

The embedding of journalists with the military in Gulf War II has provoked discussion about its success from both the media and the military/ government perspective. A key question is to what degree did reporters identify with the troops? Writing about the Falklands conflict, Morrison and Tumber stated:

> The journalists not merely observed their subjects, but lived their lives and shared their experiences, and those experiences were of such emotional intensity that the form of prose which journalists use to take the reader into that experience – the 'I was there' form – provided not only a window for the reader, but also a door for partiality irrespective of any desire to remain the detached professional outsider. (1988: 96)

The experience of those reporters stationed in the Gulf provides an opportunity for comparison with previous conflicts. Some high-profile journalists, such as Ted Koppel of ABC, embedded with the US 3rd Infantry Division, were enthusiastic about the chance to go to the Gulf. Koppel stated:

> I feel about as well informed as anyone out in the field. I've just been astounded at the level of access. If the principle here is that a free people have a right to know what the military is doing at a time of war, we are putting that principle to the test. I am trying to be responsible about it and handle it in a serious way. (Cited in Bauder, 2003b)

On being questioned regarding what was the best thing about being an embedded, Bob Franken of CNN responded:

> You were there. You were there. You experienced everything. That was part of it. The other part of it is that the military people got to see first hand that we weren't just a bunch of lazy pencil necks, to use the expression, who would sit at our desks in Washington drinking coffee and reporting ignorantly. One of my proudest moments came when this marine colonel, a John Wayne type if there ever was one, came up to this riff-raff group of reporters, all of us dirty, none of us had bathed, we were all eating the MREs, all that type of thing. And he said, 'You guys are like the Marines.' I was embedded with the marines. 'That is to say, you'll do whatever it takes to get the job done. Whatever it takes, no excuses.' That was a high compliment, but it also does speak to the great tradition of journalism that we were able to practice out

there. And I'm sure we'll have a chance to talk about some of the limitations of all this. But, of course, the obvious advantage is we were there and covering the war from as close up as you possibly can get in a particular unit's case. (Franken, 2003)

He also saw limitations in the embedded role:

The limitations were, to be very blunt about it, that a lot of the military people need to be better trained on the role of the media. There was frequently a belief on the part of the military that we were there to represent the home team. Some of us bought into that, and, of course, that's not what we do. We are there to, as dispassionately as possible, as objectively as possible, report on the bad and good of what's going on.

I was very fortunate. I was with a unit, a Marine unit, with a very enlightened commander, a very enlightened general over that commander who had taken the time prior to the war to send people to some media training. I think there's a huge need for more of that so that the next time around we can build on this experience and the war coverage can be better and we can have, I think, improved access on many occasions. (Franken, 2003)

Jim Landers of 'This Morning News' was with the 1st Marine Division when it led the ground invasion of Iraq:

We were in the back of the amphibious armed vehicle a couple of hundred yards behind a wall of tanks fighting their way across Iraq. We could see the muzzle flashes, we had people shooting at us, we had artillery landing around us. It was as if they had put journalists in the landing craft at D-Day and we had been filing reports from the beach as it happened. When you have access like that I don't know what more you want. (Cited in Swanson, 2003)

Landers was also positive about the military co-operation:

Almost everyone I have approached has been willing to talk with me pretty candidly. (Cited in Swanson, 2003)

CNN anchor Bill Hemmer believed that reporters embedded with military units made the television coverage of the war different from any other previous conflict.

Commenting during the conflict, Hemmer said:

To have journalists in with these Marines and tell us first hand by way of telephone, video or satellite image that the Marines are hunkered down in bunkers wearing gas masks and chemical suits . . . that is priceless information . . . it's given our viewers a tremendous vantage point, and gave those of us anchoring the story the opportunity to gather information first hand and fast . . . without those reports we would never have an opportunity to find out what was going on in there. (Cited in Deggans, 2003)

Hemmer anchored CNN's war coverage for several hours from the balcony of a hotel in Kuwait City.

Some journalists, though, defended themselves from the criticism made by their colleagues about the embedding process. The charge was that they might be dependent on the military for their stories and their safety, that they identified with the military and abandoned their professional detachment, allowing themselves or socialising themselves into being co-opted into reporting more favourably and less sceptically than facts might warrant. But for journalists like David Shaw, access and information are the profession's lifeblood:

How can one complain about too much access? (Shaw, 2003)

And quoting ABC's Ted Koppel:

Embedding with the frontline units is a 'reporter's dream'. (Shaw, 2003)

Shaw went on to defend journalists' possible vulnerability:

I see nothing wrong and a great deal right with real time television stories and pictures and next day newspaper accounts of individual battles and triumphs, tragedies and daily routines of individual soldiers. Nor am I terribly concerned with reporters falling prey to some more or less beneficent version of the Stockholm syndrome and identifying with the soldiers they're accompanying. (Shaw, 2003)

Some British journalists were also positive about the process. In a report of a *Media Guardian* forum on war coverage held in June 2003, Roy Greenslade stated:

Gavin Hewitt, the BBC correspondent attached to the US 3rd Infantry Division, was unequivocal. He didn't have a minder, he wasn't censored and he was allowed to broadcast live from the battlefield. He wasn't blind to the difficulties. He conceded that by travelling with a unit there is 'a powerful bond' between reporter and soldiers. (Cited in Greenslade, 2003b)

It was impossible to stop and talk to the local population. He realised that he had only a partial view of the war. ITN's Bill Neely, embedded with a unit of British marines, similarly understood that his reports were 'only one piece of the jigsaw'. He had originally planned to un-embed himself once Basra had been taken but, in spite of obvious hostility to his presence from the commanding officer, he stayed on once he realised he wasn't being censored. The *Guardian*'s Audrey Gillan, embedded with the Household Cavalry, said she did suffer from censorship, though her examples – such as being asked to change 'running' for cover to 'dashing' – were hardly draconian. 'It was irritating,' she said, 'but I still saw it as a positive experience. I got good access and I did discover what it's like being a soldier – the boredom, the fear, the awful conditions' (Greenslade, 2003b).

As we pointed out in Chapter 1, praise for the embedding process came from senior military figures. General Tommy Franks, commander central command, speaking on Fox Television was an important proponent:

I think I said very early in this effort, I'm a fan. I'm a fan of media embeds, and it's for a very simple reason: I believe that the greatest truth that's available to the world about what's going on is found in the pictures that come from the front lines where the war is being fought. I believe that every step we remove ourselves from the fact of the picture, we become less precise in our description of what's happening. And so, if we believe in the First Amendment to our Constitution, and if we believe in the power of having our country know the truth, then the embeds have carried us a long way in the direction of making that happen. (Franks, 2003)

And Colonel Arthur Haubold of the US air force's public affairs office said:

One of the driving reasons we elected to embed so many journalists with front line troops was to have them there as third-party observers. We expect the Iraqis to put out untrue stories claiming various abuses or atrocities. And we want journalists there to provide some level of unbiased reporting to counter Iraqi accounts. (Cited in Swanson, 2003)

## Identification

It was not long after the start of the war before warnings of possible identification were being aired. Jeff Gralnick, a journalist with experience in Vietnam, warned of the dangers facing the embedded reporters and likened them to the fate of hostages with their captors:

. . . But that is not, as we know, why you've opted to be embedded. Not for combat. Not that. You're all going over to report. Truth. Honesty. The real story. But that is going to be difficult because once you get into a unit, you are going to be co-opted. It is not a purposeful thing, it will just happen. It's a little like the Stockholm syndrome.

You will fall in with a bunch of grunts, experience and share their hardships and fears and then you will feel for them and care about them. You will wind up loving them and hating their officers and commanders and the administration that put them (and you) in harm's way. Ernie Pyle loved his grunts; Jack Laurance and Michael Herr loved theirs; and I loved mine. And as we all know, love blinds and in blinding it will alter the reporting you thought you were going to do. Trust me. It happens, and it will happen no matter how much you guard against it.

Remember also, you are not being embedded because that sweet old Pentagon wants to be nice. You are being embedded so you can be controlled and in a way isolated.

Once you're in the field, all those officers and commanders you now hate, because you love your grunts, you will hate even more because they will have total control over where you can go, what you can see and what you can do. Vietnam was easier, we came and went – serial embedees – essentially uncontrolled, which made for a great deal of reporting the Pentagon would rather have buried. And this embedding plan, which is being adopted now like war summer camp, has been put together by guys, now senior officers, who were burned or felt burned by the press as juniors 35 or so years ago. Fool me once. (Gralnick, 2003)

And Clarence Page of the *Washington Times* gave this warning:

Journalists who travel with troops need not only to stay out of the way but also to avoid being so seduced by their camaraderie with troops, even while under fire, that they lose sight of what their audience back home needs to know. 'Embedded' should never mean 'in bed with'. (Page, 2003)

Recognising the dangers of becoming too close to the troops, some journalists like Bob Franken of CNN tried to maintain a distance between themselves and the troops in order not to become a cheerleader for the military. Franken expanded:

I've always been worried on occasion in Washington where the beat reporters become cheerleaders for the institutions they cover. And I think that it's perfectly similar. The good journalist has an obligation, from my point of view, to make sure that everybody he covers remembers we have different interests here. You don't have to explain that to somebody like Torie [Victoria Clarke]. She knows that big time. But often times you do have to explain that. I made it a point in fairly blunt language to see to it that my hosts, so to speak, out there in the desert daily got a dose of that. As a matter of fact, I don't know if you've read it or not, but the guy who was the PAO for the Marines wrote about it, and he writes about this particularly irritating guy, and I'm very proud to tell you that was me . . . And I also had a little speech when I was in a dangerous situation where I would say to the unit leader, I'd say, 'Look, let's get this straight. It's not your responsibility to protect me. Obviously if I'm in danger, I would expect you to do it as a human being, and if you're in danger, I'll do it as a human being. But you have no obligation to me.' I'm not sure I meant it, but I would go through that. It was really important that that separation was maintained, just as it was when I covered Congress. And anybody who was not able to withstand the Stockholm syndrome, as I called it before, probably isn't doing his job or her job as much as he should. I think that most of my colleagues did. (Franken, 2003)

And on whether he succeeded or not (as an embedded reporter) in avoiding being co-opted and not pulling his punches, Franken stated:

I don't feel I did, bluntly, but I had to keep reminding myself that I was there to report on them, not us. I, quite frankly, think that some were. There was a sort of Stockholm syndrome. It's very tempting to become a part of the unit . . . (Franken, 2003)

The sympathies of Mike Cerre of Globe television, embedded with Fox Company, 2nd Battalion, 5th Marines, towards the troops were obvious, as shown in the following excerpt from his war journal:

> . . . you must be careful not to lose your objectivity when a 19-year-old lance corporal offers you his goggles and scarf when a sudden sandstorm starts giving you an unexpected facial scrub. You've also got to be very careful with the Marine officers and non-commissioned officers who will insist that you eat before them, along with the junior enlisted men, in case there is not enough hot food to go around, which is often the case when an errant meal truck finally makes its way out to your position. Any self-respecting reporter with fears of a government manipulation and long-held beliefs that military people couldn't possibly have opinions, insights and perspectives their viewers and readers could possibly find more profound than their own, must be especially careful. They are about to get some sand kicked in their face. (Cerre, 2003)

The closeness developing between the journalist and the troops was sometimes exhibited in shared emotions, a feature similar to the experiences of journalists attached to the Task Force during the Falklands conflict (see Morrison and Tumber, 1988: Ch. 6).

Jim Axelrod, CBS news correspondent, described how for a few hours each night, when his news organisation's satellite dish was put up to feed video, a phone was attached giving the soldiers five minutes each to call home. Some of the soldiers had not talked to their families since arriving in January 2003, two months earlier:

> I just watched Army Specialist Oscar Barretto Jr. find out that he was a father. Little Oscar III. 7 pounds, 11 ounces. 20 inches. And very cute, his father tells me.
>
> It's a marvellous, moving thing to watch. And a bit Pavlovian. As soon as they hear the generator rumble, indicating the satellite dish is going up, the troops start to line up. In the brutal sun. In the freezing night. Even as a sandstorm bore down on us. They don't move. When they get their turn, they sort of turn their backs on the line, put their heads down, cock them to one side and try to create a little private space to steal a private moment in the midst of these close, communal quarters.
>
> Ten seconds into his call, Specialist Barretto let out a 'whoop'. The rest of the soldiers started badgering him: 'What happened? What happened?' After he told them, a huge cheer exploded across the quiet camp. Now even when I'm not in a war zone, I'm not exactly what you'd call 'steely' when it comes to emotions. Wedding pictures, baby videos, certain reruns of 'The Wonder Years', they can all knock me for a loop. But watching Specialist Barretto sent me over the edge.
>
> His news came on the eve of breaking camp and heading for the border. Everyone was feeling a little tight. Ready to break the long, mind-numbing routine of training, but making acquaintance – many for the first time – with the uncertainty, anxiety and apprehension of approaching combat.
>
> I made a deal with myself to try to avoid thinking too much out here. Save

the deep thoughts for when I get back home. But there it was – laid bare in the Kuwaiti desert. The pure joy of birth. The pure dread of death.

Whatever I see in the next few weeks, watching Specialist Barretto's phone call will remain among the most indelible images. Happy birthday, Oscar III. You should have seen your dad's face when he found out you were here. (Axelrod, 2003b)

Keith Harrison, of the Wolverhampton Express and Star, reporting from Umm Qasr, admitted to the quickness of the socialisation process:

It's been less than a week, but already the experiences of the war have had a startling effect on everyone taking part – and those reporting on it. In our combat kit, we look and sound like soldiers, which is a tribute to the army's embedding system, in which journalists are trained and attached to military units for the duration of a campaign. We answer to the Commanding Officer, we follow orders, we share the rations, we eat where the soldiers eat and we sleep where they sleep. The Royal Logistic Corps – where they go, we go. The military language that first seemed like talk from another world is now our mother tongue. Terms like 'sitrep' (situation report) and 'be advised' have not so much crept into our language as carried out a military coup. Place is now location. Car is always vehicle. Pardon has become 'say again'. ETD, ETA and IAD – estimated time of arrival/departure and immediate action drill – are now used almost constantly as we communicate with the soldiers and officers of the RLC. We know that 'dobhi' is laundry, 'gash' is rubbish and 'chogie' is an is an affectionate term for the local workers. We say ablutions, not toilets, and put up with flies, food and facilities that we would have sniffed at just three short weeks ago. Sniffing at the toilets today would be extremely unwise. The novelty of the American MRE (Meals Ready to Eat or Meals Rejected by Everyone) has long since worn off, but at least we're now experts in heating the food with the chemical packs involved. We're becoming indoctrinated and recognise the sights and sounds of army life instantly. We've endured no fewer than 30 air raids since war began. Many have been false alarms – others have carried the chilling threat: 'Incoming ballistic missile! Take cover! Missile in air!' . . . Hours earlier, when we left our US base, we were given lengthy and frankly disconcerting farewells from those staying behind in reserve. As our vehicle was being prepared, television pictures showed an Iraqi bunker being blown to smithereens at close range by a US tank and I found myself cheering along like a bloodthirsty Dallas cowboy. (Harrison, 2003)

Identification as an issue arose long before the outbreak of the war in March 2003. In November 2002, the Pentagon held the first in a series of week-long training seminars for journalists at a Marine corps base in Quantico, Virginia. More than 50 members of news organisations attended the course, which included staged hostile environment scenarios and instruction on chemical weapons protection.[1] The problem, as Jay de Foore commented, was that:

. . . the course raises as many questions as answers about objectivity, safety and access. (de Foore, 2003)

The *Washington Times* photographer Gerald Herbert was present at the November boot camp and told how the journalists at first enjoyed getting their hands on the new toys, but then some of them quickly realised the dangers of donning all that military gear (de Foore, 2003).

De Foore tells of one incident at the boot camp when, after a demonstration on weaponry, one of the participating photographers took a picture of UPI reporter Pam Hess wearing full battle fatigues and holding an M16 rifle, while a marine at her side gave instructions. When the picture ran in the *International Herald Tribune* the next day, some boot campers began to worry about how they had been perceived by the outside world. Some feared the picture would fuel suspicions that American journalists were working in concert with the American military, a danger made all the more real by the murder of *Wall Street Journal* reporter Daniel Pearl last year (2002) in Pakistan. According to de Foore, on the final night of boot camp the journalists learned they were about to become the subjects:

> . . . in a massive photo op organized by the military. The thought of marching five miles in full gear with still and television cameras documenting their every move spooked many of the journalists there. So before the big event, many decided to present themselves in more of an independent light when the time came for their pictures to be taken. (de Foore, 2003)

As Gerald Herbert commented:

> All of a sudden the media were trying to spin the media. That question was nagging me all week long. It came to a head that day: at what point are we observing and at what point are we participating? (Cited in de Foore, 2003)

According to Herbert some of the journalists used white tape and black markers to designate themselves as press, while others wore jeans and one guy even drew a peace symbol on his shirt:

> In the back of your mind you're wondering how much is too cosy and when do you become your subject. It's a very difficult line and it's still something people are trying to sort out. How much do you assimilate into the military's mode and how much do you maintain a profile of visual separation? (Cited in de Foore, 2003)

The problem of visual separation presented a Catch 22 for embedded journalists. De Foore posed the dilemma:

> If they blend in too much they could be seen as doing the military's bidding, but if they stand out visually they could be an easier target for opposing forces and possibly endanger certain missions. (de Foore, 2003)[2]

According to Victoria Clarke, the Pentagon spokesperson, military units would be making their own rules about how embedded journalists could distinguish themselves. Her ultimate concern was to keep both the media and the military safe.

> An injured journalist is just as much a concern as an injured service member. (Cited in de Foore, 2003)

Jeff Gralnick, a former network news executive who covered the Vietnam War for CBS, thought that the reports from the embeds lacked depth:

> It's a lot of breathy reporting with gas masks on, gas masks off . . . they're saying, the grunts are great and we are moving across the desert at 55 miles per hour. It is very exciting but it doesn't add up to much. (Cited in Swanson, 2003)

Gralnick believed that journalists were embedded in order to be controlled and in a way isolated. Other journalists, though, particularly the ones who were embedded themselves, were much more supportive of the operation.

And James Poniewozik, writing in *Time*, pointed out that many important early operations, like special forces missions, went on without media witnesses and although many of the embedded reporters gave very personal and frightening glimpses of the immediacy of war, all it:

> . . . objectively told us was that somebody somewhere was shooting at someone or something. All that live video sent the stirring message that the planes were unleashing hell, Saddam's palaces were burning, and that Caissons were rolling along. The first days of war, it didn't show us what was behind those telegenic, orange cotton–candy fireballs: dead Iraqi soldiers and civilians. Nor did it answer the big question: was the war going well? Military leaders saw little reason to supplement the television images with concrete information. (Poniewozik, 2003)

Journalist and author Haynes Johnston commented that perspective is something that journalists would have got round in the Falklands by writing books about it afterwards but:

> American correspondents went in with the troops. They landed with the troops. They shared the foxholes and so forth. They went off on bombing runs. Cronkite made bombing runs over Germany. What's different about this, then they could leave and move from place to place. Embedding means you're restricted to one particular unit. In other words, you can't just move back and forth as they did in Vietnam where you go out with the troops. But the American correspondents always went until recently with the troops. That's where you wanted to be. Then you could step back and write an armchair piece of great theory and strategy . . . I think to the Pentagon's credit, they're smart to do it. Have access. The pictures are dramatic. The people are there. We will get stories that we will find out what was happening in the individual units. They won't tell us the whole story of the war. (Online NewsHour, 2003)

But historian Michael Beschloss warned of the dangers should one of the well-known journalists get killed:

> Ernie Pyle was killed in World War II and God forbid if something happened to David Bloom or one of these other embedded reporters that we've seen on television every single day rolling across the desert. Think of what that can be on American support for this war, someone that they have had a emotional connection with, suddenly something horrible happens. It would have an inordinate effect on the way that Americans look at this war and whether we should be there.[3] (Online NewsHour, 2003)

Beschloss makes a very interesting point because previous discussions about the battle for public opinion centred on the dangers of seeing soldiers killed and the effect that may have on the public back home and the degree of support for the war. The constant reporting by journalists 24/7 brings another dimension to the analysis of public morale should a journalist be killed, and especially one who was appearing nightly on the news (see Chapter 3).

The main danger, of course, was that the reporters became so clearly identified with the troops that they began to identify too closely and their reporting became subjective and 'unprofessional'.

A report from the Project for Excellence in Journalism (PEJ) argued that the embedding process was a giant step forward in access, particularly in comparison with the previous conflict in Afghanistan and Gulf War I in 1991. Tom Rosenthal, Project Director, argued that 'On balance this suggests it's a wonderful tool but like any tool you can use it well and you can use it not so well' (PEJ, 2003).

The study looked at more than 40 hours of news coverage on ABC, CBS, NBC, CNN and Fox News and conducted a content analysis of the embedded reports on television during three of the first six days of the war. The coverage, according to the study, was largely anecdotal, and, as one would expect, lacked context, but according to the project study, was unusually rich in detail. The study found, in particular, that:

1  In an age when the press is often criticized for being too interpretative, the overwhelming majority of the embedded stories studied, 94%, were primarily factual in nature.
2  Most of the embedded reports studied – six out of ten – were live and unedited accounts.
3  Viewers were hearing mostly from reporters, not directly from soldiers or other sources. In eight out of ten stories we heard from reporters only.
4  This is battle coverage. Nearly half of the embedded reports – 47% – describe military action or the results.
5  While dramatic, the coverage is not graphic. Not a single story examined showed pictures of people being hit by fired weapons. (PEJ, 2003)

The report came down in favour of the embedding process. They concluded that 'on balance Americans seemed far better served by having the embedding system than they were from more limited press pools during the Gulf War of 1991'[4] (PEJ, 2003: 1).

The report did admit to the problems over whether journalists are 'capable of fully contextualising the news they report', for example in the reports of Oliver North, working for Fox News, in which he talked about remarkable displays of humanitarianism by US armed forces, or remarkable displays of military prowess on the part of Marines.

> The problem is that the embedded reporter surrounded by US troops may need to be careful about adopting terminology carefully chosen by military strategists to win hearts and minds. (PEJ, 2003)

An additional problem is that:

> . . . the challenge for news organisations and for viewers is knowing how to leaven the embedded reporting with the other information available. (PEJ, 2003)

To a large degree the networks were able to do this in their traditional half-hour nightly newscasts. The PEJ report acknowledges that the PBS's 'NewsHour' with Jim Lehrer was particularly effective in doing this by using repeated summaries during the newscast to remind viewers of the larger developments of the day. The challenge is obviously far greater for the cable channels and easiest for print.

Citing ABC News, who began to produce promotions for its evening newscast by advertising that ABC News was covering the war 24-hours a day, but that viewers could get that reporting on 'World News Tonight' in 30 minutes, they said:

> In the age of the new media culture, not being on 24-hours a day is now offered as a value.' (PEJ, 2003)

## Post Assessment

Commenting on coverage of the war, Victoria Clarke confirmed that Pentagon officials were pleased with the results of embedding about 700 journalists with troops in Iraq and would like to see the programme in future conflicts.

> 'I am quite confident that people feel so good about this process that they want it to continue, we are aware that military officials liked having reporters along because it allowed the American public to get a better view of what was happening and a better appreciation for the military. The reporting also countered Iraqi propaganda and dampened certain guessing of the war by American commentators'. (Cited in Kelley, 2003)

The government and military will no doubt conduct further evaluation of the embedding process. One thing they have received is the thumbs-up from the public relations (PR) industry. Kate Delahaye Paine, writing in the *International Newsletter of PR Measurement,* stated:

> The current war has been called the best-covered war in history, and certainly the visuals and reports from 'embedded' reporters have been spectacular, bringing war into our living rooms like never before . . . this is a brilliant strategy and could well change the face of PR forever. After less than desirable coverage during Desert Storm and disastrous coverage of Mogadishu, the Department of Defense learned from its mistakes: 'No comment' is the wrong answer. So, starting with the war in Afghanistan, the army began opening its kimono more and more to the media.
>
> And the embedded reporter tactic is sheer genius. Most journalists go into their profession because they want to know what's really going on behind the scenes. And there's nothing that brings out the lust for behind-the-scenes knowledge like a war.
>
> Taking reporters from behind the lines and putting them on the front lines was an offer the media couldn't resist. They went through the basic training and are now reporting back from within the armed forces. The sagacity of the tactic is that it is based on the basic tenet of public relations: It's all about relationships. The better the relationship any of us has with a journalist, the better the chance of that journalist picking up and reporting our messages.
>
> So now we have journalists making dozens – if not hundreds – of new friends among the armed forces. And, if the bosses of their new-found buddies want to get a key message or two across about how sensitive the US is being to humanitarian needs or how humanely they are treating Iraqis, what better way than through these embedded journalists? As a result, most (if not all) of the dozens of stories being filed contain key messages the Department of Defense wants to communicate . . . The truth is, it's a win–win situation. We are getting more and better coverage of war than ever before, journalists are getting better access than ever before and the coalition is getting more messages across than ever before . . . The lesson here is the same for business as it is for the military: treat reporters as human beings, train them, give them access, let them develop the relationships – and chances are good you'll get your messages across. (Paine, 2003)

The embedding process was carefully managed and well prepared. It was planned long in advance of Gulf War II, and evaluations and refinements are already under way for future conflicts.[5]

In October 2003, the United States Army War College's Centre for Strategic Leadership conducted a workshop entitled 'Reporters on the Ground: The Military and the Media's Joint Experience During Operation Iraqi Freedom.' The discussions focused on three main areas:

1  The military–media ground rules, building trust, and the consequences of breaking that trust between soldiers and reporters.

2 The military's use of the media in the conduct of information operations.
3 'Battle After Next' as a dispersed battle space with heavy use of robotics and aerial manoeuvres.

Brigadier General Vince Brooks, US Central Command spokesperson during the conflict, addressed the workshop and Major General J.D. Thurman, chief of operations for the land component commander, presented his view of the strategic aspect of the media-military relationship during the planning for and execution of Operation Iraqi Freedom. The workshop made five recommendations:

1 *Ground Rules*  All parties – military and media alike – concluded the 'eight page' list of ground rules was too lengthy to be of practical use. Most felt that a simple discussion between public affairs officers, their commanders and their embedded media representatives could identify workable parameters. In fact, most present indicated that was what they did anyway. The group recommended that embedded journalists write a follow-on set of rules distribute them to all participates to review and subsequent DoD approval.
2 *Training*  Recommendations were made from both military and media representatives to toughen the predeployment media training and to make it available to potential embeds quarterly. This recommendation seeks to build a bench of qualified reporters who are certified to deploy on very short notice. An associated recommendation is for units to invite media members to embed with them during training at both their home station and the National Training Center to begin to build the trust that is so important to the process.
3 *Media self-policing*  The issues of censure and discipline of the news media (embedded and unilateral) was discussed several times. In all discussions, the point that the media is better at this task than the military was driven home; however, self-censure by non-US journalists was not discussed. It was recommended that the media continue to develop procedures that could be accepted and implemented industry-wide within the US, and perhaps internationally. All media present were unanimous in their support for this concept.
4 *Permanent Embedding*  Recommend that the military follow the examples of police departments, sports teams and political campaigns and have permanently embedded reporters. None of the embeds seemed to think that this would compromise their objectivity. Cost to media companies may restrict participation with units.
5 *Military Casualty Reporting*  The now-instantaneous nature of communications and reporting and fellow soldiers with access to e-mail and satellite phones have challenged the military's very deliberate casualty reporting and notification system. First reports can be wrong; however, the military needs to review the technology available today to improve the notification process.

The conclusion stated:

> The embedded media program placed journalists, soldiers, and marines together in the same environment. Under such circumstances whether reporters can or cannot be objective may be irrelevant. What is important is the trust and confidence built between those embattled soldiers and the embedded media that accompany and report on them and their actions. This unique kind of war reporting appears to have won the trust and confidence of the American public. Such success increases the burden on both the military and the media to ensure continued integrity of the reporting within a program that has heightened the expectations of the American public. (CSL, 2003)

Whether reporters can or cannot be objective is, of course, not irrelevant at all. The public need to be aware under what conditions and circumstances they receive information. The integrity of that information is important for both news editors and the public. The danger for journalists in becoming participants as opposed to observers is how to respond when events in the course of a conflict force a choice between a professional commitment and loyalty to the troops.

The well-known war correspondent Chris Hedges believes that the 'participant journalist is structurally and socially inevitably becoming an additional agent of the lies that characterise information in wartime'. Talking of the embedded journalists, he wrote:

> These journalists do not have access to their own transportation. They depend on the military for everything, from food to a place to sleep. They look to the soldiers around them for protection. When they feel the fear of hostile fire, they identify and seek to protect those who protect them. They become part of the team. It is a natural reaction. I have felt it.
>
> But in that experience, these journalists become participants in the war effort. They want to do their bit. And their bit is the dissemination of myth, the myth used to justify war and boost the morale of the soldiers and civilians. The lie in wartime is almost always the lie of omission. The blunders by our generals – whom the mythmakers always portray as heroes – along with the rank corruption and perversion, are masked from public view. The intoxication of killing, the mutilation of enemy dead, the murder of civilians and the fact that war is not about what they claim is ignored. But in wartime don't look to the press, or most of it, for truth. The press has another purpose.
>
> Perhaps this is not conscious. I doubt the journalists filing the hollow reports from Iraq, in which there are images but rarely any content, are aware of how they are being manipulated. They, like everyone else, believe. But when they look back they will find that war is always about betrayal. It is about betrayal of the young by the old, of soldiers by politicians and of idealists by the cynical men who wield power, the ones who rarely pay the cost of war. We pay that cost. And we will pay it again. (Hedges, 2003)

When journalists are embedded with the military their future becomes entwined with that of the troops they are accompanying. What becomes important to the troops also matters to the journalists. Morrison and Tumber related the experiences of journalists during the Falklands conflict:

> It was not just a question of sharing the moods of the troops through shared experience, but of actively beginning to identify with them by being part of the whole exercise. Consequently, although some of the journalists disagreed with the decision to send the Task Force, once it was likely that there would be a battle, they felt an affinity with the troops, a shared determination to see the venture through to the end. (Morrison and Tumber, 1988: 97)

For some of the reporters in Gulf War II, like their predecessors in the Falklands, their experiences living alongside the military were reflected in their copy. Chris Ayres of *The Times* recognised his emotions and the impossibility of remaining detached. In writing about Marines shooting Iraqis who failed to stop at a checkpoint, he wrote:

> To the Marines – and to me – there was nothing gung-ho about it. It was simply survival. Of course, I was hardly objective: as a journalist embedded with a frontline artillery unit, my chances of avoiding death at the hands of suicide bombers were directly linked to the Marines' ability to kill the enemy. (Cited in Mangan, 2003: 7)

In effect, what was happening to Ayres and other journalists was similar to what happened to some of their professional colleagues in previous conflicts. Their professional requirement to cover a story in a detached way was slowly being swamped by the very real, human need to belong, to be safe (see Morrison and Tumber, 1988: Ch. 6).

Journalists were slowly being enveloped into an unfamiliar occupational world of the military from which there was no chance of distancing themselves. And that is when problems emerge. The values that normally provide journalists with a protective shield are replaced with kindred values grown of closeness, and that means entering a world of professional uncertainty.

## Notes

1 Some news organisations eschewed the military sponsored training camps and sent their correspondents to those run by private companies. See Chapter 4.
2 For first-person accounts of journalists' experiences at 'boot camp', see Arsenault, 2002 Parts 1, 2 and 3; Koopman, 2003; Mazzetti, 2003; Schlesinger, 2003; Yago, 2003.
3 Tragically David Bloom of NBC died of a pulmonary embolism two weeks later whilst working in the war zone.
4 The study examined stories from embedded reporters on three of the first six days of coverage, 21, 22 and 24 March. They examined the traditional key viewing hours for news each day, 7 a.m. to 9 a.m. on the three major broadcast

networks and two cable channels, as well as the evening news programmes for the broadcast networks and the analogous hour-long evening news programmes on cable.

5   See, for example, 'Embedded Media Travel – Embedding Rules', written in 1998 at http://call.army.mil/products/trngqtr/tq4-98/duckwrth.htm.

# 5

## INFORMATION MANAGEMENT

Information planning by the US government before the war was based on a 24-hour news cycle, a kind of global PR network to be activated from different parts of the world, from the Pentagon, from Qatar and from the embedded journalists.[1]

Suzy DeFrancis, President Bush's deputy assistant for communications, outlined the media relations that were to be introduced:

> When Americans wake up in the morning, they will first hear from the [Persian Gulf] region, maybe from General Tommy Franks, then later in the day, they will hear from the Pentagon, then the State Department, then later on the White House will brief. (Cited in Quenqua, 2003)

Before anyone went on air, the White House Press Secretary, Ari Fleischer, would set the day's message with an early morning conference call to Alastair Campbell (Tony Blair's then Director of Communications and Strategy), a conference call to White House communications director Dan Bartlett, State Department spokesperson Richard Boucher, Pentagon spokesperson Victoria Clarke, and White House Office of Global Communications (OGC) Director, Tucker Eskew. This was a routine that was similar to the procedures introduced during the conflict in Afghanistan (Quenqua, 2003).

In the UK the Ministry of Defence (MoD) cemented its existing media staff in the MoD headquarters and throughout parts of the forces. Lt Colonel Angus Taverner, the director of news media operations policy, had a remit to co-ordinate the military and civilian press functions within the MoD. The MoD then set up a core press office of 24 people in London headed by Director of News Pam Teare with, according to reports, more than a hundred media reservists called up with secondary roles to act as media operators when needed. Some of these worked in UK operations while others were deployed to the Middle East as part of a 160-strong public relations office contingency (Williams, 2003).

According to Taverner, the MoD was torn between fulfilling its public duty to keep the British public informed and that of keeping issues of national security closely guarded:

> We learned in Kosovo, when there were a lot of incorrect accusations made against NATO by the Milosovic regime, that the media won't wait, and the timeliness of our response is key. The one battle we lost in the Falklands was

the media battle, and it produced a lot of work in its wake. By the time we got to the last Gulf War, people thought we had come a long way but we still haven't got everything right. (Cited in Williams, 2003)

It is evident that the experiences of the government and military in Kosovo were important in the operations developed for Gulf War II.

According to James Reuben, the North Atlantic Treaty Organisation (NATO) developed a number of techniques to co-ordinate the management of mass information, which have since become standard practice. Among the most notable is the conference call involving ministers and press secretaries from five or six countries who would speak a couple of times a day in a bid to keep 'on message'.

Some people were too quick to put out information that was proven to be inaccurate – we learned that the key was to take a deep breath, get all your facts straight and then explain it. We realized later that we should have had the briefing centres based with the military rather than NATO. The military tend to be the best briefers – they are very comfortable and explain the details in useable form and tend not to cover the facts. (Williams, 2003)

The main source of complaint from journalists was the US Central Command at Camp As Sayliyah, Qatar. The US military set up a $1.5 million briefing centre complete with plasma screens, mini studios and banks of phones. The Pentagon enlisted one of Hollywood's top art directors, George Allison, to create a set for General Tommy Franks and other US commanders to give their daily updates.

White House and Pentagon correspondents also felt irritations with the information flow, as is apparent from this attempt to deflect them. On 20 March 2003, at the start of the US-led campaign, Ari Fleischer, the White House press spokesperson, in reply to reporters' questions stated:

Let me back up one step. I've been getting many questions from the press, as is appropriate at a time like this for what the press calls tick-tock, or what people understand as tell us everything that happened and every step along the way, how decisions were made, which, of course, is an issue of very important historical value. As you can imagine, the military planners – Secretary Rumsfeld, Dr Rice, the Vice President – the people who are in the room with the President for these meetings are focused on other things right now. They are focused on winning a war. That's their first mission and that's where their time is being spent. I have confidence that at the appropriate time, we will have sufficient information to pass along, more of a tick-tocky nature that is appropriate and is important, and it's the White House's determination to try to provide it. But at this point, I'm very constrained in how much detail I can get into as a result of what the principals are spending their time on. (Fleischer, 2003)

Information management at the media centre in Doha, Qatar, did not get off to a very auspicious beginning. It was some days into the conflict before the first briefing took place and it was held on the Saturday following the start of the bombing of Baghdad on early Thursday morning (20 March). Journalists were warned by US Navy Captain Frank Thorp, Central Command spokesperson, that even once the briefings started journalists should not expect them to be able to confirm or deny every report from the field. He added that spokespersons at Central Command would not be able to keep up with the frenzy of site-specific information coming from embedded journalists (Bauder, 2003a).

In Doha, each briefing session began with a 'bullish statement' about the state of the war and videos depicting precision bombing by US forces. Questions on reports from the battlefield by senior US officers concerning stretched supply lines, troop numbers and Iraqi resistance either went unanswered or were contradicted in Doha by junior officers (IPI, 2003).

Brigadier General Brooks, the chief US spokesperson at Central Command in Qatar, fronted the briefings and as Richard McGregor who reported from there for the *Financial Times* remarked:

> So metronomically on message was Brooks that you felt as if you might have found a cyborg inside if you opened him up. (McGregor, 2003: 8)

Journalists became very irritated and critical of the media centre operations. In a piece for the *New York Review*, Michael Massing describes the frustrations experienced by the correspondents based there:

> The Coalition Media Centre, at the Saliyah military base in Doha, Qatar, seems designed to be as annoying and inconvenient as possible for reporters. To get there from the centre of town, you have to take a half-hour ride through a baking, barren expanse of desert. At the gate, you have to submit your electronic equipment to a K-9 search, your bags to inspection, and your body to an X-ray scan. You then have to wait under the scorching sun for a military escort, who, after checking your credentials, takes you to the press bus. When the bus is full, you're driven the 200 yards to the media centre. The bus lets you off in a concrete courtyard surrounded by a seven-foot high wall topped by barbed wire. If you stand on a ledge and look out, you'll see two rows of identical warehouse-like buildings – the offices of General Tommy Franks and the US Central Command. Journalists, though, never get inside these buildings, for they're restricted to the windowless media centre, which is 60 feet long, brightly lit, and heavily air-conditioned. (Massing, 2003: 16)[2]

Access to the media centre for journalists was gained via a military pass which could have been withdrawn at any time.

Jeff Meade, the Sky News correspondent based in the Qatar centre, similarly described how they would have to spend the first hour of each day going through security checks which included full body x-ray scrutiny by dogs trained to sniff explosives. He also described the atmosphere as a sense of unreal detachment in the million pound air-conditioned media suite compared to what was happening in Iraq's towns and deserts 600 miles to the north. Most of the time they spent talking to one another or watching everybody else's stories on television.

Meade remarked on the hierarchical nature of the seating plan in the hi-tech briefing centre at Central Command. According to Meade, front row chairs under the eye-line of the generals at the gun-metal grey podium were the most prized, with those front row chairs going mainly to the television broadcasters:

> In a pecking order as precise and closely studied as the place cards at a royal banquet, the prime spots go to the international television news agencies, serving hundreds of channels and millions of viewers but without resources to send around crews. Then, counting outwards are the five US networks. British are next, as befits the biggest of the four partner nations allied in the American-led war. I inhabit the part of the front stalls earning a reputation as the awkward squad. My name/neighbour is Omar Assaweh, of Qatar-based al-Jazeera. On the other side is ITV News's Kevin Dunn. (Meade, 2003)

Network correspondents sitting in the front rows of the briefing room were allowed to ask the first questions. After that:

> Brooks skilfully employed affirmative action, picking out reporters from more obscure regions who had their questions bounced by satellite around the world. (MacGregor, 2003)

Some blamed the fact that the central command in Qatar was run by the US military and that if the British had been in charge things would have been done differently. Meade, for example, contrasted the highly-structured and restrictive American approach to dealing with journalists compared with the British.

> Broadly they tell us nothing, preferring we should focus all our enquiries on the hour-long news conferences, becoming a live broadcast feature in each day of the war. The British officers' good humour and greater approachability has made them as much favourites with the media as their on-camera spokesmen have become with audiences at home . . . it's often true, the Brits do not actually say much more than the Americans and are too professional ever to reveal more than they intend. But their impromptu corridor conferences are always well intended even if their office, next to the ever busy lavatories, doesn't enjoy the most fragrant location. It is obviously a testing and tiring time covering a fast changing story with 24-hour outlets. To keep our spirits up there is an in-house cappuccino bar, and even a souvenir shop. (Cited in Meade, 2003).

David Howard of the UK Ministry of Defence more or less agreed:

> Central Command in Qatar was clearly an American-led operation. We admit there are issues arising out of Qatar, that's why we're looking at that at the moment. If we'd been a UK command we would have given context-setting briefings. We believe there are lessons we need to learn from the way the

operation ran, we need to look closely at it. There are issues about the quality of make up of our media personnel. (Cited in Byrne, 2003d)

Paul Adams of the BBC, describing his frustrations in Doha, also remarked that he was more fortunate (in information terms) than his US colleagues. In his reporter's log he wrote:

Others will have dug themselves foxholes, seen soldiers physically sick with fear, felt, seen and heard the reality of war. But some of us have led a very different existence these past weeks. A daily shuttle, hundreds of miles from the action, from a comfortable hotel to the press centre at the drab As-Sayliyah military base, home to CentCom's forward headquarters. And while we allowed ourselves to say 'here at CentCom', we knew that we were being held at arm's length. We were rarely allowed to stray from the spartan warehouse with its hi-tech briefing room and cramped, woefully inadequate work-spaces. The real business of running the war was taking place in other, equally spartan warehouses some distance away in this vast, faceless facility. It is an odd way to cover a war, and some wondered if it was really worth it. But while our American colleagues tore their hair out at the lack of information beyond the daily – and rather anodyne – briefings from the unflappable Brigadier-General Vince Brooks, we in the British media were more fortunate. We were extensively briefed, on and off the record, in a way that enabled us to gain some precious appreciation of what was going on in Iraq. So for weeks, I strained to hear what my 'embedded' colleagues were saying from their grubby foxholes, and tried to marry that with notes taken during furtive conversations held in the shade of the concrete blocks that hemmed us into our media pen. By and large, it worked. I felt I understood what was going on. At times, I was given fascinating – and not always reportable – insights into the campaign. And as events unfolded far to the north, I did not feel so disconnected after all. (Adams, 2003)

However, comments about the information coming from the British were often less than complimentary too. According to reports, journalists from Britain felt so starved of information that they put up a sign with a recurring remark uttered in briefings by British forces commander Air Marshal Brian Burridge:

We don't do detail. (IPI, 2003)

The general complaint amongst journalists at the US Central Command in Qatar was that they got more spin than news. After a while journalists, openly contemptuous of the daily proceedings that US General Tommy Franks called a 'platform for truth', began to withdraw (IPI, 2003). Alan Sipress of the *Washington Post* put it down to information management:

At daily news conferences and private briefings, senior Central Command officials have been more determined to paint Iraqi forces in the darkest light possible than to shed light on the embattled progress of the military campaign. (Cited in IPI, 2003)

Whilst acknowledging the obfuscation of the military command, Jeff Meade drew a distinction between what he viewed as his and his colleagues' own robust approach to journalism and the more polite enquiries of the American correspondents:

> 'Much more of that, and you'll be at the back with the French and Germans,' muttered one colleague after my question challenged coalition commander General Tommy Franks about how bombarded civilians were expected to greet his forces as liberators. (Meade, 2003)

## War on the Media: Casualties and Prisoners of War

Whilst journalists in Qatar were experiencing the frustrations of trying to gather information and were involved in arguments with the military about the lack of information, a large public row over media coverage was taking place back in the US and the UK. If the first media skirmish of the war was about the presentation (or lack of it) of the 'big picture' (see Chapter 2), one of the major media battles centred on the graphic portrayal of casualties and prisoners of war.

At a meeting on 27 February – before the invasion began – the US Department of Defense spokesperson Bryan Whitman alerted bureau chiefs that the reporting of coalition causalities was the most sensitive area of news from the government's perspective:

> The issue has to do with the timing and identification of casualties. In the ground rules your reporters will see that reporting on casualties obviously is permitted, but there are safeguards and conditions within the ground rules to try to prevent identification of battlefield casualties in real time. In other words, the sensitivity here is trying to allow the next-of-kin procedures to be able to get to family members and notify them of injured or killed family members prior to the first notification of it being in real time in the television coverage or a news story or a wire story that goes out there.
>
> So we've tried to strike a balance that allows you to cover those varied realities of warfare and combat. But we've asked you to do it in a way that is sensitive to our needs to be able to communicate to our family members those type of tragic incidents that might occur on the battlefield. (Whitman, 2003b)

It was not long before controversy arose. The US and British governments attacked news organisations and in particular al-Jazeera for showing pictures of two dead British soldiers and two British prisoners of war. The soldiers were said to have been killed and captured around the town of al-Zubayr. Al-Jazeera showed two dead bodies in military uniform lying next to a vehicle in a road, and two live men out of uniform in a room full of Iraqis.[3] Tim Howell-Lockwood, a British military spokesperson in Qatar, criticised the broadcasting of the footage, saying:

I find the pictures abhorrent. It is against all protocols of the Geneva Convention . . . I hope very much it is pulled immediately. (Cited in BBC News, 2003b)

Tony Blair, the British prime minister, condemned the showing of these pictures, expressing horror at the deaths and the decision to broadcast footage of the corpses. In their defence, a spokesperson for al-Jazeera stated:

The way we assess news is very simple. Its news worthiness is assessed first then it's put through a process of verification to check its authenticity. Then it's checked for relevance. We do not broadcast footage for any other reason than news worthiness and relevance and certainly not for the hell of it. When that footage was originally broadcast it was deemed to be news worthy and relevant. As for showing it again, that will also depend on news worthiness and relevance. We have lots of news of more immediate relevance and we won't be running it for the hell of it, it will depend on the view of the senior producer at the time. (Cited in Deans, 2003a)

The controversy started a few days earlier when al-Jazeera relayed footage of Iraqi television interviews with five captured American soldiers. The US Defence Secretary Donald Rumsfeld, condemned the broadcast as a breach of the Geneva Convention. Al-Jazeera was also criticised for showing pictures of injured and dead civilians – casualties of the American attacks on Iraq.

The International Committee of the Red Cross (ICRC) condemned the footage of captured US soldiers, originally broadcast on Iraqi television, stating that it violated the Geneva Convention. ICRC also condemned the showing of Iraqis surrendering to American and British forces by news organisations. However, the British Defence Secretary Geoff Hoon drew a distinction between the pictures shown by Iraq and western news organisations:

There is an enormous difference . . . between the factual photographs, very often of the backs of prisoners surrendering (as US forces show) as against the barbaric behaviour of Iraqi forces dealing with American prisoners. (Cited in BBC News, 2003b).[4]

The Pentagon had requested US networks not show any video footage of dead and captured American service personnel.

Out of respect for the families and consistent with the principles of the Geneva Convention, we request news organisations not to air or publish recognizable images or audio recordings that identify POWs. (Cited in Wells and Campbell, 2003)

Most western broadcasters conceded to requests from the Pentagon not to show pictures until the families of soldiers had been informed.[5] As names leaked out or relatives identified themselves, some footage was shown and

CNN decided to show brief audio and video footage while avoiding images which they said would distress relatives. The *New York Times*, *Washington Post*, *Philadelphia Enquirer*, *Boston Globe*, and *USA Today* were among those declining to run photos from the al-Jazeera videotape of the captives. However, other newspapers, including the *Washington Times*, *New York Daily News*, the *Chicago Tribune* and *Los Angeles Times*, used the photos (Kurtz, 2003b).

Welsey Pruden, chief editor of the *Washington Times*, justified the publication on the grounds that:

> It shows the American public the true face of the enemy, who we're dealing with that they would take these pictures and treat them like that. (Cited in Kurtz, 2003b)

And John Carroll, *Los Angeles Times* editor, insisted on even-handness:

> We've run pictures of prisoners taken by both sides, it's a war, and we're supposed to cover the whole thing, not just part of it. (Cited in Kurtz, 2003b)

Other editors, though, were more reluctant to show the pictures. *Washington Post* editor Leonard Downey was circumspect on the issue:

> We are relatively conservative here, period, about pictures of dead people, people under duress of any kind. We're always having to make decisions of that kind . . . I think: try to behave like someone's house guest. (Cited in Kurtz, 2003b)

Downey's reluctance, though, only lasted a day once notifications to the family had taken place.

CBS played the video tape of American prisoners of war that had been made available by al-Jazeera. On the programme 'Face the Nation', Donald Rumsfeld had been denying media reports that at least ten American soldiers were captured or missing in Iraq. It was at that point that CBS played the video tape and Rumsfeld was asked by the interviewer Bob Schieffer what he made of that: 'I've no idea,' Rumsfeld replied. During a commercial break, Victoria Clarke, the Pentagon spokesperson, asked CBS executives to blur the soldiers' faces, which the network did during the second airing. The episode sparked self-examination on behalf of CBS. Schieffer said:

> I think in retrospect we should have waited. We probably shouldn't have shown the faces and allowed [one soldier] to say his name. It was just one of those split second decisions you make in the news business. (Cited in Kurtz, 2003a and b)

The episode sparked disagreements within ABC. Anchor Charles Gibson told viewers that it was disrespectful to show the dead bodies whereas Ted Koppel, the well-known ABC journalist embedded with the troops, argued:

> Because the media are 'jimmyin up patriotic feelings' before a war, I feel we do have an obligation to remind people in the most graphic way that war is a dreadful thing . . . young Americans are dying. Young Iraqis are dying. To turn our faces away from that is a mistake . . . to sanitize it too much is a dreadful mistake. (Cited in Kurtz, 2003b)

Some commentators in the US condemned al-Jazeera as more of a political organisation than a media outlet. One commentator called it 'Jihad TV'. Walid Phares, a professor of Middle East studies at Florida Atlantic University, has called their operations 'an electronic Fatwa' (Phares, 2003). Images are always very contentious in times of war because of concerns over public opinion. Some newspapers were criticised by readers for showing pictures of Iraqi military and civilian deaths on the grounds that they were too sympathetic to the Iraqi cause. John Woolcott, Washington bureau chief for Knight Ridder newspapers, argued:

> Our reporters are encouraged to cover everything they see. It is our responsibility to show the face of war no matter what it looks like. (Cited in Strupp, 2003b)

Tim Connolly, international editor of the *Dallas Morning News*, defended his editorial position over the page one photo of the market bombing in Baghdad that his paper had run:

> We have gotten some criticism that our coverage is too sympathetic to Iraqi civilians. I have heard comments that we should pay more attention to our troops. Some people view coverage of the victims of war as being anti-war, but we think it is something we've got to report on. (Cited in Strupp, 2003b)

Other newspapers took a similar stance. *USA Today*, for example, had a number of complaints after it had run a picture of dead Iraqi soldiers on its front page on 23 March. Several of the readers had asked why the paper did not replace it with the inside photo of a US soldier walking with several smiling Iraqi children (see Strupp, 2003b). In response, Brian Gallagher, *USA Today* executive editor stated:

> We looked at both photos, one showed a bloody scene and the other was very benign. Given the bloodshed that day we did not think it was very responsible to show the more benign photo on page 1. (Cited in Strupp, 2003b)[6]

Attitudes towards dead Iraqi civilians or troops could not be more different from attitudes towards coalition casualties and prisoners of war. When al-Jazeera showed such pictures, they were accused of violations of the Geneva Convention; when US media showed them, they were accused of sympathy for the enemy.

Arguments over the showing of casualties and prisoners of war frequently arise during war and conflict. The battle for public opinion is the key element in the information war. In the following chapters we explore this further by examining media coverage through three stages of the conflict.

## Notes

1  Psyops campaigns were also in operation by US and UK governments; see, for example, BBC News 2003d; Edwards, 2003; Knightley, 2003. For discussion of psychological operations during operation Enduring Freedom; see Taylor, 2003; for discussion of propaganda and persuasion during Gulf War I, see Taylor, 1997; and for discussion of British propaganda during the twentieth century, see Taylor, 1999.

2  See also Michael Wolff (2003a; 2003b) for accounts of life at the Media Centre in Doha.

3  Richard Sambrook, head of BBC News, stated that when the BBC was carrying live reports from embedded journalists in the Gulf, it had the option of introducing a 30-second delay to prevent graphic images being broadcast (Deans, 2003c).

4  Article 13 of the Geneva Convention states 'prisoners of war must at all times be protected, particularly against acts of violence or intimidation and against insults and public curiosity'.

5  One view is that the relevant part of the Geneva Convention about Article 13 of the Third Convention only applies to states and since al-Jazeera and other news organisations are not states, then the Article does not apply to them. The argument becomes a moral one rather than a legal one. This is an argument in regard to the showing of the prisoners at Guantanamo Bay where the US classified them as unlawful combatants, thereby bypassing the cover of prisoners of war under the Geneva Convention.

6  Tim Goodman argues that it's the print reporters that are providing the flesh and blood stories, the quotes and descriptions that sear. 'When television says four Americans died in a firefight, it's the print reporters who end up with the details: bullet in the neck, shot in the hands, back and head; blown apart by rocket-propelled grenade. That's what sticks with you. Or a snapshot of a limbless child. Television somehow lost its visceral connection to the home' (Goodman, 2003).

# PART II

## Media Coverage

In this part, the focus changes from institutional arrangements for reporting war to media coverage of the Iraq crisis. Most of the data refer primarily to the UK press; however, there is analysis of the television news coverage of the military phase of the conflict (Chapter 7), and reference is also made to elements of media coverage in other nations' media systems.

The analysis is divided into three time periods: the pre-invasion phase (November 2002 to March 2003); the invasion phase (20 March to late April 2003); and the post-invasion phase (1 May 2003 onwards).

The analysis of the pre-invasion period is both quantitative and qualitative. The quantitative analysis considers the extent to which the UK press was favourable or unfavourable to the policy initiatives that came from Washington, initiatives which were largely adopted by the UK government. Analysis is restricted to the UK press, and to the period beginning with the preparations for the UN resolution that demanded Iraqi compliance with weapons inspections (Resolution 1441) and that finished at the point when it became clear that the divergence between UK/US and French/German/Russian policy would prevent a second consensual resolution being passed (early March 2003).[1] This analysis essentially seeks to assess to what extent the UK press was supportive of US/UK policy. The qualitative analysis extends the quantitative analysis by exploring details of certain dominant themes in the reporting, as well as some near-silences. Here the primary focus is the internal articulation of the thematic material and inter-channel differences that cannot be observed through the quantitative indicators.

Analysis of media coverage of the invasion phase of the crisis is primarily quantitative, and considers a sample of both UK television news and the UK national press. Quantitative analysis was the main research tool for various reasons. First, research assistants were used in the data gathering, and the instructions to them needed the type of precision associated with quantitative analysis. Second, analysis of both broadcast and print media demanded an analytic scheme capable of delivering comparability. Third, various other quantitative analyses were published during the preparation of this book, and comparisons between the data sets is useful: while it is true that these coding schemes were not identical (and in one case is a commercial secret), a comparison between quantitative analyses is more consistent than a comparison between quantitative and qualitative analyses.

The analysis of the post-invasion phase is entirely qualitative. The focus is primarily on the selection of themes that constitute the main emphases of reporting, and especially on the way in which they relate to each other. The output of a sample of the UK national press for the months of May and June has been systematically analysed, and other elements of media output appear as they became relevant to the themes under analysis. The sample of titles is the same as for the pre-invasion phase (*Daily Mirror*, *Daily Mail*, *Daily Telegraph*, *Guardian* and their Sunday equivalents). Inevitably, the choice of themes was in part dictated by the events that acquired significance in the period of preparation of this book. In this way, it has been possible to use retrospection to illuminate the significance of elements of media reporting that might not have been visible in the analysis if a quantitative scheme had been adopted at the outset, which would have set exclusive parameters.

## Note

The analysis of the pre-invasion phase was commissioned by the Belgian journal *Médiatiques* as part of a comparative international study. The research question ('What is the image of the USA in national media system x?') was devised by the editorial board and common to all the studies. The study was to be delivered by the end of April, 2003 for publication in the summer (Lits, 2003a). This origin explains certain features of the design of the quantitative analysis reported here, especially the time sample. The qualitative analysis considers the coverage in a wider frame.

# 6

## THE PRE-INVASION PHASE

The following pages show the results of a quantitative and qualitative content analysis carried out on a sample of the UK national press during the period November 2002 to March 2003. Titles used as the basis of the sample were: *Daily Telegraph*, *Guardian*, *Daily Mail* and *Daily Mirror*. This sample is representative of the nationally-circulating press in terms of spread of political alignment and distribution by media sector. All articles mentioning the word 'Iraq' during the stated timeframe were downloaded from a web version of the titles. Many of these articles only mentioned Iraq in a marginal fashion, in the context of a theme other than the crisis; the percentage of all articles mentioning Iraq, but not mainly about the Iraq crisis, ranged by title from 40% to 60%. These articles were excluded from the analysis.

The analysis records the numbers of positive/negative mentions of US policy and related matters during this period in a stratified sample of articles which had the Iraq crisis as their main theme; the sample amounts to approximately 10% of articles having the Iraq crisis as their main theme, in each title. Articles are drawn from both news reporting and comment/analysis pages. The analysis sets out the distribution of these positive/negative mentions across four identified sub-themes:

1  Policy options.
2  US motives.
3  US relationships with allies.
4  Outcomes of US policy.

### Negative and Positive Mentions of US Policy

Table 6.1 shows the overall distribution of all negative and positive mentions by title, and shows that the political alignment of the newspapers is associated directly with the balance between negative and positive mentions of US policy. It is also striking that during this period the left-wing titles consistently gave more space to the Iraq crisis than did the right-wing papers.[1] The distribution by media sector (broadsheet/tabloid) reveals no intra-sector common features in this respect.

If we aggregate the left and right titles, the pattern is more visible (see Table 6.2). Looking at Tables 6.1 and 6.2 together, the two right-wing titles

**TABLE 6.1** All mentions, negative and positive, by title. Percentage distribution

|  | Negative % | Positive % | Total n |
|---|---|---|---|
| Daily Telegraph | 43 | 57 | 915 |
| Guardian | 55 | 45 | 1771 |
| Daily Mail | 41 | 59 | 652 |
| Daily Mirror | 70 | 30 | 1025 |

Note: One mention = one paragraph.

**TABLE 6.2** All mentions, negative and positive by political alignment. Percentage distribution (averages of Table 6.1)

|  | Negative | Positive |
|---|---|---|
| Left (Guardian, Daily Mirror) | 62.5 | 37.5 |
| Right (Daily Telegraph, Daily Mail) | 42 | 58 |

show a very similar pattern – each is within 1% of their average in both positive and negative distributions; however, the left-wing titles are rather divergent in this respect: the balance between positive and negative mentions in the *Guardian* is very different from that in the *Mirror* (the divergence = 7.5%), even though both are predominantly negative. The *Mirror* is by far the most negative of the titles analysed, reflecting a clear editorial decision to campaign directly against US policy from an early stage of the crisis. Thus editorial policy, in association with long-term political alignment, is clearly a determinant of the balance between positive and negative mentions in this matter.

## Thematic Analysis

Support for/criticism of the US position on Iraq is clearly related to political alignment and editorial policy. However, support and criticism can also be seen in relation to the spread of thematic material that constituted the 'story' of the Iraq crisis in general. The content analysis was based upon the distribution of four themes, which were partly *a priori* in the sense that they could apply to more or less any similar crisis (themes 1, 2 and 4), and were partly derived from a preliminary scan of the press material collected for this analysis (theme 3). The themes, and the principles distinguishing negative from positive mentions, are shown in Table 6.3.

The purpose of division of material into themes was to see if any correlations – by title, political alignment or media sector – emerged from the analysis, and to examine what aspects of the crisis most attracted press attention.[2]

**TABLE 6.3**  Thematic coding devices, negative/positive mentions

| Theme no. | Negative/unsupportive of US | Positive/supportive of US |
|---|---|---|
| 1 Policy options | Policy options criticised, or different (set) of policy option(s) outlined. Discussion of alternatives, alternatives presented as equally/more valid. | Policy options outlined uncritically in line with US policy. No discussion of alternatives, or rejection of them. |
| 2 US motives | US purposes queried/criticised. | US purposes/motives accepted. |
| 3 US/UK relationships | US/UK and/or Europe and/or other normally allied countries (Israel, Turkey) relationship seen as problematic. | US/UK and/or Europe and/or other normally allied countries (Turkey, Israel) relationship seen as unproblematic. |
| 4 Outcomes of US policy | Negative outcomes predicted or observed, or problems in implementation. | Positive outcomes predicted or observed, no problems of implementation. |

## Distribution of Themes by Title and Media Sector

Tables 6.4a and 6.4b show the distribution of positive and negative mentions of the thematic material by title. Distribution is shown both by n and by percentage. The purpose of the n table is to show the dramatically different levels of attention given to themes by different titles.

**TABLE 6.4A**  Distribution by theme (negative and positive mentions) and by title: n

| Title | Theme 1 | Theme 2 | Theme 3 | Theme 4 | Total n |
|---|---|---|---|---|---|
| *Daily Telegraph* | 238 | 177.5 | 174 | 325.5 | 915 |
| *Guardian* | 589 | 193 | 344 | 645 | 1771 |
| *Daily Mail* | 487.5 | 44 | 82.5 | 38 | 652 |
| *Daily Mirror* | 771 | 134.5 | 54 | 65.5 | 1025 |
| Total n | 2085.5 | 549 | 654.5 | 1074 | 4363 |

Note: The fractional units represent mention units evenly divided between themes.

**TABLE 6.4B**  Percentage distribution by theme (negative + positive mentions) and by title

| Title | Theme 1 | Theme 2 | Theme 3 | Theme 4 | Total % |
|---|---|---|---|---|---|
| *Daily Telegraph* | 26% | 19% | 19% | 36% | 100% |
| *Guardian* | 33% | 11% | 19% | 36% | 99% |
| *Daily Mail* | 75% | 7% | 13% | 6% | 101% |
| *Daily Mirror* | 75% | 13% | 5% | 6% | 99% |
| Theme % | 48 | 13 | 15 | 25 | 101 |

From tables 6.4a and 6.4b, it is clear that the theme which attracted most attention was American policy (theme 1). After this, most attention was paid to the predicted or observed results of that policy (theme 4). American purposes (theme 2) and relations with allied nations (theme 3) attracted far less attention than the other two themes that between them attracted the clear majority of attention. However, if we aggregate these figures by media sector, we can see that there are two distinct patterns of attention (see Tables 6.5a and 6.5b).

**TABLE 6.5A**  Percentage distribution by theme and by media sector

| Sector | Theme 1 | Theme 2 | Theme 3 | Theme 4 | Total |
|---|---|---|---|---|---|
| Broadsheet | 31% | 14% | 19% | 36% | 100% |
| Tabloid | 75% | 11% | 8% | 6% | 100% |

**TABLE 6.5B**  n distribution by theme and by media sector

| Sector | Theme 1 | Theme 2 | Theme 3 | Theme 4 | Total |
|---|---|---|---|---|---|
| Broadsheet | 827 | 370.5 | 518 | 970.5 | 2686 |
| Tabloid | 1258.5 | 178.5 | 136.5 | 103.5 | 1677 |
| Theme n | 2085.5 | 549 | 654.5 | 1074 | 4363 |

It is clear from the total number of mentions (n) of themes 3 and 4 that the broadsheets gave substantially more attention to these themes than did the tabloids. Moreover, it is clear that these sector averages are close to the individual distribution by title within each media sector: the two tabloid titles each show close to the same pattern of distribution by theme, likewise the broadsheets; or at least the broadsheets are closer to each other than to either of the tabloids where this distribution is concerned (Tables 6.4a and 6.4b). Within each sector case, the similarity of percentage distribution by title is not affected by the widely diverging n. In other words, where patterns of attention are constituted by choice of thematic material, they vary with media sector rather than by political alignment.

This pattern of distribution by media sector is even clearer in an aggregation of the four themes into two macro-themes, according to a principle that underlies their construction. Themes 1 and 2 are broadly concerned with matters of principle, or even – insofar as the term is applicable to the world of politics, diplomacy and international relations – of morality. Themes 3 and 4 are more pragmatic in their orientation: they are concerned with the results of political action (theme 3 is effectively a sub-set of theme 4, as it consists of a particular set of such results). The distribution of attention by media sector and by principle/pragmatism is shown in Table 6.6.

**TABLE 6.6**  Percentage distribution by macro-theme and by media sector

|  | Macro-theme 'principle' Themes 1 and 2 | Macro-theme 'pragmatism' Themes 3 and 4 | Total |
|---|---|---|---|
| Broadsheet | 44.5 | 55.5 | 100 |
| Tabloid | 85 | 15 | 100 |

This distribution by media sector suggests two different news agendas. The tabloid agenda is driven by hard news values, dictating a focus on the major facts of any set of events, with a low degree of analysis of related material but with a relatively strong focus on the main principles that drive policy, whereas the broadsheet agenda is also driven by a desire to present maximum possible background and analytic material.

## Distribution of Themes by Negative/Positive Mentions

Finally, the distribution of positive and negative mentions across the themes can be examined. If all titles are aggregated to show only the correlation between positive/negative mentions and themes, the results will be as shown in Table 6.7.

**TABLE 6.7**  All mentions by theme and by negative and positive: percentage distribution

|  | Theme 1 | Theme 2 | Theme 3 | Theme 4 | Total |
|---|---|---|---|---|---|
| Negative | 25 | 6 | 10 | 12 | 53 |
| Positive | 22 | 6 | 5 | 13 | 46 |
| Theme %* | 47 | 12 | 15 | 25 | 99 |

Note: *Inconsistencies between this row and Tables 6.4a and b are due to re-calculations based on n and rounding to the nearest whole per cent.

As we would expect, having seen the widely different distribution of thematic material by media sector, and knowing that the balance between negative and positive mentions is consistent with political alignment, Table 6.7 is not very informative by itself. It shows that the treatment of three of the four themes was roughly balanced across the four titles, but that theme 3 was predominantly negatively treated, regardless of media sector and political alignment. We shall see below the extent to which this negativity was universal across titles. This overall distribution can also serve as a benchmark for assessing various margins of divergence from it by title, political alignment and media sector.

The patterns of distribution of negative and positive mentions by theme and by title are revealed through separate analysis of each theme.

## Theme 1

**TABLE 6.8** Percentage negative and positive mentions of theme 1 by title

| Title | Negative | Positive | Total |
|---|---|---|---|
| Daily Telegraph | 34 | 66 | 100 |
| Guardian | 60 | 39 | 99 |
| Daily Mail | 33 | 67 | 100 |
| Daily Mirror | 66 | 34 | 100 |

It is clear that the distribution of positive and negative mentions of theme 1 (which is the theme to which most attention is given overall) follows the political allegiance of the media titles, as shown in Table 6.8. The extent of the convergence and divergence by political allegiance of the media titles can be demonstrated by considering the margins of difference in Table 6.9.

**TABLE 6.9** Theme 1: percentage positive and negative mentions and divergence by political alignment

| Title | Negative | Positive |
|---|---|---|
| Daily Telegraph | 34 | 66 |
| Daily Mail | 33 | 67 |
| Divergence within right-wing press | 1 | 1 |
| Guardian | 60 | 39 |
| Daily Mirror | 66 | 34 |
| Divergence within left-wing press | 6* | 5* |

Note: *Error caused by rounding to nearest whole number.

Table 6.10, an aggregation of the left/right media title figures and the divergence between them, shows figures that are way in excess of the divergence figures in Table 6.9:

**TABLE 6.10** Theme 1: percentage divergence between left- and right-wing press

| | Negative | Positive |
|---|---|---|
| Left-wing press | 63 | 36.5 |
| Right-wing press | 33.5 | 66.5 |
| Divergence | 29.5 | 30 |

From Table 6.10, it can clearly be seen that the similarities and differences in distribution are associated directly with political alignment. Indeed, the left/right emphases with regard to theme 1 are close to direct inversions of each other.

## Theme 2

**TABLE 6.11**  Theme 2: percentage negative and positive mentions by title

| Title | Negative | Positive | Total |
|---|---|---|---|
| Daily Telegraph | 38 | 62 | 100 |
| Guardian | 50 | 50 | 100 |
| Daily Mail | 41 | 59 | 100 |
| Daily Mirror | 71 | 29 | 100 |

If the figures in Table 6.11 are analysed by political alignment and by degrees of divergence between titles (Table 6.12), the pattern is less clear than in the case of theme 1.

**TABLE 6.12**  Theme 2: percentage negative and positive mentions by title – divergence

| | Negative | Positive |
|---|---|---|
| Daily Telegraph | 38 | 62 |
| Daily Mail | 41 | 59 |
| Divergence within right-wing press | 3 | 3 |
| Guardian | 50 | 50 |
| Daily Mirror | 71 | 29 |
| Divergence within left-wing press | 21 | 21 |

Additionally, theme 2 can be considered in terms of left/right divergence, based on aggregated figures for the two political alignments:

**TABLE 6.13**  Theme 2: percentage negative and positive mentions – aggregated divergence by political alignment

| | Negative | Positive | Total |
|---|---|---|---|
| Left | 39.5 | 60.5 | 100 |
| Right | 60.5 | 39.5 | 100 |
| Divergence | 21 | 21 | |

From Table 6.13, it can be seen that the divergence between the aggregated left- and right-wing press is the same as the divergence between the *Guardian* and the *Daily Mirror*. This indicates that political alignment does not predict accurately the treatment of theme 2, although the right-wing press also shows a high degree of coherence *a propos* theme 2. Although the coding scheme does not capture this feature of the treatment of themes, it is likely that the difference between the *Guardian* and the *Daily Mirror* derives from the fact that the *Mirror* chose to campaign on the Iraq issue, and its treatment of the topic in question (US purposes) is overwhelmingly cynical (this is not shown by the quantitative analysis, but can be seen through qualitative interpretation). The *Guardian*, in contrast, despite its clear editorial insistence that the war was wrong in principle, nonetheless reported American purposes in a more balanced fashion, regularly allowing US spokespersons – as well as the UK politicians who followed largely the same line – to speak in their own voices.

### Theme 3

**TABLE 6.14** Theme 3: percentage negative and positive mentions by title

|  | Negative | Positive | Total | n |
| --- | --- | --- | --- | --- |
| *Daily Telegraph* | 57 | 43 | 100 | 174 |
| *Guardian* | 73 | 27 | 100 | 344 |
| *Daily Mail* | 66 | 34 | 100 | 54 |
| *Daily Mirror* | 94 | 6 | 100 | 83 |

All titles treat theme 3 primarily negatively, but by different margins (see Table 6.14). Indeed, it is obvious that the left-wing titles are more inclined to see the subject of US/UK relations with other countries more negatively (average negative mentions 83.5%) than the right-wing ones (average negative mentions 61.5%), by a clear margin. To this extent, political alignment is a clear indicator of treatment of theme 3. However, it should be remembered that all titles gave this topic a relatively low degree of attention. No doubt this is partly because the questions involved (the possibility of a Franco-German veto, the difficulties in Turkey over US troops using their bases) either did not arise before the New Year 2003, or became much more prominent after it. Indeed, given the importance of the likely Franco-German veto in the Security Council in late February/early March 2003, it is difficult to see how any news reporting of theme 3 could fail to be mainly negative during the time period selected. This is an inevitable result of the coding device in question: any non-evaluative mention of the possibility of the Franco-German veto, or of Turkish lack of co-operation with the coalition, counts as a negative mention of US policy. In the qualitative analysis (see below), important differences between the left- and right-wing titles' treatment of this theme will be seen. However, the greater prominence given to negative interpretation by left-wing newspapers cannot be explained by the nature of the events in question, nor by the nature of the coding device. What is clearly revealed is that the left-wing (primarily, the *Guardian*) titles chose to give more prominence to theme 3, even in its 'objective' form, than did the right-wing titles.

### Theme 4

Theme 4 was far more widely reported in the broadsheet press than in the tabloid press, and the most significant feature of the media representation of theme 4 is certainly this sectoral distinction (Tables 6.5a and b). However, we should nonetheless consider the meaning of the balance between negative and positive mentions of this theme.

**TABLE 6.15**  Theme 4: percentage negative and positive mentions by title

| Title | Negative | Positive | Total |
|---|---|---|---|
| Daily Telegraph | 44 | 56 | 100 |
| Guardian | 43 | 57 | 100 |
| Daily Mail | 95 | 5 | 100 |
| Daily Mirror | 92 | 8 | 100 |

Table 6.15 shows that media sector is a better predictor of negative and positive mentions of theme 4 than political alignment. However, it is possible that this is an artefact of sampling, as the very low level of attention given to this theme by the tabloids (Tables 6.4 and 6.5) may have a distorting effect on the results. It is also striking, however, that the broadsheets show a pattern that is similarly different from the usual distribution by political alignment that has been seen elsewhere. It seems likely – though this aspect of the reporting is not captured by the coding scheme – that the broadsheets gave far more attention to the likely future events in Iraq than did the tabloids, and that both broadsheet titles saw the ousting of Saddam Hussein as a positive outcome of US policy, despite differences of editorial line with respect to most of the other aspects of US policy.

## Discussion and Conclusion of the Quantitative Analysis

On the majority of the indicators presented here, the UK press divided clearly along left/right lines on questions of policy: the left-wing titles clearly opposed, and the right-wing titles clearly supported, US policy. This is evident in the overall balance between aggregated negative and positive mentions of the four themes analysed, and is reflected in both news reporting and comment/analysis pages. Put crudely, it shows that left-wing papers looked for bad news about American policy, whereas right-wing papers looked for good news. The only major difference within these indicators is the divergence between the *Daily Mirror* and the *Guardian*, deriving from the former's campaigning editorial policy with regard to the crisis; however, this difference does not affect the basis of the left/right division.

Where the division between themes covered is concerned, differences by political alignment are still visible, but differences by media sector are also visible and the balance between positive and negative mentions is somewhat ambiguous.

Coverage of the themes classified as 'matters of principle' (1 and 2)

shows a clear distinction by political alignment. Despite the *Guardian's* balanced approach to the question of US purposes (Table 6.11), the left-wing titles nonetheless are largely negative about both the matters in question, whereas the right-wing titles are positive.

However, where the 'pragmatic matters' themes are concerned, the clear pattern shown so far breaks down. As far as distribution of overall coverage of themes is concerned (i.e., positive and negative mentions), the titles within each media sector show a striking similarity, whereas between media sectors they are visibly different (Tables 6.4a and b). Broadsheets give a relatively high level of attention to these matters, whereas tabloids give a low level of attention. Tables 6.5a and 6.5b show that broadsheets distribute attention more or less equally between US policy and its results, whereas tabloids focus massively on the policy itself. There is a similar distribution of attention to the outcomes of the invasion of Iraq (see Chapter 8): tabloids pay relatively little attention to the situation inside Iraq (one of the main results of US policy) when compared with levels of broadsheet attention.

Where the distribution of negative and positive mentions of themes 3 and 4 is concerned, the pattern of division by political alignment is still clear in the case of theme 3 (US/allied nations relationship). The negative treatment by all titles notwithstanding, left-wing titles treat theme 3 more negatively than right-wing ones. However, in the case of theme 4, broadsheets treat the theme more positively than negatively, whereas tabloids are overwhelmingly negative. We shall return to this matter in the qualitative analysis.

## Qualitative analysis

While the quantitative analysis reported above gives clear overall indications of the major features of coverage and editorial policies of the titles in question, it probably underestimates some important features of the pattern of reporting to be found in the UK press, some of which can be better accessed by qualitative analysis.

UK opinion polls showed that there was substantial opposition to the war, especially before it began.[3] Since the left-wing press was overwhelmingly opposed to US policy, it is to be expected that this opposition would be registered in their pages. However, qualitative analysis of news and comment columns shows that right-wing titles also registered and clearly recognised the depth of public opposition to US/UK policy. Letters to the editor no doubt revealed the spread of opinion among their readers to individual editors, and a poll subsequently corroborated this when it correlated political views with newspaper title preference: substantial proportions of the right-wing titles' readers opposed the war (Greenslade, 2003a). Editorial acceptance of this fact in the right-wing press was especially obvious around the middle of February 2003, the time of a second massive public anti-war demonstration. The acceptance of readers' stance occurred despite editorial support for the policy and a tendency to find positive aspects to events in news page reporting (for example, giving space to US spokespersons rather than to anti-war movement representatives). While this recognition is not explicitly caught by the coding devices, it is visible to qualitative reading, and may explain a substantial part of the negative coverage of US policy found in these titles; for example, the *Daily Telegraph* covered *in extenso* Norman Mailer's speech in which he accused the Bush administration of imperialism (21.2.03). Even the *Daily Mail* (14.02.03: 6 and 13) published articles favourable to the anti-war cause. Conversely, the *Guardian* recognised that the likely regime change in Iraq had a positive side as well as a negative one: some of the paper's columnists argued forcefully that the left should *not* oppose the war on the grounds that getting rid of Saddam was a benefit to the Iraqi people that outweighed considerations of sovereignty and the role of the UN. Such articles, in combination with balanced reporting of US war aims, appear to have contributed substantially to the level of positive mentions of US policy in this title; the contrast with the *Daily Mirror*, which was routinely cynical about US war aims, is clear and supports this reading.

The coding devices used in the quantitative analysis miss an important aspect of the reporting of the relationship between the UK and the US: the extent of possible divergences between the two countries' vision of the role of the UN. Whatever the reality of the UK's role in persuading the US to 'go down the UN road' in the winter of 2002–03, the UK press overwhelmingly accepted that the Blair government had played a substantial role in the process (see, for example, *Guardian*, 9.11.02: 21 and 14.11.02: 26; *Daily Telegaph*, 8.11.02: 16, 29; *Daily Mail*, 9.11.02: 2). Details of such negotiations and possible splits inside the US administration on this issue figured in the reporting.[4]

Specifically, the coding devices do not allow any analysis of inter-title differences in the treatment of the protracted process of negotiation at the UN and in the reporting of the UN mission of arms inspections in Iraq and its reports to the UN Security Council. In the interests of consistency of coding, all mentions of the inspection process which simply recorded events in a neutral way were assigned to the category of positive mentions of US policy, since at the time US administration policy was indeed to accept the validity of the inspection process as the right way forward, despite frequent expressions of frustration at the tone of voice of the reports, which were – they argued – insufficiently negative towards Iraq. To the extent that US negativity towards the UN processes caused problems for the UK government domestically, reports of this fall-out figure negatively under theme 3 (relationships with allied countries).

Qualitative analysis of these matters shows significant inter-title differences. In the case of UN Resolution 1441 (voted on 8.11.02), there were similarities in the overall pattern of reporting, with all titles trailing the resolution and discussing the negotiations that led up to it during the preceding day. All titles agreed that it was a 'tough' resolution and that it represented a victory for US and UK diplomacy. However, while the *Daily Mirror* stressed the decisive role given to the UN weapons inspectors in the final decision over war (9.11.02: 8), and the *Guardian* stressed the ambiguities and 'fudge' involved in the details of the resolution, the *Daily Mail* declared that Saddam Hussein was 'looking down the barrel of a gun' (9.11.02: 2). The *Daily Telegraph* emphasised President Bush's interpretation of the situation (war would result from the 'slightest defiance' from Saddam) (9.11.02: 1) and reported (in two separate articles on p. 21) that the Bush administration was sceptical about the inspection process.

Dr Hans Blix's report to the UN Security Council on 27 January 2003 was reported by all titles (28.1.03), but with different emphases and interpretations:

- The *Daily Mirror* in its leader argues that the Blix report did not justify war on Iraq; the news page reports (pp. 4–5) on the Security Council meeting highlight the need for more time for inspections and the negative responses by UN diplomats to its implication for US and UK policy, but also includes an article by an ex-inspector which stresses the need to make Iraq accountable. On 29 January the paper published a long anti-war article by the campaigning journalist John Pilger and more details of the paper's own 'Not in Our Name' campaign.
- The *Guardian's* coverage on its front page stresses that the US and the UK interpreted the Blix report as justification of their policy, and the leader (p. 21) condemns this 'pre-scripted' use of the report and rejected the US and UK interpretation as 'mendacious spin'. The front page coverage also notes that the Blix report is an 'outspoken attack' on the veracity of the Iraqi regime, but emphasises that the report's implication is that more time should be given to the inspections process. Further articles on news pages report ambiguous responses internationally and give a panel of independent experts' judgment on the details of the Blix report.
- The *Daily Telegraph* leader states that the Blix report supports US and UK policy, and the front page report emphasises that Dr Blix 'unequivocally' states that Iraq has failed to disarm. Further news reports from the US say that the report offers 'more than enough ammunition' to the US and UK case, that the 'predicted ambiguity' of the report has given way to a 'devastating catalogue of violations' by Iraq, and trail Bush's next day State of the Union address which makes the case for war. The paper also reports parliamentary opposition to the government's interpretation of the report (p. 14).
- The *Daily Mail* leader says that the Blix report does not reveal a 'smoking gun' in Iraq, and condemns the 'rush to war'. However, the news pages' coverage (pp. 4–5) asserts that the Blix report provides 'devastating ammunition for the US and Britain' and that it is a 'damning verdict' on Iraq. This incoherence is no doubt due to the paper's strident hostility towards the Blair government; on 29 January

a long piece examines the consequences of the US/UK policy and declares that it will be 'the still-birth of a common European foreign policy' (another policy that the paper opposes).

With the exception of the *Daily Mail's* editorial incoherence, these 'angles' are largely in line with the left/right division noted above. It is worth remembering how positive the right-wing press's reception of the Anglo-US interpretation of the Blix report was at this time, since in the post-military phase these titles started to condemn the Anglo-US misuse of intelligence to support war aims (see Chapter 9).

As is commonly the case in quantitative content analysis, many important details of coverage get lost in the coding devices. This time was no exception. Here are some examples:

- Starting on 8 January, the *Guardian* created a special heading for the reports about the crisis, in the form of a small graphic panel containing the words 'Threat of War'. The choice of terminology is a powerful semantic relay, encouraging the reader to see what is said below in a way that corresponds to the notion of threat.
- On 15 February, a *Guardian* report of Tony Blair's arguments in favour of an invasion of Iraq characterised them as 'freshly minted'. The cynical phrase inflects the meaning of the facts reported.
- A BBC report of a UN speech by the French Ambassador, Dominique de Villepin, stressed the favourable reception he received by including audience applause in the video tape of the report. That this was deliberate was stressed by the BBC newsreader George Alagiah in a lecture at London Metropolitan University (6.3.03).

Qualitative analysis suggests that such editing tends to be in line with an overall editorial position; for example, Alagiah stressed that the decision to include the applause at the end of de Villepin's speech derived from the recognition that world opinion was deeply divided, and that the BBC had a duty to give due weight to different elements in opinion in the UN.

The quantitative analysis of the Franco-Russian-German initiative (intended to avoid an invasion, or at least to postpone it and make it a last resort) records it as negative towards US policy, on the grounds that it was indeed in opposition to it – hence the derisory US comments about the 'axis of weasels' and 'cheese-eating surrender monkeys'.[5] While the content analysis device is valid, it fails to capture differences in UK press reporting, that is, that the left-wing titles broadly welcomed this initiative, while the right-wing titles were negative to the point of derision (for example, *Daily Telegraph*, 4.2.03).

Where domestic UK politics were concerned, all titles analysed the importance for the Blair government of obtaining a second UN resolution mandating direct intervention in Iraq. This insistence on the importance had the implication that the existence of weapons of mass destruction

(WMDs) became central to the politics of the situation in the UK; indeed, the government had already made WMDs a central issue by issuing a dossier in September 2002 focusing on Iraqi possession of them.[6] Consequently, the failure of the UN resolution process caught UK media attention and brought out varied evaluations of the situation. All titles were also alert to the fact that the Blair government started to shift ground in its rhetoric at around the time the UN process started to run into real difficulties, when it began to insist less on the UN resolution and more on the morality of regime change for the benefit of the Iraqi people. It is likely that this negative attitude to such changes of policy direction and the problems later incurred by the government in this respect are due to the fact that the government had no 'friends' in respect of this crisis among the newspaper titles surveyed. The right-wing titles were at best ambiguous about the Blair government in general, and the left-wing titles both opposed the potential war on principle.

It was widely noted in the media coverage of the pre-invasion phase of the crisis that various individuals and organisations had predicted a variety of disastrous outcomes to the war. Among the most frequently reported in the UK press were predictions by the UN that the war would create a large number of refugees both inside Iraq and across its borders. Speaking on the BBC on 27 December 2002 Ruud Lubbers, the UN high commissioner for refugees, predicted a 'humanitarian disaster' and was widely quoted in the press to predict around one million refugees, a figure subsequently used by both the former Labour Minister Mo Mowlam and Clare Short (the then secretary of state for international development) in arguments about the war. Subsequently, unnamed UK immigration officials predicted a 'significant increase' in refugees to the UK, and an Italian minister predicted the arrival of millions of Iraqi refugees in Europe, in the event of war (both quoted in the *Daily Mail*, 22.2.03, which had been campaigning on the asylum seeker and refugee issue for some time). The *Daily Telegraph* reported that camps were being set up all around the Middle East to accommodate the expected exodus of two and a half million Iraqis (10.2.03). The *Guardian* (19.2.03) printed an article by Caroline Lucas MEP predicting both a humanitarian disaster ('11 million' in need of aid), as well as 'devastating' environmental effects from burning oil wells. The 11 million figure appears to be based on a 'secret' UN report noted by the *Guardian* (15.2.03), which predicted that if the war lasted three months, 10 million Iraqis would be displaced. An international medical charity, Medical Action for Global Security, had claimed that there would be 0.5 million deaths and 'millions' of refugees if there was a war, including between 48,000 and 260,000 civilian deaths, and 200,000 deaths from disease and hunger in the aftermath (quoted *Guardian*, 13.12.02). A *Guardian* report during the war (23.3.03) expressed some surprise at the lack of refugees crossing from Iraq to Jordan.

Whether or not these predictions were accurate (largely they were not), it is noteworthy that in the aftermath of the war there was little reference to them. While Mark Steyn (*Daily Telegraph*, 1.6.03), William Shawcross (*Guardian*, 17.6.03) and Julie Flint (*Observer*, 6.10.03) subsequently refer scathingly to their inaccuracy, near-silence seems to have been the preferred way of handling this material.[7] It is also noteworthy that the treatment of these predictions was made to conform to the papers' policies towards the conflict and/or other matters. In the *Daily Mail*, mentions of these predictions are fitted into a pattern of denunciation of the government's handling of the refugee 'problem' in the UK. In the *Guardian* and *Daily Mirror*, they are part of the pattern of denunciation of the war aims and likely consequences.

Two elements of the press reporting attracted less attention than their importance might lead one to expect. While we cannot speak of symptomatic silences in this respect, it is arguable that more attention should have been given to such significant matters.

First, the alleged links between the Saddam regime and Osama bin Laden (or more generally Islamic terrorism) were largely taken for granted in US opinion, and were constantly asserted by the administration as a valid motive for the invasion of Iraq. Indeed, the link was already made in the autumn of 2001, when responsibility for the anthrax attacks in the US was alleged to be Iraqi (Waisbord, 2002: 209–11). One linkage between President Bush's State of the Union address and Colin Powell's subsequent UN presentation of the intelligence dossier proving that Iraq had not disarmed, was the al-Qaida link to Iraq (*Daily Telegraph*, 30.01.03: 17). Indeed, long after the war President Bush was still asserting the existence of links between Saddam and al-Qaida, even while admitting that Saddam Hussein had no personal ties to the September 11 terrorist attacks on the US (bbc.co.uk/news, dated 18.9.03).[8] Before the invasion, UK press coverage was mainly sceptical of this argument. In the *Daily Mirror* on 3.12.02, John Pilger accuses the Bush administration of trying to make nonsensical claims about the links, and Tony Blair of colluding in this propaganda. The *Daily Mail* (13.02.03: 12) condemns Colin Powell's attempt to use an al-Jazeera broadcast of a bin Laden tape to assert a link between the latter and the Saddam regime; it also calls attempts to assert the links 'risible' (14.01.03: 14). The *Daily Telegraph* and the *Guardian* either refer to UK intelligence sources' scepticism on this issue, or provide direct refutations. The government's own statements on the subject are somewhat equivocal. In his speech to the Lord Mayor's Banquet on 11 November, Tony Blair made an 'explicit link' (*Daily Mail*, 12.11.02: 2) between Saddam and al-Qaida. However, close analysis of the details presented in his speech shows no evidence of an actual link, only of potential ones, whereas both the *Daily Mail* and the *Daily Telegraph* refer to the link as a reality; however, neither the *Guardian* nor the *Daily Mirror* do. The *Guardian* editorial (12.11.02) suggests that Blair's emphasis in this speech on the threat from al-Qaida may be motivated by the possibility of war with Iraq. On 14 and 16 January, Blair is quoted as saying that all the evidence suggests that sooner or later 'there will be links' between Saddam and the terrorist organisations, and that his weapons of mass destruction are likely to fall into terrorist hands. On 30 January, Blair is quoted as asserting that there are links, even if their extent is not known. The *Daily Telegraph* reports this mainly uncritically, but notes briefly that UK intelligence sources dissented and the *Guardian* notes the assertion and gives substantial negative assessments of its plausibility (p. 5). Thus government statements are reported in different lights depending on the political allegiance of the title in question.

There is also the question of the treatment of other government warnings about the threat of terrorist attacks, which were – in its words – not directly linked to the question of Iraq. On various occasions during the winter of 2002 the government issued warnings about the possibility of such attacks, and on one occasion ordered military mobilisation around Heathrow Airport. There was some cynicism about the timing of these warnings in the press, which argued that the essential point was to use public fear of terrorism to increase support for the Iraq policy (see, for example, *Daily Telegraph* 13.02.03: 6). Any such cynical use of potential links was denied by government.

Arguably, news media could have said more about this issue, given its centrality to US motives for war. Of course, this is in part a matter of professional judgment. It is difficult for news media to report that nothing is happening unless a story has already got such massive attention that even 'no development' is a significant update on the topic. In this case, it is arguable whether periods of silence from political leaders on the subject are worth extended media attention or not. However, given editorial will, journalistic enterprise can usually be guaranteed to produce some newsworthy intervention in a matter like this if sufficient effort is put into evoking it.[9]

The second instance of matters attracting less press attention than their importance might lead one to expect is the question of the US motives for going to war. Although major media attention was given to this question – as shown in the quantitative analysis – this attention was largely presented through either reports of stated US motives (for example, WMDs, UN resolutions) or cynical counter-interpretations (notably, Iraqi oil reserves). There was little mention of the US Republican administration's long-term commitment to a fundamentally new doctrine in foreign policy – the possibility of unilateral action being preferable to multi-lateral, temporary 'coalitions of the willing' and so on – encapsulated in the *Project for a New American Century* and similar documentation (for example, see *Guardian*, 22.01.03: 6; 24.01.03: 22; 26.02.03: 15 and *Daily Telegraph*, 31.1.03; 6.2.03). Again, it is arguable that more attention should have been given to such a fundamental matter.

Both of these last matters figure in post-invasion reporting, although again at levels that suggest that they were not considered newsroom priorities. The cause of this relative inattention cannot be assessed on the basis of content analysis alone. Access to editorial decision-making processes is necessary to understand it, and probably also knowledge of patterns of source access.

Finally, another matter marginalised in both the present analysis and press coverage: the impact of the sanctions and other international pressure brought to bear on Iraq during the decade separating the two Gulf Wars. The impact of sanctions was reported throughout the decade; in particular the continuation of low-level military activity over Iraq was reported, if not in a lot of detail.[10] Debates about how effective sanctions had been in containing Iraq's weapons programmes were reported. However, the extent to which these events may have contributed to making Saddam's regime what it was accused of being was relatively little discussed. When it was reported, it was usually in terms of the repression of the rebellions against Saddam following his retreat from Kuwait. The dearth of reporting is in part a result of the dearth of information due to the successful information control from Baghdad. Nonetheless, the appalling human rights record of the Saddam regime could have been contextualised in this manner. An account of these events might have made the post-invasion situation more comprehensible to the UK public.

## Conclusion

The analysis shows the extent to which coverage of the pre-invasion phase of the crisis conformed to a pattern of political allegiance, with some significant differences by media sector. While some of the differences can be accounted for by editorial and comment pages, it is clear (as seen in the qualitative analysis) that elements of news reporting also fit the differences driven by political allegiance. Perhaps titles tended to find – or even to seek – facts that fitted their predispositions, or to interpret the facts in the light of their overall commitment. But equally, journalists take their information from sources, and it is in the interaction between the two that definitions arise. If a source is saying the same thing to a number of journalists, and the reports differ in the way that we have seen, then clearly editorial interpretation is responsible. However, it is equally possible that different journalists have different sources, or even that the same source responds to slightly different questions from different journalists in different ways. In short, there are many variables in the news gathering and production process that might be responsible for the differences observed here. Nonetheless, there were significant title differences in both the reporting and analysis of essentially the same set of events, and they cannot be solely ascribed to the nature of the events themselves. Thus our data support the contention that news is not exclusively event driven, but is also driven by interpretation. Indeed, this is inevitable given that news judgment involves contexts: news is that which is important (or interesting) and timely *in some context*. In the relationship between event and context, it is inevitable that interpretation comes into play.

However, it is also true that there was remarkable homogeneity in press assessments of what was significant in the events that preceded the invasion, with the overwhelming focus on the political and diplomatic processes. Inevitably, inter-sectoral differences in news values created great differences in levels of attention to these matters, though it is clear that the basic editorial decisions about which events were significant in some measure not very varied. No doubt this is due to the nature of the events in question, in which international diplomacy was taking the lead role. Under these circumstances, the range of relevant sources is more limited than in other cases, as is the range of journalists who are available in the arenas in question. But it must be stressed that there are two important exceptions to this observation. The first is the attention given (or not given) to the anti-war movement, both in terms of quantity of attention and in terms of how its significance was assessed; and secondly – in particular – the *Daily Mirror's* active campaigning stance, which drove its coverage in a fundamentally different direction to that of other titles.

In general, the account of this phase of the crisis that can be derived from the UK press overall (as opposed to any particular title) gives a version of events that is sensitive to different currents of opinion and to the various forces at play in the situation. We make this assertion in full recognition that those in the peace movement would certainly criticise the UK press for not paying enough attention to radical alternatives to the range of policy options discussed. If it is clearly evident that some agents get more attention than others, nonetheless the way in which they are treated is subtle and subject to critical distance. References to policy disagreements between major players were frequent, for example, as the negative mentions of themes 3 and 4 in our quantitative analysis show. This overall account reveals different results from those found in studies of the US media coverage of the pre-military phase of Gulf War I (quoted in the Introduction) where there is general agreement that it was favourable to US policy development. Specifically, the range of policy options discussed was limited to the alternatives that the US administration wanted considered (Bennett and Manheim, 1993); media coverage of Saddam's regime in Iraq was sporadic, negative and largely devoid of contextualising elements (Lang and Lang, 1994); and although there was reporting of elite policy disagreements, the supportive material was more prominent than the 'most pertinent criticisms' (Entman and Page, 1994: 84). None of these conclusions apply to the UK press coverage of the pre-invasion phase of the Iraq crisis in 2003.

## Notes

1 A *Daily Telegraph* journalist perceptively commented that Iraq was 'the defining issue today ' for the Left (Born, 2003). The *Guardian* entitled its book about the crisis *The War We Could Not Stop*.

2   Although this book does not explicitly use framing theory, a consistent pattern of media attention would amount to a media frame.

3   See, for example, the ICM polls commissioned by the *Guardian* at www.icmresearch.co.uk.

4   We shall see in Chapter 8 that the role of the UN becomes an issue again after the invasion.

5   'Axis of weasels' is said to have been invented by the website scrappleface.com and subsequently popularised by the *New York Post* (in February 2003); 'cheese-eating surrender monkeys' derives from a character in 'The Simpsons', but was popularised by the conservative controversialist Jonah Goldberg (www.nationalreview.com/goldberg/goldbergprint04060.html); see also *The Age* (www.theage.com.au/articles/2003/02/11/1044927597014.html).

6   See the Prime Minister's press briefing: http://www.number-10.gov.uk/output/page2485.asp. The dossier itself is at: http://www.number-10.gov.uk/output/page271.asp.

7   See below, Chapter 8.

8   Long after the invasion was complete, surveys by the University of Maryland's Program on International Policy Attitudes (PIPA) and Knowledge Networks, as well as the results of other polls, found that '48% of the public believe US troops found evidence of close pre-war links between Iraq and the al-Qaida terrorist group'. Viewers of Fox Television were the most likely to think this (Lobe, 2003).

9   For example, in December 1993 in the immediate aftermath of the *News of the World's* revelation of UK Conservative Minster Timothy Yeo's extra-marital fatherhood, the *Daily Mail* and BBC Radio 4's 'Today' programme put extended effort into producing a newsworthy reaction, which duly succeeded; this played a significant role in the extension of the 'Back to Basics' scandals in December, 1993/January, 1994; see Palmer (2000: 72). See also Boorstin, 1961: Ch. 1.

10  Summaries at: www.globalissues.org/Geopolitics/MiddleEast/Iraq.asp.

# 7

# THE INVASION PHASE

There has already been both public controversy about and academic analysis of the coverage of Gulf War II. Systematic analysis has come from the German-based media consultancy Media Tenor,[1] and from a team from Cardiff University.[2] Both of these studies consist of quantitative content analysis: Media Tenor was commissioned by the *Frankfurter Algemeine Zeitung* to do a comparative, international analysis of television coverage of the conflict; the Cardiff team analysed UK television news coverage. Our analysis is also primarily quantitative, with some brief qualitative material to illustrate particular points.[3]

Common to the Media Tenor and Cardiff University analyses of media output is a concern about two central elements of the coverage: whose voices were heard, and were they represented in a positive or negative manner? Additionally, there is concern about the themes of reporting (for example: attention to Iraqi civilian casualties, or to the balance between Iraqis welcoming/not welcoming the coalition forces). Clearly, the choice of such thematic material is related to the question of positive/negative representations. Unsurprisingly, levels of media attention to such themes are the subject of debate and recrimination in partisan analyses. For example, a decision to focus reporting on Iraqi or coalition casualties rather than on military advances obviously plays into the positivity or negativity of the profile of the events in question, and into the development of public opinion in the countries involved; no doubt this is why President Bush expressed his frustration at media reporting of these matters in the second week of the invasion.[4]

Levels of media attention to such issues can be assessed in terms of the degree of objectivity/bias shown in reporting; for example, the *Guardian* presentation of the Cardiff University media analysis appears under the headline 'Biased broadcasting corporation', with the sub-head 'A survey of the main broadcasters' coverage of the invasion of Iraq shows the claim that the BBC was anti-war is the opposite of the truth' (4.7.03). However, all of these studies – including our own – are based on inter-channel comparisons, not upon some independent, external benchmark; thus all judgments about objectivity are comparative, not absolute.

The Media Tenor analysis compares a sample of German television news across three channels with the BBC's main evening bulletins and the US ABC news.[5] It analyses:

- the balance between negative and positive *commentary* about the political and military activities of the coalition partners over an extended time scale;
- the balance between negative and positive *information* about American military activity during the first two weeks of the conflict (this analysis excludes the BBC);
- the balance between positive and negative evaluations of UK military activity during the same time period;
- the balance between attention to coalition and Iraqi casualties; and
- coverage of the anti-war movement.

Their findings are as follows:

- The balance between positive and negative *commentary* favours the coalition on ABC news, is substantially anti-coalition on German television (the margins are roughly inverted in the two cases) and the BBC is absolutely even-handed in this respect.
- The balance between negative and positive *information* shows that there was not a big difference between the channels analysed during the first few days of the conflict, but from the end of the first week there was a significant divergence: the German channels were on average more negative than positive, whereas the US channel became increasingly positive over time.
- In their *evaluation* of UK military activity, the German channels were on average a little more negative than positive, but by a small margin (3%), ABC was massively positive (25% positive/10% negative), and the BBC was marginally more negative (by 2%).
- In attention to 'our/their' casualties, German television paid extensively more attention to Iraqi suffering than to coalition casualties, ABC massively favoured attention to coalition casualties, and the BBC paid somewhat more attention to coalition casualties than to Iraqi ones, but by a far narrower margin than ABC.
- Coverage of the anti-war movement was most developed on German channels, least on the BBC, and had a substantial presence on ABC.

What does this analysis indicate? First, it shows large international variations in the profile of the war. Second, on three out of five indicators, the BBC comes out as *relatively* even-handed, but very (*relatively*) silent on the subject of the anti-war demonstrations. Third, it is clear that German television was predominantly anti-war; this is unsurprising given the known state of German public opinion and the position of the German government. Fourth, it appears that ABC is substantially more pro-war than the channels with which it is compared.[6]

The final point in the Media Tenor study was used by David Miller (Stirling University Media Research Institute) to show that the BBC had seriously misrepresented the level of public opposition to the war in the

UK, arguing that this derived from an inability to adapt its news and comment procedures to these circumstances:

> The level of public opposition to the war in Iraq was difficult for the BBC to navigate. The war exposed a serious disconnection between the political elite and the public, so the usual method of ensuring 'balance' – interviewing politicians – was never going to be enough. Other channels, including even ITV's lightweight 'Tonight' programme, tried new ways of accessing opposition, while the BBC cautioned its senior management, in a confidential memo dated 6 February, to 'be careful' about broadcasting dissent.
>
> Once the war began, the BBC restricted the range of acceptable dissent yet further. The network's head of news, Richard Sambrook, said this is 'partly because there is a degree of political consensus within Westminster, with the Conservatives supporting the government policy on the war and the Liberal Democrats, while opposed to the war, supporting the UK forces'.
>
> The BBC thus turned a blind eye to divisions in the country. (Miller, 2003)

While Miller's point, in combination with his other arguments, is indeed demonstrated by the indicator in question, it is worth noting that the other indicators used by Media Tenor suggest the opposite – that the BBC is *relatively* impartial, in comparison with the other channels analysed here.[7]

The Cardiff University study compares the coverage of the war in the four main UK news channels' bulletins (BBC, ITN, Channel 4, Sky). They use four main indicators in their comparison:

- UK government sources as a percentage of sources used;
- the percentage of reports referring to Iraqi civilian casualties;
- the percentage of reports in which Iraqis are shown welcoming the invasion; and
- the percentage of reports in which Iraqis are shown as unhappy about the invasion.

UK government sources appeared *more* frequently on the BBC than on the other channels, and it was also the channel that referred *least* frequently to Iraqi casualties. The BBC appeared around average in its mentions of Iraqis welcoming the invasion. While all four channels mentioned Iraqi discontent with the invasion in approximately equal proportions, the BBC scored lowest on this indicator by 1%.

These indicators justify the Cardiff team's conclusion that the BBC was far from anti-war, *contra* claims allegedly made by the UK government (and referred to in the *Guardian* presentation of the Cardiff research (Lewis, 2003a)). Indeed, according to the Cardiff survey, the government's complaints would have been better directed against Channel 4, which emerges as significantly more unfavourable to coalition policy than the BBC.[8]

However, *all* UK channels were more likely to show Iraqis welcoming the invasion than not welcoming it, by an average margin of 19%. Indeed, with the exception of Channel 4, the channels were remarkably similar in their levels of attention to these two possibilities: 'welcoming' gets between 31% and 37% of relevant mentions from the BBC, Sky and ITN, but only 20% from Channel 4; 'not-welcoming' gets between 11% and 13% from all four channels. In this respect, Channel 4's low level of attention to Iraqis welcoming the coalition forces is exceptional. We repeat: these are inter-channel comparisons, not comparisons with an external benchmark; who is to say who got it right in this respect? To illustrate this point, the BBC reporter Ben Brown who accompanied UK forces when they took Basra said that as he walked around the city in the immediate aftermath of the UK forces' arrival, he saw few manifestations of joy; while he was aware of other pictures which recorded it, he decided not to use them in his report as on balance he thought they were an inaccurate record of the population's reactions.[9] As we shall see below, the UK press varied in its attribution of joy in the local population at that moment, but there undoubtedly were photographic records of popular pleasure. The figures in the Cardiff survey record the cumulative product of many such decisions by reporters and editors, often on the basis of very partial evidence. While they may legitimately be interpreted to show a consistent profiling of events, this does not necessarily allow any evaluation of the profile, since there is no external benchmark of accuracy.

The indicator referring to casualties is consistent with the Media Tenor finding that the BBC paid more attention to coalition casualties than to Iraqi ones. The other indicators are not comparable between the two surveys, except in the most general fashion. If the German analysis indicates that the BBC is relatively even-handed, the Cardiff one places it as among the more pro war channels in the UK. However, the bases of the comparison are so different that it is difficult to use it to sustain any more detailed claims.

After the combat period, the UK regulatory body the Independent Television Commission surveyed audience responses to UK media portrayals of the war (Sancho, 2003). Just as before the invasion,[10] public opinion was still clearly divided over the morality of the invasion, with 43% condemning it to a greater or lesser extent, and 58% in favour to a greater or lesser extent (2003: 12). Opinion was divided about whether the level of television coverage had been too much or about right: 37% felt it was about right, 34% thought it was a bit too much and 27% far too much; a small minority wanted more (2003: 14).[11] Where impartiality was concerned, the great majority (72%) thought the UK terrestrial channels' news had been fair to all parties; around one-fifth thought they had been biased towards the coalition position.[12] Lewis (2003b) finds that respondents thought the BBC more trustworthy on this subject than the other UK channels. Both Lewis (2003b) and Sancho (2003) find that the overwhelming majority wanted impartiality in broadcast news.

Our analysis of the media coverage of the combat phase of the crisis is based on the following coding devices as indicators:

■ The balance of attention between the conduct of the war and attention to its long-term political purposes or outcomes.
■ Which sources are quoted or directly referred to in reports; they are categorised as follows:
  – Coalition military and government;[13]
  – Coalition other/civilian and NGOs;
  – EU institutions, government and military;[14]
  – United Nations;
  – EU other/civilian, for example, opinion polls, newspapers;
  – Middle Eastern governments or military;
  – Iraqi government or military; and
  – Iraqi civilian (including Iraqi political exiles).
■ Positive/negative mentions of the activities of the coalition partners; this indicator is sub-divided into the categories of 'military' and 'political'.
■ Tone of voice of the reports: objective, sceptical or 'heroic', in other words couched in the kind of language that is supportive of, or celebrates, military achievements.

All indicators are used for the purpose of inter-channel comparisons.

All devices are unitised as mentions, of any size; mentions are not weighted for emphasis. The media sample consisted of : BBC1 6.00 p.m. news and ITN 6.30 p.m. news, with some additions from Sky News and BBC News 24 (a total of 196 bulletins); and national newspapers: the *Sun*, the *Daily Telegraph*, the *Daily Mirror* and the *Guardian*. All media were analysed from the first day of combat (20.3.03) to 17.3.03; the purpose of this timeframe was to see in what ways (if at all) news frames changed after the fall of Baghdad. The selection of reports was made on the basis that each had the war in Iraq as its main theme (that is, ignoring articles in which it was only mentioned in passing or only in some other context, for example, stock market prices).

In the television news bulletin sample, all reports coming into this category were analysed in respect of all four indicators. The press sample was further sub-divided by time. All articles in the sampled titles in the first five days of combat, which had the war in Iraq as their main theme, were analysed. However, due to the quantity of material generated by the UK press, from 25.3.03 to 17.4.03 only the front page and a selection of articles from the 'dedicated' inside pages were used;[15] this sample amounted to approximately 10% of the total output of reports having the war in Iraq as their main theme.[16] Additionally, both the press and the broadcast samples were divided again at the fall of Baghdad (the night of 6/7 April). A comparison is made between the different distributions of some indicators before and after this point.

## Balance Between Conduct of the War and its Purposes/Outcomes

In the previous chapter, we saw the extent to which different UK press titles focused on the details of US/UK policy in the Iraq crisis, its purposes and its predicted or observed results. Only the broadsheet press paid any substantial amount of attention to the likely or observed *results* of policy, although all titles paid substantial attention to the *motives* of policy. Now the analysis considers the extent to which the purposes and/or results of warfare continue to be the focus of attention once combat had started, especially since in the pre-war period the UK press was clearly divided about the morality of the war and its purposes.

The first level of analysis addresses the extent to which reports focused on both combat and its purposes/outcomes together, inside the same frame. Each report is coded according to whether it had only a principal theme, or both a principal and secondary theme. As can be seen in Table 7.1, only a minority of sampled reports had two themes.

**TABLE 7.1** Percentages of reports with a secondary theme

| Sun | Daily Telegraph | Daily Mirror | Guardian | BBC | ITN |
|---|---|---|---|---|---|
| 17 | 15 | 14 | 13 | 5 | 9 |

Note: Television sample: all reports 20.3.03–6.4.03; press sample: 20–24.3.03 incl., all reports.

Unsurprisingly, given the compression typical of television news, the broadcast average is below the press average, and even below the tabloid press average. The sample size means that cross-tabulations of these reports are unlikely to be significant, and there are no other significant forms of correlation between principal and secondary themes. Nothing more will be said about secondary themes.

**TABLE 7.2** Conduct and purposes as percentage of principal theme mentions

| | Conduct | Purposes | Total |
|---|---|---|---|
| Sun | 83 | 17 | n = 71 |
| Daily Telegraph | 55.5 | 44.5 | n = 146 |
| Daily Mirror | 53 | 47 | n = 70 |
| Guardian | 68 | 32 | n = 105 |
| BBC | 92 | 2 | n = 61 |
| IIN | 93 | 5 | n = 56 |

Note: Sample: all television reports 20.3.03–6.4.03; all press reports 20–24.3.03 incl. Data omits TV reports with neither as main theme.

Table 7.2 shows the distribution of the principal themes of reports. These figures demonstrate that the press was paying very substantial amounts of attention to the purposes and outcomes of the war even during the first days of combat. Insofar as the press plays a role in the formation of public agendas, the focus of knowledge of the war was not exclusively on the battlefield, but also substantially on the political and moral frame within which the war was being fought.

Since the press sample includes the first morning of the war, when the press are effectively still reporting on the pre-war period, and the distribution of material is biased towards outcomes in all titles, the attention to outcomes is slightly over-represented in the press figures. However, no adjustment for this bias can account for the disproportion between press and broadcast reporting in this respect. While nothing in the data provides an explanation of this distribution, the answer may lie in another feature of the sampling procedure. The press sample includes all articles in the news and comment/analysis pages of the titles, whereas the television sample consists entirely of news bulletins. Insofar as it is possible to make equivalences between press and television editorial structures, the television bulletins are analogous to the news pages of the press, and a broadcast equivalent to comment and analysis pages would be found in current affairs programming. Whether broadcast organisations also paid attention to these matters is not recorded in our data. However, those members of the public who got news about the war exclusively from broadcast news bulletins would have seen the war in a largely decontextualised manner.[17] As soon as Baghdad was in the hands of coalition forces, the focus of television reporting switched dramatically, as can be seen in Table 7.3.

**TABLE 7.3** Conduct and purposes as percentage of principal themes of television reports, by period. Reports with neither as main theme omitted.

|  | Conduct | | Purposes/outcomes | |
| --- | --- | --- | --- | --- |
|  | 20.3–6.4.03 | 7–17.4.03 | 20.3–6.4.03 | 7–17.4.03 |
| BBC 1 | 92 | 23.5 | 2 | 76.5 |
| ITV 1 | 93 | 27 | 5 | 73 |

These figures show a massive and clear change in focus, as television reporters switch their attention from the conduct of the campaign (which was still going on during all the period surveyed) to matters related to the effects of the military campaign. Data presented below, derived from other indicators, will be seen to correlate with this shift in focus. The sample of press data for this period has a very limited validity, due to its random nature, and inferences should be treated with caution; however, it seems clear that there is no such dramatic shift of focus in the press coverage at the point where Baghdad falls into American hands. Substantial numbers of articles about both the conduct of the military campaign and its outcomes and purposes are still to be found in the press titles.

## Whose Voice?

The question of whose voices dominate reporting of warfare is an ongoing concern in both academic and practitioner analysis. Table 7.4 shows the distribution of voices across the sampled channels/titles.

**TABLE 7.4**   Voices 20.3.03 – 7.4.03: percentage distribution of mentions (TV, 6.4.03).

|  | Sun | DTel. | DMi. | Gdn | BBC | ITN |
|---|---|---|---|---|---|---|
| Coalition g/m [UK + US, etc.] | 65 | 57 | 54 | 54 | 58 | 66 |
| US + EU civ/NGOs | 14 | 16 | 16 | 14 | 10 | 10 |
| EU states g/m | 3 | 5 | 4 | 6 | 2 | 0 |
| UN | 0 | 3 | 3 | 3 | 1 | 0 |
| Arab (non-Iraq) | 2 | 4 | 5 | 7 | 1 | 3 |
| Iraq g/m | 11 | 9 | 10 | 12 | 10 | 9 |
| Iraq civ | 5 | 6 | 8 | 5 | 17 | 12 |
| Total | 100 | 100 | 100 | 101 | 99 | 100 |
| N = | 166 | 428 | 226 | 434 | 87 | 90 |

Note: g/m = government and military; civ = other, NGOs, etc.; Arab (non-Iraq) = all Middle East nations, including Turkey and Iran; US, UK and other EU nations are amalgamated in row two, as there were only a maximum of 1% mentions of EU civil/other/NGOs voices in any channel. Iraq civ includes Kurdish fighters. Any report may contain multiple voices.

What is striking here is that the rank order of access to media space is virtually identical across channels: coalition official spokespersons and representatives of government and the armed forces dominate by a large margin in all cases. Second in rank order comes other voices from the civil society of the coalition and EU nations, including non-governmental organisations (NGOs) such as the Red Cross. However, these figures include attributions of information to other journalists, where they are cited as sources – for example, Reuters and al-Jazeera reporters in Baghdad. Therefore, the level of attention to public opinion in the form of NGOs, polls, vox pop, and interviews is somewhat less than these figures suggest. Bodies to which quite substantial levels of attention were given in the pre-war period – EU governments, the UN – are very marginalised by the course of events and the editorial decision to focus on combat. The levels of attention given to official Iraqi sources and to Iraqi civilians are quite consistent, except that television appears to favour Iraqi civilians substantially more than the press does. The coding device for recording the presence of voices in this analysis is based upon direct attribution of material to a category of person. Press reporters may have simply recorded attributions of material to civilians less frequently than television reporters did, as scenes of Iraqi civilians' reactions to events made good television footage. However, this would not explain the fact that television news appears to have given more attention to Iraqi civilians than to Iraqi official spokespersons, whereas the opposite is true of the press.

Insofar as sourcing is a valid indicator of balance or partiality, the data suggest that all sampled UK channels were about equally balanced. These findings are not compatible with the Cardiff University study, which found the opposite in two respects. First, according to their figures the BBC was more likely than ITV to use UK government sources whereas our data show that the two channels were even-handed in this respect: the disaggregated figures for the UK and US personnel show that 32% of the BBC's quoted sources in our sample were UK government or military personnel, and in the case of ITN the figure was 33%. The Cardiff study also finds that the BBC was slightly more likely than other channels to use UK military sources, therefore it is not possible to explain the discrepancy on the grounds of different definitions of UK personnel quoted. Second, these findings are incompatible with the Cardiff study where the use of material attributed to official Iraqi spokespersons is concerned: according to our data, the two television channels common to both studies are more or less equal in their attribution, but the Cardiff team find significant differences. The data as recorded offer no explanation of these differences.

Analysis of the distribution of sources in the period following the fall of Baghdad shows only one important difference: all channels (bar one) increase their attention to the voices of Iraqi civilians. Table 7.5 shows the change in levels of attention to them brought about by the fall of Baghdad.

**TABLE 7.5**   Levels of attention to Iraqi civilians before and after the fall of Baghdad

|        | Sun | Daily Telegraph | Daily Mirror | Guardian | BBC 1 | ITV 1 |
|--------|-----|-----------------|--------------|----------|-------|-------|
| Before | 5   | 6               | 8            | 5        | 17    | 12    |
| After  | 5   | 13              | 13           | 9        | 39    | 44    |

Note: Figures are % of mentions of all sources.

It is striking that although all press titles and television channels (except the *Sun*) increase their attention to these sources, the margin of change is dramatically different: the television channels not only more than double their attention, but in both cases (these figures are not shown here) these sources become the single biggest quoted source, outnumbering even coalition government and military sources. This figure no doubt correlates with the shift in attention from the conduct of the campaign towards its outcomes, as seen in Table 7.3, whereas the press titles continue to pay more substantial levels of attention to official coalition voices.

## Positive and Negative Mentions

The third indicator shows to what extent television channels perceived events in a positive or negative light. Of course, this is in some measure event driven. It is impossible to present a 'friendly fire' accident in a positive light, for example. In the second week of the war, coalition spokespersons complained that media were presenting events in a negative light by concentrating on the fact that the war was apparently not going according to plan (see Chapter 2). Nonetheless, since it was in theory the same set of events that were being reported, inter-channel differences in emphasis on negative and positive aspects must be explained either on the basis of random differences in reporters' experiences of the war, or on different interpretations of events (or both, in some combination). Because of the restricted validity of the press sample, only television channels will be compared in this respect; however, qualitative analysis (see below) will show substantial differences in press interpretations of the same set of events.

**TABLE 7.6** Good and bad news as percentage of all mentions 20.3.03–6.4.03; all television reports

|  | Military good | Military bad | Political good | Political bad | Total |
|---|---|---|---|---|---|
| BBC 1 | 35 | 60 | 3 | 2 | 100 |
| ITV 1 | 43 | 53 | 4 | 0 | 100 |

Table 7.6 shows that there was a substantial degree of difference in the even-handedness of the two television channels analysed here. While both were more prone to see bad news rather than good, the margins between the two are clearly different. There is nothing in the data that allows an interpretation of this difference; however, it is in line with reports of partisan accusations that the BBC was excessively negative about the coalition military efforts (see Chapter 9). Other studies analysed above do not have comparable data with which a comparison could be made. The low level of attention to political news in reports about Iraq, however it is interpreted, is striking, and no doubt is a product of the same set of editorial decisions which marginalised material concerning the outcomes and purposes of the war.

## Tone of Voice

Qualitative analysis (see below) shows that the reporting of events in the press and television news bulletins used a wide range of stylistic devices, which may amount to a difference in 'tone of voice' between channels/titles. In order to see if there were any *consistent* differences between channels/titles in this respect, quantitative data were collected based on the following coding devices:

- An objective tone, corresponding to the textbook 'normal', factual way of writing news by marginalising value-laden or emotive terms.
- A positive, supportive tone, celebrating heroism, lamenting the suffering of troops and/or adopting their terminology.
- A sceptical tone, where either overt doubts about the events were expressed, or juxtapositions of conflicting information left the reader in no doubt that two versions or evaluations of the events were possible.

Table 7.7 shows the results of the analysis of the sampled press titles up until the moment of the fall of Baghdad. The first five days of the war have not been analysed separately in this section of the analysis, as no important differences were found between the two periods in each of the titles' reporting. In each case, the rank order of the tones of voice was the same across the two periods. There are no data about the tone of voice of television reporting, as it was overwhelmingly objective; other features of television reporting language will be discussed later in a purely qualitative manner.

**TABLE 7.7**  Percentage of reports by title according to tone of voice, 20.3.03–7.4.03

|  | Objective | Heroic | Sceptical | Total |
|---|---|---|---|---|
| *Sun* | 32 | 52 | 16 | 100 |
| *Daily Telegraph* | 66 | 17 | 17 | 100 |
| *Daily Mirror* | 54 | 14 | 32 | 100 |
| *Guardian* | 58 | 2 | 40 | 100 |

Here a clear pattern emerges: the right-wing press is less likely to be sceptical than the left-wing titles, and more likely to adopt a positive, supportive tone of voice. However, the element of 'heroic' material in the reporting is very different by media sector (broadsheet/tabloid) in both the right-wing and left-wing titles. No doubt this corresponds to editorial decisions about support for 'our boys at the front'.

## Qualitative Analysis

A small number of examples of news reports were also analysed in a non-quantitative manner. The purpose of this analysis is to access elements of news reporting that are difficult to observe through quantitative data of the variety used here (and indeed in other analyses referred to above), even if it cannot be asserted that they are necessarily representative of any wider pattern.

The first example is the press reporting of the events of the weekend in which Basra fell to UK forces, and the US army made its first incursions into Baghdad (5–7.4.03). This example was chosen on two grounds: first, in order to test the extent to which events that were clearly (in all the usual military terms) good news were reported in different ways by titles with different editorial policies towards the war; second, in order to see to what extent inter-channel differences, and any other element of reporting that were not accessible through quantitative coding devices, could be observed. News reports are in fact very varied in their approach to these events. In part this is a question of style, in part a question of editorial scepticism about the actual events.

In the incursion into Baghdad, the *Sunday Telegraph* and the *News of the World* (6.4.03) largely accept the US version of what happened. The front page of the *News of the World* has a picture of a shattered Iraqi tank with the headline 'In the Bagh', whereas the *Sunday Telegraph* uses more sober language: 'Endgame in Baghdad'. But the message in the two cases is essentially the same, since both papers largely accept US sources' account of what happened. The *News of the World* says 'Allied tanks sliced the city in two yesterday – and their crews were greeted as heroes. Families . . . cheered and waved. US armour took an astonishing cruise through the city. Some surrendering Iraqi soldiers leapt on to the tanks, begging to be made prisoners of war'. The *Sunday Telegraph* says the US troops 'battled their way' and in a second report on page 2 quotes a US soldier who boasts 'We'll cross the river and barbecue [Saddam's] ass . . .'; it also refers to 'hundreds of triumphant American troops . . .'.

The *Sunday Mirror* published a report of the US incursion which stresses how easy it had been and how many Iraqi soldiers had died, but the leader page emphasises that the military advance was 'the easy bit', probably to be followed by intense street fighting which would be more difficult for the coalition forces. Another report on the same page reinforces the number of Iraqi civilian casualties. The *Observer* has three reports on the incursion into Baghdad. In one, a correspondent located on the Iraqi side of the lines reports driving around Baghdad and finding little trace of the American army; the report concludes that the incursion was only a small one, which only probed at Iraqi defences. Iraqi military were present in large quantities, and the correspondent concludes that the Americans have lost the advantage of surprise. However, a parallel report in the *Observer* gives the same version of the event as found in the *Sunday Telegraph* and the other papers: it was a substantial attack, Fox television news was with the army, 1000 Iraqis died in fierce firefights, numerous suicide attacks were repulsed. In a report inside the same paper, civilian deaths and casualties are the main focus. The headline is 'The moment young Omar discovered the price of war', accompanied by a picture of a boy whose family were all dead as the result of a misunderstanding with US soldiers at a checkpoint.

Both in terms of stylistic devices and editorial approach to the reporting of the events, there are clear differences between the titles analysed here. The stylistic differences between the *News of the World* and the *Sunday Telegraph* are those commonly associated with the differences between tabloid and broadsheet style. Considered from a purely informational point of view, these stylistic differences may be considered relatively unimportant; however, the constant use of stylistic devices which express enthusiasm for military effort constitute an incitement to vicarious pleasure in warfare.[18] This is analogous to the widely-criticised use of military footage of 'smart' weapons in Gulf War I which was said to give the impression of sanitised warfare.

On the following day (7.4.03), British forces finally captured Basra. The siege of Basra was already controversial in reporting terms, as its capture had been announced several times well in advance of its actual fall; according to the *Columbia Journalism Review*, it was first announced on

23 March, some two weeks before its actual capture.[19] Also, on 26 March various UK press titles announced that there was an uprising against the Saddam regime in Basra, which in fact never happened. On 27 March, the Prime Minister referred to it in a speech despite the fact that the *Guardian* had already noted (26.3.03) that the al-Jazeera correspondent in Basra had said that he had seen no sign of an uprising. The BBC correspondent Ben Brown, who reported from the Basra siege, said in a public lecture that he wondered whether the military-sourced reports of the uprising were in fact an attempt by the military to encourage locals to rebel.[20] Certainly, on 27 March US military officials are quoted (in the *Guardian*) as saying to a radio reporter that they are trying to encourage locals in another town to rebel. In general, UK and US forces expected that the Shia population of southern Iraq, which had suffered terrible repression under Saddam after 1991, would actively welcome the coalition forces.

It is in this context that the entry of UK forces into Basra on 6 April was reported. The *Sun* gave very positive, supportive coverage to their entry. The front page has a large photograph of military vehicles and Iraqi civilians waving to them, and the report states 'Grateful civilians welcomed [the UK forces] who liberated Basra'. The Desert Rats 'seized control . . . in a classic pincer movement'. The fuller report on pp. 2–3 opens with a letter from an Iraqi to the UK troops, which refers to their ' brave . . . great and human action . . . forgetless [sic] deed', under the headline ' You Brits are brave. Iraqi's tribute . . .'. Although there is still resistance to the UK forces, it is described on p. 1 as 'pockets of resistance from desperate Iraqis'; on pp. 2–3 the letter is quoted to the effect that there is no resistance, as contact with Baghdad has been cut off. The claim that Saddam's local commander 'Chemical Ali' has been killed is also reported.

The letter quoted is important not only because of the actual words used, but because it is a demonstration of welcome from the local population, in line with earlier predictions that this would occur.

The *Guardian* also puts this story on p. 1 and gives it a more sceptical turn: 'Forces loyal to Saddam Hussein appeared last night to have lost control . . . after columns of British troops poured into [Basra] . . . Some Iraqis were reported to have cheered and waved . . . while others began looting' (6.4.03). The phrases 'appeared to' and 'were reported to' serve as distancing devices, which give the event a partly different profile to that promoted by the language used in the *Sun*. The mention of looting serves to reduce the celebratory tone too, although the emphasis on looting and the breakdown of law and order which came to typify much reporting of the post-war situation (as we shall see later) is not well established at this early stage of the process. According to the UK chief of staff, the Iraqi armed forces have 'departed', but Ba'ath Party loyalists and Fedayeen are 'still a threat', an emphasis which is less thoroughly optimistic than 'pockets of resistance from desperate Iraqis'. The end of the *Guardian* report notes that 'some Iraqis' cheered the British arrival, and the paper uses the same agency-derived photograph as the *Sun*; the letter given pride of place in the

*Sun* report is placed briefly at the end of the *Guardian* report, which also reports that Chemical Ali's fate is still uncertain.

The *Daily Mirror*, preferring to emphasise the negative side of the conflict, focuses more on another incident in the war than the other papers. It gives front page treatment to the friendly fire incident in northern Iraq in which the BBC correspondent John Simpson was injured and his interpreter killed. The front page mentions the capture of Basra, but only in terms of the deaths of three UK soldiers in the operation. The full report of the assault on Basra is relegated to pp. 6–7, while the full report of the friendly fire accident is on pp. 4–5. The report on Basra opens with 'Allied troops took most of Basra but three British soldiers were killed'. The photographs show children greeting the British troops and commandos in action. Apart from the mention of the deaths in action, the report is positive in tone, but less enthusiastic than the tone of voice used in the *Sun*.

The *Daily Telegraph* places the capture of Basra on the front page under the headline 'The Desert Rats 'storm' into the city'. The paper notes there was heavy fighting and that 'Some Iraqis cheered and waved . . .'. In general this report is positive in tone but without the emphasis favoured by the *Sun*. It includes a story about a British soldier whose life was saved by a colleague, also used in the *Daily Mirror*, and presumably on the basis of a common source. On p. 2 there is a further report on the capture of Basra, under the headline 'Everyone smiles and cheers, but thirst is now more pressing than liberty'; this headline is an accurate reflection of the overall tone of the report. Among other things, it notes that the city was defended for longer than expected, and that the tactics of delay and the form of attack used were in part based on concern for civilians, which was necessary in order to lay the grounds for future trust and co-operation. This theme is picked up in a separate article by the defence correspondent who argues that such tactics are necessary in order to win hearts and minds, stating that this approach is typical of UK forces, but that it is questionable whether US forces are used to it.

In these summaries, we can see differences in approach to reporting likely to be the result of consistent editorial choices: the *Guardian* and the *Daily Mirror* have both adopted an approach and a tone of voice that reflects their basic scepticism about the morality of the war. The *Sun* is directly supportive and the *Daily Telegraph*, while generally supportive, does not hesitate to note that problems lie ahead. The argument about the relationship between tactics and long-term strategic purpose is in line with much military-sourced reporting both during and after the invasion, which stresses the UK forces' commitment to winning hearts and minds.[21] As coded in our quantitative analysis, all four papers' reports would figure predominantly under the heading 'military good news', as this is indeed the main thrust of the information contained there. At the same time, they would also be distinguished by the tone of voice coding. Such codings, while giving an overall summary of the different titles' approach to the war, reduce the attention we can pay to the detail of reporting.

Another episode from the war that received extensive coverage was the toppling of a statue of Saddam Hussein by an Iraqi crowd helped by an American military vehicle in al-Firdoz square, which was broadcast live. This event was hailed as a moment of symbolic significance; US Secretary of Defense Donald Rumsfeld likened it to the fall of the Berlin Wall (quoted ABC News, 9.4.03). Similar comparisons are to be found in press comment:

> This joyous moment recalls the deposition of scores of statues of Lenin all over eastern Europe at the end of the Cold War. (*Daily Telegraph*, 10.4.03)
>
> [L]ike newly-freed Russians pulling down the statue of the hated secret police chief in Dzerzinsky Square, the newly-freed Iraqis toppled the figure of their tyrant and ground their shoes into the face of Saddam Hussein. (William Safire, *New York Times*, 10.4.03). (Both quoted in Brown, 2003)

Television news hailed it in similar terms:

> Saddam statue toppled in central Baghdad. Crowds cheer as a statue of Saddam Hussein falls. (CNN, 9.4.03)
>
> A giant concrete and metal statue of Saddam Hussein with his arm outstretched pointing across Baghdad was pulled down in a dramatic scene. And in the same way that the destruction of the Berlin Wall became a part of history in 1989, these pictures will become historical. They will signal the end of Saddam's 24-year rule. (BBC 'Newsround', 9.4.03)
>
> Beginning of the End? Saddam statue – and Regime – toppled, but US doesn't declare victory. Iraqis had only a noose and single sledgehammer when they tried to topple a giant statue of Saddam Hussein in the heart of Baghdad, but the monolith – and the Iraqi dictator's reign – only fell today after US forces tore it down . . . A frenzied mob roared and jumped and danced on the fallen statue. (ABC News, 9.4.03)

This statue was located in a square in front of the Palestine Hotel, used by most western journalists as a base, and it was filmed using cameras in the hotel. The scene has been accused of being staged for television: '. . . the most staged photo-opportunity since Iwo Jima' said Robert Fisk.[22] The television coverage used both close-up shots of the statue and its immediate surroundings, and long shots that show the whole square. The close-up shots give the impression that the whole square is filled with jubilant Iraqis; however, in the long shots it is clear that the crowd is small and most of the square is empty.[23] While it is no doubt legitimate to interpret the scene in symbolic terms, regardless of how it was created, the television presentation certainly frames it in a way that strengthens the symbolism.

A shift in the UK government's justification of the invasion has already been noted: although the original justification – framed by the terms of UN Resolution 1441 – was the existence of WMDs, the UK press noted a shift in government rhetoric towards the record of human rights abuses by the Saddam regime. During the invasion, evidence of these abuses started to come to light, and journalists brought public attention to them. At an infamous prison in Baghdad (BBC1, 17.4.03), Fergal Keene speaks of 'electrocution, murder, rape: all the weaponry of terror' and shows us the gallows 'where the nameless thousands vanished'. His guide, a former political prisoner, cries but is ready 'to forgive Saddam'. Bill Neely (ITV1, 2.4.03) refers to 'the repressive and brutal state that is Saddam's Iraq'. In such comments, the link between human suffering and those responsible for it is made explicit, in line with the new rhetoric of purpose. However, in celebrated cases where western forces made great efforts to save the lives of Iraqi civilians, especially children, who had been severely wounded by coalition bombs, the link between suffering and responsibility is occluded in favour of a rhetoric of humanitarian effort (ITV1, 14 and 16. 4.03; BBC1, 14.4.03). While no-one doubts that the human rights accusations against the Saddam regime were justified, or that the humanitarian efforts to help child victims were genuine, the clear attribution of responsibility in one case contrasts directly with its occlusion in the other.

## Conclusion

The international comparative surveys of television coverage (taken in conjunction with surveys of UK television) suggest that UK television channels were less anti-war than some others – for example, German channels – and less pro-war than US channels. The internal UK comparisons show some clear differences between channels. Our own survey of television news bulletins shows substantial homogeneity between the two main terrestrial channels' bulletins. Although such differences and similarities are often interpreted in terms of bias, it should be remembered that all such surveys operate by comparison between channels only, not by reference to some external benchmark. Our own survey of television news shows a high degree of homogeneity between the two main terrestrial channels except in one respect: the BBC appears to have been more alert to things going wrong militarily than ITV, although both gave more attention to bad news in this respect than to good. All the indicators we have used show that both channels switched focus in the same way after the fall of Baghdad.

Because the regulatory pressures towards impartiality and objectivity are greater on broadcast news than on print media, it is normal to expect higher degrees of partisanship in the latter, especially where opinion and analysis pages are concerned. Indeed, the 'tone of voice' indicator suggests that this is so, and this indicator is supported by qualitative analysis of reports of two significant military events. Elements of the reporting which are directly visible in quotation conform closely to the quantitative indicators. Where patterns of sourcing are concerned, the distribution by title is remarkably homogeneous, across the divisions both of political allegiance and media sector. Although there are clear differences in the degree of focus on the battlefield between press titles, no clear pattern emerges. However, the difference between press focus and television news bulletin focus is very clear in this respect. This is no doubt due to the separation in the television sample between news and current affairs, which is not a feature of the press sample.

## Notes

1 We have accessed this in the form of a CD-ROM PowerPoint presentation, also in a brief outline commentary in *Media Tenor*, 2003,2: pp. 1, 39–43. The full report is obtainable from the company, and will be more fully reported in a future edition of *Media Tenor*.

2 Presented in outline in the *Guardian*, 4.7.03; results of another element of their study were presented in the *Guardian* on 30.9.03 (Lewis, 2003a, 2003b).

3 Notes on methodology and coding sheets can be found at www. lgu.ac.uk/sjcda/department/mediat.html

4 CNN 28.3.03, quoted www.globalissues.org/Geopolitics/MiddleEast/Iraq/ Attack.asp. See Chapter 5 for the argument about showing the injured on TV.

5 It also includes comparative material from two other nations, which we are omitting for the sake of simplicity.

6 However, since ABC was one of the main targets of conservative accusations of bias (see Introduction, note 16), we can assume that a comparative content analysis of US channels would not place ABC at the most pro-war end.

7 A point made by Mark Damazer of BBC News in a reply to Miller published on the *Guardian* letters page.

8 cf. Miller's comment *a propos* a particular incident that 'It was almost as if the BBC and Channel 4 News were covering different wars' (Miller, 2003).

9 In a public lecture at London Metropolitan University, 14.10.03.

10 See Chapter 6, note 4.

11 Comparable figures are to be found in Gunter et al. (2003).

12 These figures are averages based on the terrestrial channel figures in Sancho, 2003: 27, Table 5.

13 The reason for this coding device is explored below. The data as recorded distinguish between US and UK personnel, and the figures are also disaggregated for the purposes of comparison with another study.

14 Including states joining the EU and – for the purposes of this analysis – Russia, since in the pre-combat phase of the crisis Russia sided with France and Germany over the war; in practice there were few mentions of any source in this category except the French government.

15 By 'dedicated' we means pages with a heading indicating that the overall content of the page is Iraq.

16 This sample was used to generate material in respect of only some of the indicators, where a substantial, randomised sample is no less valid than one made representative through stratification.

17 Post-war surveys of public access to news about the war give contradictory results: a survey by the ITC suggests that the overwhelming majority of the population (67%) got their international news primarily from television, and only 16% from newspapers (Sancho, 2003: 19); another survey gives the figures

as 37% and 23% respectively (Gunter et al., 2003). Such a discrepancy may be an artefact of sampling, or of the questions asked.

18   For analyses of tabloid language and other stylistic elements, see Palmer, 2000: 43–4; Engel, 1996.

19   www.cjr.org/issues/2003/3/standard-smith.asp.

20   At London Metropolitan University, 14.10.03.

21   This is especially prominent in the reporting of the deaths of a group of UK military police after the major combat period. See Chapter 8.

22   Quoted www.informationclearinghouse.info/article2838.htm.

23   The shots of the square can be seen at www.informationclearinghouse.info/article2838.htm. It has also been alleged on this website that the square was sealed off by US troops and that the men pulling down the statue were members of an Iraqi militia force flown to Iraq by the US military. The evidence is on the website. If it was staged in this way, it was carelessly arranged, as the US soldier who attached the hawser that pulled the statue down also put a US flag on its head, in direct contravention of military orders (ABC News, 9.4.03). According to CNN: 'About the same time, a marine draped the American flag over the head of the statue – a gesture that drew a muted reaction from the crowd, gasps in a Pentagon briefing room and anger from a commentator on the Arab news network al-Arabiya'. (http://edition.cnn.com/2003/WORLD/meast/04/09/sprj.irq.statue). An Arab-edited comment on the Arabic satellite channel coverage of the war comments: 'The image of an American flag draped over Saddam Hussein's statue was transmitted to tens of millions of Arab viewers and contributed to a sense of the humiliation of their Arab brothers and their fears of American imperialism. This is an excellent example of the power of transnational satellite broadcasts – one soldier makes an individual gesture and an entire region watches in astonishment' (Amin, 2003).

# 8

## THE POST-INVASION PHASE

In this chapter, the analysis moves to the post-invasion phase of the conflict. The following themes are elements of the post-invasion phase of the Iraq crisis that we identify as the main potential candidates for media attention:

- The situation inside Iraq.
- Other nations' policies towards the situation in Iraq.
- The relationship between Islamic fundamentalism – or 'the war on terror' – and the post-conflict situation.
- The domestic political situation in the countries in question (here, the UK and – because of the nature of the crisis coalition – the US and Australia).
- Diplomatic and political relations between nations involved in one way or another in the Iraq crisis – in the UK case, this involves primarily the EU nations, the US and Russia; however, the nations denounced by President Bush as members of the 'axis of evil' are potential candidates, as are also neighbouring Middle Eastern states.
- The impact of the end of the war on the economies of the West.
- Re-evaluation of the war and its representation – that is, the question 'what really happened?'.

The pattern of reporting observed in the UK press suggests that the focus of analysis should be the balance between reporting of the post-conflict situation in Iraq and elements of the domestic political situation in the UK, in particular the dispute over the status of the weapons of mass destruction (WMDs) allegedly held by Iraq. However, given that the war on terrorism was also alleged as a justification for the war (as well as the WMDs) – especially in the US – we must see to what extent reporting focused on the relationship between Islamic terrorism and the post-conflict situation, and in what terms. The US and UK governments also promoted the alleviation of the condition of the Iraqi people by removing the Saddam regime as a justification for invasion, and therefore it is legitimate to see to what extent this theme, as it appears in post-war reporting, justifies the pre-war insistence on its legitimising function.

## The Post-invasion Situation Inside Iraq

On 1 May 2003 President Bush declared in a speech, made on board an American aircraft carrier returning to base, that major military action in Iraq was over. This statement was adopted as the basis of policy decisions by the US government about how to act inside the occupied country. However, since other parties to the conflict – whether it was the remnants of the Saddam regime or other elements of the Iraqi population – refused to recognise this new definition of the situation, a measure of ambiguity arose both in media coverage and in reality over the status of the current situation inside Iraq.

An article in *Le Monde* (19.8.03) about a series of recent events in Iraq provides an indicator of this definitional problem. Headlined 'Sabotage and anti-American attacks divert hopes of reconstruction in Iraq', the piece starts with a series of questions about the significance of these events:

> Who damaged a pipeline of drinking water in north Baghdad on Sunday 17 August, risking thirst for tens of thousands of Iraqis? Who, the day before, dynamited the oil pipeline that takes Iraqi crude to the port of Ceyhan, interrupting exports for a good week, causing a loss of US$7m a day? To whom should we attribute the regular sabotage, at different points in the country, of the electrical network cables? Who fired a mortar shell at the Abu-Ghraib prison in Baghdad, killing six Iraqis held by US forces and wounding 60 others? Who is attacking US forces, especially in Baghdad and its periphery, also British soldiers (but less frequently) in the south of the country? So far no one has laid claim to these acts of sabotage (Naim, 2003).

*Le Monde* gives a wide range of possible answers, citing a number of different interpreters of the situation, from Iraqi citizens writing opinion columns in the Arab press, to the US forces and their supporters in Iraq. Perhaps it is elements loyal to Saddam, possibly co-ordinated by him or those close to him; perhaps it is a group linked to al-Qaida; perhaps it is ordinary Iraqis acting out of a sense of shame at occupation, they say. The range of answers is less important than the fact of asking the question.

Our interest in the patterns of media coverage lies in the range of answers – explicit or implicit – to the question of how is the situation post-invasion interpreted? Is it simply eliminating the remains of the Saddam regime (as was largely said by both journalists and coalition spokespersons in the early days of the post-invasion phase), albeit a process that is taking longer than expected? Or is there a new state of affairs, in which protracted organised resistance can be expected? Or even, indeed, is there still a war? How did journalists interpret this situation? At what point did different press titles think that there was any ambiguity in the situation (if they ever did)?

In examining the coverage of the circumstances inside Iraq, there are four major themes that dominated the reporting of the first weeks of the coalition occupation. These are: dealing with the remnants of the Saddam regime; reconstruction; continuing violence; and Iraqi politics. The benefit of hindsight clearly shows the extent to which these themes are linked to each other. In the initial coverage (late April and May), these themes were largely treated as distinct, separate matters, which suggests that either journalists or their sources considered them as separate issues. Arguably, the relationship between these four themes is important and constitutes a major stake in how the events are interpreted and presented by the media.

### The remnants of Saddam's regime

Dealing with the remnants of the Saddam regime was initially (in April and early May) presented as a relatively simple matter. It was said to consist of 'mopping up' the last 'pockets of resistance' (ITV1, 10.4.03; BBC1, 14.4.03) and the capture of leading figures. The coverage singled out Saddam and his immediate family – encapsulating this in an easily communicable way via the 'pack of cards' of wanted men issued to US troops. Further communications by Saddam through video tapes and letters to Arab media were reported in all sampled press titles, as were their obverse: arrests of important figures. Since Saddam's continued 'presence' weighed heavily on the occupying powers, proof of his continued 'existence' through communication via the media, became a major part of the post-invasion situation. The role of Arab media was thus important:

> Not ten days had passed [after President Bush's declaration of an end to combat on 1 May] that the Iraqi President appeared on video tape broadcast on Arab satellite channels, to declare the continuation of fighting and calling for 'jihad'. Preachers, during their Friday sermons, followed in this incitement campaign and adamantly asked to resist the occupation and not to submit to American hegemony. Immediately, their followers in Najaf, Nassiriyah and Fallujah carried out their demands by killing three soldiers. (Nassar, 2003)

While we may doubt that the causality was as direct as this writer maintains, it is clear that transnational Arab media have continued to provide a communications presence that is less amenable to control by western governments than are the western media. The importance of these Arab media was later underlined by the decision of the provisional Iraqi governing council to expel these channels from their country, a decision later modified to banning them from government buildings and press conferences (*Guardian*, 23 and 24.9.03). The grounds for their objection was that the material constituted an 'incitement to violence'.[1] However, apart from broadcasting messages by Saddam and Osama bin Laden, the transnational Arab media also regularly published information about attacks on coalition forces that differed from reports in western media based on coalition sources. For example, in mid-September 2003 al-Jazeera reported an attack that left eight American troops dead, whereas US sources 'insisted' that only two US soldiers had been wounded (quoted *Guardian*, 23.9.03). Without judging which version is accurate, it is significant that the two versions systematically differ.[2]

The captures of members of the Saddam regime represent victories for the coalition *provided that the captures are publicly known*. The reporting of the deaths of Saddam's two sons in August 2003 is an especially clear illustration of how important the public information flow is under such circumstances. The US administration decided to publish the photographs of their corpses because, according to Secretary of Defense Donald Rumsfeld, Iraqis deserved the certainty of their deaths.[3] According to the BBC, the US military hoped that confirmation of their deaths would act as a deterrent to attacks on US forces, (BBC News, 24.7.03). However, this was a vain hope – three more attacks occurred within hours (BBC News, 24.7.03) and attacks have continued until the time of writing. The photographs were quickly broadcast on Arab satellite channels, and on the BBC television news, where vox pops suggested some acceptance and some rejection of the authenticity of the images by Iraqis.[4]

For the coalition, central to dealing with the remnants of the regime was the capture of individuals, documents or objects that might lead to finding the elusive weapons of mass destruction that subsequently came to occupy centre stage in mediated accounts of the post-invasion phase in UK media. However, suggestions by coalition political leaders that these arrests would probably lead to solid information about the WMDs came to nothing. This negative outcome was not widely reported, although the publication of the Iraq Survey Group's interim report on 2 October 2003 led to comments on the lack of information derived from captured Iraqi scientists.[5] Similarly, following the arrest of Saddam's personal secretary Abid Hamoud Mahmoud in mid-June 2003, US military sources were publicly optimistic that his arrest would enable them to find Saddam and his sons. This was widely reported in US media (for example, www.cnews.canoe.ca and CNN on 18.6.03; see also *Sunday Telegraph*, 22.06.03 and 29.06.03). The *Mail on Sunday* (22.6.03) quotes anonymous sources saying that Mahmoud had brought Saddam's surrender terms with him, a possibility mentioned as 'one theory' in the *Sunday Telegraph*, but which disappeared into silence thereafter. A strike on a convoy of vehicles heading for Syria some days later was attributed to intelligence from him (CNN, 24.6.03; *Daily Telegraph*, 24.6.03: 12). However, no-one in the convoy was a high-ranking member of the Saddam state. Subsequent references to Mahmoud's arrest only mention the original event, or retrospective claims by US military sources that raids based on his intelligence were 'near-misses' on Saddam (quoted, for example, CBS News, 29.7.03; *Die Welt*, 18.9.03). The attack on the convoy and the deaths it caused then disappeared from the news. While the actual surrenders or captures of ex-regime personnel are regularly reported, there is little media follow-up of the results. This may be due to source reticence, or to journalistic indifference, or both. No substantial reporting of any outcomes from the capture of Iraqi scientists or military personnel was evident.

Widely noted in all sampled media was the discovery of the mass graves of Saddam's victims, evidence of the human rights abuses that had become – perhaps by default – one of the political justifications of the invasion, as was evidence of Saddam's 'theft' of bullion and bank notes. Journalists were clearly alerted to these finds by military or other occupation personnel, and it is clear that such events are unproblematic negatives about the Saddam regime.

Reports during May 2003 in the *Daily Mirror* and the *Daily Mail* dealing with the remnants of the regime concentrate largely on the captures and the graves. However, in broadsheet reporting more complex matters are also found. The *Daily Telegraph* notes that the education system, the police force, the staffing of the new ministries, local government, even the local Olympic committee are all problematically linked to the old regime (7.5.03, 10.5.03, 15.5.03, 24.5.03, 29.5.03). The *Guardian* notes the same transition problems, but pays less attention to them than does the *Daily Telegraph*. The difference in news values between tabloid and broadsheet titles is a likely explanation for the lack of complex matters in the tabloids. The tabloid reports comprise the hardest of hard news: relatively brief statements of verifiable facts taken from reliable sources.[6] The broadsheet articles involve journalists on the ground seeking out relatively non-standard sources (primarily relatively 'junior' Iraqi sources) and using the information to illustrate the overall situation in Iraq. These reports frequently refer to the relationship between dealing with the remnants of the regime and the process of reconstruction (for example, *Guardian*, 17.5.03).

In June 2003, reports of the discovery of new mass graves occasionally occur, reminding the reader of the 'human rights/regime change' justification for the war. Reports of captures of members of Saddam's regime are accompanied by reminders of the fact that Saddam and most of his inner circle are still missing, and that this may account for lack of co-operation by many Iraqis and may hinder the hunt for WMDs (for example, *Guardian*, 5.6.03, 19.6.03). In an optimistic version of this scenario, an Iraqi scientist is reported to have handed over nuclear material he buried in his garden many years ago on Saddam's orders (*Guardian*, 27.6.03; *Daily Mail*, 26.6.03). In June 2003, the tabloids give little space to this matter, except to the possibility that Saddam's ex-wife and daughters may seek asylum in the UK, to which the *Mail* devotes six reports between 3 and 14 June. The tone of these reports ranges from factual to outraged, and is clearly more motivated by domestic political concerns (opposition to the current asylum policy) than by the situation in Iraq. Also reported, but as a matter of human interest with no apparent political meaning, is the re-appearance of the former Iraqi Minister of Information, nicknamed 'Comical Ali'.

## Reconstruction in Iraq

In May 2003, the coverage of reconstruction in Iraq in the UK media contains a lot of material whose common theme is 'life is returning to normal', for example, the re-opening of the UK embassy in Baghdad and the announcements of new ambassadorial or other administrative appointments. Clearly, the purpose of these announcements by the UK and US governments was to stress that the war was over and its purposes about to be achieved. However, one of these diplomatic changes involved the return to Washington of the two senior US administrators originally appointed to oversee the reconstruction (General Jay Garner and Barbara Bodine). This was interpreted in UK media as a sign of failure in the reconstruction efforts, despite US diplomatic denials to the contrary. US broadcast reports appear to have been more neutral in their evaluations (CNN, 11.5.03; PBS, 12.5.03).

Tabloid reporting of reconstruction is either reports of new appointments or largely negative reporting of failures. The *Daily Mirror* takes every opportunity to condemn 'American blunders' for the observable chaos, and the *Daily Mail* notes the same level of chaos. In both cases, relatively little background information is made available. The *Daily Telegraph's* coverage of reconstruction, by contrast, contains a lot of optimistic material including, for example, an account of the regeneration of the marshlands drained by Saddam for military reasons and the skill and devotion of Iraqi oil engineers, while at the same time the paper recognises the continuing problems resulting from lack of security, fear and damage. The *Guardian's* coverage of the process of reconstruction is overwhelmingly negative, with extensive attention given to the alleged looting of the National Museum (which is blamed on American carelessness). The paper loses no opportunity to present material showing American management of the reconstruction process in a negative light. A further example is a leading article about President Bush's declaration of the end of combat operations, which is interpreted as a way of giving US forces more latitude in their suppression of any opposition (2.5.03: 29). From an early stage of the post-invasion phase, the *Guardian* presents the military victory as the starting point of political problems, both in Iraq and internationally. An article about US policy on internal security in Iraq pointedly says that the chief administrator, Paul Bremer, 'admits' that it is a serious issue, and this 'admission' is interpreted by the paper as an indication that Washington sees the situation in Iraq as out of control (16.5.03). The *Daily Telegraph*, in contrast, interprets Bremer's statements as a 'promise' of more security against the regime remnants (16.5.03). Another *Guardian* article, summarising the situation in Baghdad, reports that there is little optimism about reconstruction, no sense of security, and substantial warning signs about continued military opposition to the coalition presence (9.5.03). This overwhelming negativity contrasts dramatically with the more upbeat information gathered and reported by the *Telegraph*. This may be due to choice of sources, with their varying perspectives, made by both papers. The *Telegraph* sources many stories from within the UK military, whereas the *Guardian* appears to use more information from aid agency personnel.

In June 2003, the *Guardian's* account of reconstruction continues to be largely (but not entirely) negative. Articles by Naomi Klein argue that US 'De-Ba'athification' policy in Iraq is disguised privatisation, an argument picked up and reinforced in comment pieces (5.6.03, 19.6.03).[7] The 19 June article is an overwhelmingly negative analysis of the post-combat process suggesting that: the occupation has gone 'spectacularly wrong'; there is 'Iraqi resistance' that amounts to 'insurgency'; and the new power in Iraq is 'anti-democratic and colonial'. The *Daily Telegraph* continues to print more optimistic reports and comment pieces which outnumber the pessimistic ones produced in the paper during May and June 2003. An especially upbeat report on 1 June claims that there are no refugees in Iraq, the looting was only of state or Ba'ath Party property, the water is perfectly drinkable and the hospitals are empty. The topic of reconstruction is close to absent from the *Daily Mail* in June: three articles use it as their main theme. The first is about football, the second about the length of time UK troops will have to remain in Iraq, and the third a report from BP about Iraqi oil production. Reconstruction is otherwise only mentioned in passing in articles whose focus is elsewhere – for example, comment columns by Peter Hitchens about the war on terror and Blair and WMDs (8.6.03, 15.6.03). It is similarly absent from the *Daily Mirror's* pages. Four articles record the ambush on a convoy carrying Anne Clwyd (the Labour MP); the fact that US troops have killed Iraqi civilians by mistake; Greenpeace monitoring radio-activity levels in Iraq; and an entirely negative article about the chaos and lack of security in Iraq.

Attention to Iraqi politics is virtually absent from tabloid reporting. The only events noted are those linked to the alleged potential threat of a substantial Shiite presence in the new political order, sometimes labelled 'Iranian infiltration'. This interpretation is clearly linked to US policy towards the 'axis of evil' and the related fear of Iranian Shiite influence in the Middle East. The *Daily Telegraph* notes these events but in a more subtle way: if some reports are clearly oriented towards coalition denunciations of (potential) Iranian influence (for example, 30.5.03), others explore the ambiguities involved (12.5.03), for example foregrounding the Shiite clergy's apparent commitment to democracy rather than theocracy (13.5.03: 11; cf. *Guardian*, 8.5.03: 23). In June 2003, Iraqi politics largely disappears from UK media agendas: the *Guardian* notes that the return of democracy is ever-more delayed (1.6.03), and quotes warnings about Shia fundamentalism in Iraqi politics. The *Daily Telegraph* reports the return of the son of the last king of Iraq and that the return to democracy is being delayed (2.6.03). No doubt this silence is due to the mothballing of Iraqi party politics by the US administration, which leads to a relative dearth of well-sourced events to report. On the other hand, everything previously written in the UK media about the influence of the mullahs in both Sunni and Shia populations suggests that there would indeed be a continuing political life in Iraq, if not at the level of proto-Parliamentary party politics. Indeed, the murder of a prominent Shia cleric in late August demonstrates a continuing political life (*Guardian*, *Independent*, 30.8.03). The (relative) silence on this topic in the media appears to be western source-driven.

In Chapter 6 we saw, in pre-war discussions, predictions of a post-war scenario full of disaster, especially the expected tide of refugees that did not occur. No mentions of this topic at all were found in the tabloids sampled for May and June 2003. There were very few mentions in the broadsheets: the *Guardian* published an article by Baroness Amos (Clare Short's successor at the Ministry of Overseas Development) stating that 'thankfully' there had been no tide of refugees (29.5.03), and by William Shawcross denouncing silence on the subject (17.6.03), but beyond that the paper only acknowledged the topic in a report on 12.5.03 and as an aside in a Comment and Analysis piece on 27.6.03. The *Daily Telegraph* – which appeared to discount the pre-war claims – referred to the failure of the predictions in four articles in May and June. News reporting has difficulty in handling 'nothing happened', except under exceptional circumstances. It is hardly surprising, therefore, that virtually the only mentions of this non-occurrence should occur in feature pages.

## Continuing Violence

The subject of continuing violence is more complex than the previous topics, and has continued to attract substantial media attention up to the end of October 2003. In the first days of the occupation, the coalition authorities and the UK media largely attributed the violence either to 'rogue elements' of the previous regime who had not given up, or to looting (the looting of the National Museum served as an iconic summary of this).[8] However, the lethal confrontations at Fallujah around 1 May were an important turning point in coverage of the violence. From this point on, assertions about the role of the remnants, or 'rogue elements', of Saddam's regime are questioned by the media, leading to a more general questioning of the role of US forces.

The first incident at Fallujah, in which US soldiers shot dead a number of Iraqi demonstrators, occurred on the night of Monday 28 April and was reported in the following day's evening newspapers in the UK. The reports are virtually identical, using the same quotes from the same sources, and reporting that al-Jazeera had interviewed local people about the incident. The presence of al-Jazeera was crucial in establishing that there were indeed contrasting versions of events. The UK media provided both US army and local Iraqi interpretations. These diverge over the issue of responsibility for the confrontation escalating into gunfire and death. On 30 April, the UK national titles provide eyewitness accounts together with more distantly-sourced versions. The *Times* is relatively even-handed in its account, noting the underlying tensions involved in a 'conservative town' where people view the US as occupiers, not liberators. The *Guardian* and *Independent* both provide eye-witness accounts, using the same local sources. Although both papers quote the US version of events, they give more credibility and emphasis to the Iraqi version that soldiers opened fire on unarmed civilians. The *Guardian* editorial refers to 'shocking events', 'widespread popular opposition' in Iraq, and American 'staggering recklessness' (30.4.03: 25).

And a piece on its comment and analysis page points out that the usual post-military scenario does not apply:

> So the conflict must be over. Surely we are now in the 'aftermath', that less spectacular phase of war confined to the inside pages and worthy foreign policy seminars. The rest of us can doubtless tune out, unwind after a stressful few months and get ready for summer.
> Not so fast. (Freedland, 2003)

On the following day (1.5.03), the *Independent's* reporter on the scene reports that he does not believe the US version of events, calling their account 'wildly implausible and inadequate' in relation to the evidence he has witnessed.

The rest of the national press is more even-handed than the *Independent*, but only the *Sun* gives clear precedence to the US version. Even the *Daily Telegraph* is critical of the US military's handling of the situation (2.5.03: 16). The following lines from the *Daily Star* report are typical of the 'balance' achieved by other papers. Under the headline 'Troops fire on students; 13 Iraqis killed in anti-US demo', the report continues:

> US troops turned an anti-American protest into a bloodbath when they shot dead at least 13 Iraqis and wounded 75.
> The soldiers insisted they were fired on first by the crowd of protesters.
> But a cleric said: 'It was a peaceful demonstration. They did not have any weapons'.
> Arab television station al-Jazeera said the troops opened fire after someone threw a rock. (Kaniuk, 2003)

This account gives both sides of the event but puts more emphasis on the Iraqi account, as the responsibility for the incident is clearly placed on the Americans. The contrast between 'protest' and 'bloodbath' is a strong device.

On the following day (30.4.03), a further protest demonstration occurred, with more shootings by US troops. This is reported on 1 May, in parallel with the trail that President Bush would later announce an end to major military operations from an aircraft carrier – the parallel and implied contrast is made explicit in many reports. Eye-witness reports from Fallujah (*Times, Daily Mirror, Independent, Guardian*) all give more credibility to Iraqi versions of events (although the local mayor quoted by the *Guardian* does not blame the Americans, and says Ba'athists may be paying people to cause trouble). The *Daily Mirror* lays the blame on US troops, and its report is accompanied by photographs of the Iraqi victims. The *Independent* sees the events in Fallujah as a key to understanding the situation in Iraq.

The list of newspaper titles that are negative towards the US over this event is scarcely surprising, conforming to their negative stance throughout the crisis (*Guardian, Independent, Daily Mirror*). What is more surprising is that the stance of the remaining titles is either even-handed in their treatment of the event, or tilts towards an anti-US position, while observing the journalistic norms of balanced reporting. In short, it is only the *Sun* that really accepts the US interpretation of the event.

From early May, the media contain a clear pattern of attention towards the continuing violence. Throughout May and June 2003, despite repeated US military denials that the attacks have any military significance, all sampled titles are critical in their assessment of whether it is just a question of 'mopping up' the remains of the Saddam regime or something more is involved (for example, BBC News, 18.6.03).[9]

In May, the *Daily Mirror* reports the deaths of coalition troops and pays attention to what it regards as US blunders. The *Mirror's* reporting of the incidents at Fallujah is typical of its treatment of this theme in general. With only five articles in May, the *Daily Mail* devotes substantially less attention to the continuing violence than the other titles. The paper devotes twice as many articles to the story of Colonel Collins (see below) as it does to the continuing violence. Even its focus on Fallujah is pegged to President Bush's speech announcing an end to combat and only reported in passing in an article on the continued UK military presence in Iraq (1.5.03: 10 and 2.5.03: 31). Violence reappears relatively briefly in articles about the overall situation in Iraq and is dictated by Prime Minister's visit to Basra in May. This suggests the paper does not think violence is a subject that demands serious protracted attention. In the sampled broadsheets, reports of continuing violence are frequently analytically related to questions of reconstruction. Articles chiefly or exclusively about the violence do not, therefore, constitute a substantial proportion of coverage even in the broadsheet press. The difference between the two sampled broadsheet titles is that throughout May, the *Daily Telegraph* treats the continuing violence as an issue which is not a central concern in the reconstruction process, whereas the opposite is the case for the *Guardian*. This is especially noticeable in the *Guardian's* reporting of comments by American officers to the effect that they are still at war (31.5.03: 21) and that 'combat continues' against an enemy who has 'some local cohesion' (30.5.03: 6). A further example on 9 May is an article on an overview of the situation which reports on warning signs of what awaits the Americans as they trade fire every day across Iraq.

In May 2003, the overwhelming majority of reports about violence concern US troops facing fire, or the lack of security facing Iraqi citizens. Very few reports remark on UK soldiers facing armed violence. This is probably due to the lack of such incidents; however, one report notes that the local elections in Umm Qasr (in the UK sector) were postponed due to continuing disorder (*Daily Telegraph*, 24.5.03: 21). In May, many articles about the level of post-combat violence contain self-congratulatory references to the greater skill of UK troops in peace-keeping. This is contrasted with American 'heavy-handedness'. This theme is present in varying quantities in all sampled titles. However, on 24 June six UK military police were killed in southern Iraq, the first killing of UK personnel since the end of combat. From this point on, the tone of reporting on this theme changes dramatically in the tabloids.

In June 2003, the *Guardian's* coverage of the continuing violence unequivocally asserts, repeatedly, that this is tantamount to continuing warfare. In early June, the US army decides to 're-take Falluja', that is, it is reported as a continuation of combat (5.6.03: 17). By 13 June, Iraq has become a 'quagmire', a word later associated with a 'Vietnam-style quagmire' (26.6.03: 2). On the same day, the paper refers to US troops 'returning to large-scale combat' and says that 'US military figures now speak openly of a prolonged period of combat' (14.6.03: 2). On 18 June, the paper refers to the 'increasing sophistication of guerrilla fighters'. On the 23 June, it quotes a speech by President Bush in which he is 'forced to defend' the rising US death toll, for which he blames 'pockets of the old regime and terrorist allies'. In late June, the *Guardian* reports that the US administrator has announced a new crackdown on 'insurgents', which he refers to as 'pockets of resistance'. The *Guardian*, however, refers to 'fears of a long guerrilla war', and notes the difference in evaluation of the situation between 'military officials' and 'troops on the ground', stating that officials refer to 'sporadic incidents', whereas a soldier says the attacks on US troops must be 'a co-ordinated thing' (30.6.03). The *Daily Telegraph* reports the continuing violence in a predominantly negative way, but also reports US military activity in a positive manner. The paper reports that they have 'wiped out' an al-Qaida camp in the desert (15.6.03), it debates whether another US attack was a triumph or a blunder (14.6.03: 19), it notes the growing sophistication of attacks on US forces (11.6.03), and in late June voices fears that 'growing resentment could be ignited into a general uprising' (28.6.03). On the other hand, the paper regularly quotes American sources which claim there is no pattern of co-ordination in the attacks, rather they are due to remnants of the Saddam regime (26.6.03: 2; 28.6.03: 21). In the first three weeks of June 2003, the *Daily Mail* continues to pay little and irregular attention to the continuing violence, but in the last week provides far more. This follows, and may be connected to, the deaths of six UK military police on 24 June (see below). On 14 June, the *Mail* reports that US forces have wiped out 100 Saddam loyalists in a raid in the desert, but on 15 June, quoting local sources, they report what appears to be the same event as the mistaken killing of shepherds. Subsequent attacks on US forces are by 'Saddam Hussein fanatics' (17.6.03: 26), or by a solo sniper (18.6.03: 24). However, once the UK military police have been killed, the tone of voice of the paper changes: the situation is 'asymmetric warfare' that may turn into a Vietnam (25.6.03) or intensified guerrilla warfare (27.06.03). It seems that the deaths of UK personnel changed the *Daily Mail's* estimation of the nature of the situation in Iraq. The *Daily Mirror* gives prominence to reports of attacks on US troops and also to US military operations in Iraq, but whilst quoting US military sources who speak of operations against 'rebels loyal to Saddam Hussein' (17.6.03) or designed to 'root out remnants' of his regime (30.6.03), the paper also refers to a generalised resistance (14.6.03), or blames US strategy for the deteriorating situation (25.6.03).

In these newspaper titles the deaths of the UK military police are reported in a completely different way to the attacks on US troops. First, the amount of space devoted to the military police deaths is much greater than that given to the attacks on US troops, within a short space of time. More importantly, the tone of voice is different. All sampled UK titles had previously reported that the British troops were more skilled at peace-keeping and winning hearts and minds than their 'heavy-handed' US counterparts, leading UK journalists to ask how this incident could have occurred. The *Daily Telegraph*, while continuing to quote UK military personnel who insist that their tactics will not be changed by this incident, says that British self-congratulation in this respect is now misplaced. The *Daily Mail* reports this incident far more extensively than any other element of the situation inside Iraq, allowing space for 22 reports in a period of a week, as opposed to nine stories reporting on attacks on US troops in the whole of June. The *Daily Mirror* also assigns the event a high degree of prominence, stating that the implied reversal of fortune for UK forces' tactics in Iraq is 'the unthinkable' for military leaders, and at the same time continues to give prominence to UK military claims that the tactics will continue (26, 27 and 28.6.03). Both tabloids' analysis of this event contain the accusation that the government is to blame, arguing that there was no justification for the military presence in Iraq in the first place (for example, *Daily Mirror*, 26.6.03: 6–7; *Daily Mail*, 29.6.03: 29).

### Iraq and the War on Terror

During May 2003, terrorist bombs attributed to al-Qaida exploded in Casablanca and Riyadh. The Bush administration had placed considerable emphasis on the relationship between Iraq and the war on terror – indeed, President Bush referred to it again in his 1 May speech announcing an end to major combat operations, stating that Iraq had ceased to be a source of aid for the terrorists. How were developments such as these bombs presented in the press? Various interpretations are possible, for example: that there is no relationship between these events and the Iraq war; that they show that al-Qaida has not been affected by the fall of Saddam; that Islamic terrorism has been encouraged by the emotions widely aroused among Muslims by the invasion. During May 2003, the dominant feature of UK press treatment of these bombs and other elements of the 'war on terror' is uncertainty of interpretation. The bombs in Riyadh and Casablanca are sometimes highlighted in stories to show that US policy is flawed: the invasion of Iraq has allowed al-Qaida to re-group (*Daily Telegraph*, 21.5.03: 12) and fomented support for terror (*Guardian*, 19.5.03: 5), or at least distracted everyone from the war on terror (for example, *Daily Mirror*, 14.5.03: 6; *Daily Mail*, 16.5.03: 12; *Guardian*, 15.5.03: 14); but elsewhere, the opposite is highlighted: the war on Iraq helped the war on terror (*Daily Mail*, 19.5.03: 10) or that there is no link – either positive or negative – between the two (*Guardian*, 19.5.03: 17; *Daily Telegraph*, 19.5.03: 19).

In June 2003, the link between Iraq and the war on terror virtually disappears from the pages of the *Guardian*: it appears as a main theme in a single article concerning the CIA's doubts about the pre-war link between Baghdad and al-Qaida (10.6.03: 12); the *Daily Mail* picks up on the same event (10.6.03: 19). The *Daily Telegraph* reports President Bush's defence of his assertions of al-Qaida/Saddam links, *contra* a document leaked to the *New York Times* asserting that contrary intelligence had been suppressed; in its report the paper says 'it is generally accepted' that there were links between the two (10.6.03). The theme is virtually absent from the pages of tabloid reporting in June, although the *Mirror*, in an article about the 'guerrilla war of attrition' in Iraq, reports that al-Qaida is still operational (1.6.03).

The bombing of the UN mission in Baghdad on 19 August led to speculation that al-Qaida was a likely culprit. In the words of Paul Bremer, the US chief administrator in Iraq, the country was now one of the battlefields in the global war against terror; quoting his words, the *Guardian* noted acidly that one of the purposes of the invasion had been to avoid this development (26.8.03: 19, repeated 3.9.03: 21).

The link between Iraq and the war on terror is primarily event-driven in the UK press, as was the case in the pre-war coverage. It is only when spectacular events and political reactions to them drive the news agenda that any connection is made. It appears that there is not enough acceptance of this to lead journalists to look for such material. However, President Bush's subsequent admission (17 September) that there was no evidence of any link between Saddam Hussein and the September 11 terrorist attacks was widely reported. It was interpreted to confirm the constant slow emergence of evidence in the US that the links between Iraq and Islamic terrorism had been exaggerated (BBC News website, 18.9.03).

Some of the articles, in the sample mentioning Iraq, refer to the war on terror in relation to wider political developments, notably the situation in Saudi Arabia, the position of Iran, and the Israel/Palestine conflict. In an interview after the fall of Baghdad, the US deputy secretary of state for defence and a leading hawk, Paul Wolfowitz, said in a magazine interview quoted in the UK press (for example, *Guardian*, 16.5.03) that one of the motives for the invasion, which had not been widely reported *before* the war, was to enable the US to withdraw its troops from Saudi Arabia.[10] The announced withdrawal, in combination with the Riyadh bomb, led to articles in the broadsheet press analysing the situation in Saudi Arabia in relation both to al-Qaida and to the invasion of Iraq. The dominant tone in the stories is the ambiguity of Saudi Arabia due to the relationship between the regime and the Wahhabi version of Islam with its institutional influence in the kingdom.

The position of Iran is reported in many articles, most of which only make passing reference to Iraq (here we are excluding articles about the allegations of Iranian 'infiltration' of Iraqi politics), as the focus is largely on US policy towards Iran. In May 2003, stories report that US policy has recently been influenced by 'intelligence reports' that Iran has been sheltering al-Qaida people; some of the reports accept this uncritically, others note Iranian rebuttals and previous Iranian co-operation with the US in respect of al-Qaida (*Daily Telegraph*, 26.5.03; 30.5.03; *Guardian*, 29.5.03, 24.5.03). Despite previously noting links between Saddam Hussein and Palestinian organisations, most UK press reporting makes little linkage between the conflict in Israel and the Iraq war. However, the revelation that two suicide bombers in Tel Aviv were UK Muslims provoked some analysis of this relationship.

Fears of looting of Iraq's nuclear facilities linking it to the war on terror surface in some reports in the *Guardian*. On 14 May, the UN weapons inspection team is quoted as saying that the looting poses a risk of nuclear proliferation, especially of terrorists obtaining the materials to make a 'dirty' bomb. Subsequently, it is reported in the *Guardian* that the US military authorities will allow the UN inspection team to return (21.5.03: 12). Even later it is revealed that the US military have prevented them from checking the nuclear facility in question; the looting is 'embarrassing' for the Bush administration, as it risks exactly what the war was intended to avoid — terrorists obtaining WMDs (*Guardian*, 30.5.03: 4).

Finally, the sampled titles noted the relationship between the Iraq war and new anti-terrorist measures undertaken to protect Parliament. The *Daily Mail* treats the new measures in a non-sceptical way. However, in one article the paper blames the situation on the UK participation in Iraq, and in another says that the invasion of Iraq was necessary but not sufficient in the war on terror. The *Daily Telegraph* reports on the relationship in passing, and the *Daily Mirror* mentions it briefly in two articles in May. On 19 June, the *Daily Mirror* claims that the UK government attempted to deflect attention from Clare Short's attack on it by issuing the warning about terrorist activity in the UK (19.6.03).

In short, the UK press sees no consistent relationship between the war in Iraq and the threat from al-Qaida.

## The International Dimension

As shown in Chapter 6, the UK press – especially the broadsheet titles – gave substantial attention to the divisions in the UN, within the European Union, and between the coalition and other nations. These divisions were opened up by the Anglo-US drive towards war. To what extent, and in what way, did these divisions and the ongoing international relationships involved figure in post-war reporting?

First, although there is by no means silence on the subject, it is a marginal theme in relation to the most frequently treated themes. The non-coalition nations cited in the reporting are predominantly Russia, France and

Germany. There are occasional mentions of Belgium and Spain when attempts were made in both countries to launch anti-US war crimes prosecutions. Most newspaper titles commented on the US response to these nations' lack of co-operation (the view of the Bush administration) over the military phase and its preparation in the UN. The perception, as reported in the UK press, was that the US would continue to be negative in its behaviour towards these nations, except possibly Russia whose co-operation was needed in the war against terror. In the light of subsequent developments, the position of the UN is an important element in this dimension of events. As noted above, the weapons inspectors used publicity about the looting of Iraq's nuclear sites to put pressure on the occupying forces to have access in Iraq. This was part of a protracted process through which the UN's ongoing role in the country was renegotiated. In the immediate aftermath of the war, the US was averse to allowing the UN any substantial role in Iraq, and there were extensive negotiations (briefly reported) about the exact nature of this role. According to our sample, the UK press interpreted these negotiations during May 2003 as an example of US domination, and most of the media's analysis presented the new UN resolution giving a legal status to the occupying forces as a victory for US diplomacy. The media's view was that the concessions necessary to secure a vote of approval from those nations who had opposed the military phase were minor. In addition, the view was that the UN gained, at most, a contributory role in the reconstruction process, the coalition maintained control over the sale of Iraqi oil, and security remained entirely in their hands. However, to anticipate the historical sequence, by the beginning of September, the US had come to accept the necessity of UN involvement in the security of Iraq, due largely to the continuing level of violence inside the country. Indeed, in June, Donald Rumsfeld had floated the idea of an international peacekeeping force (*Guardian*, 28.6.03: 2).

Until the late summer, the newspapers paid relatively little attention to the overall nature of the UN involvement in Iraq, although they reported that it was involved in organising reconstruction and the creation of a new Iraqi political process (for example, *Guardian*, 22.7.03: 12). However, in mid-August 2003 rumours start to appear, suggesting that the US administration might be changing its mind about the role of the UN in Iraq. On 22 and 23 August, various UK titles report that the US wants a new UN resolution awarding the UN an expanded role in Iraq without handing over either military control or political power to an Iraqi administration. This follows a report in the *Guardian* (22.7.03) regarding the UN endorsement of the interim government in Iraq, stating that it 'opens the way' for the US to seek help from the UN, as it is 'keen to share financial and military costs'. By 29 August, it is reported that the US had 'abandoned its opposition to a multilateral UN force in Iraq', despite some opposition inside the Washington political establishment (*Daily Telegraph*, 29.8.03: 15). On 4, 5 and 6 September there were numerous reports about the different negotiating positions adopted in advance of a Security Council vote. Clearly the publicity given to these positions was part of the negotiating process, as the coalition leaders (especially the US) jockeyed for definitional power with France and Germany. All sampled UK titles pointed to the dramatic shift in US policy, calling it a 'humiliating climbdown' (*Daily Mirror*, 4.9.03; *Daily Mail*, 5.9.03), a 'substantial climbdown' (*Daily Telegraph*, 4 and 5.9.03), and the *Guardian* refers to the 'humiliating task' facing Bush (6.9.03). By the beginning of October 2003, when a report of the official US inspection of Iraq's suspected WMDs sites showing that no weapons had been found was published, the UN was refusing to back the new US request for substantial aid in Iraq (*Guardian*, 3.10.03).

Also discussed – mainly in broadsheet reporting – was the economic impact of the war, which in May 2003 was largely agreed to be positive – the so-called 'Baghdad bounce'. The majority of stories were confined to the finance pages, with few reports elsewhere, except in the *Guardian*, which, as well as mentioning Iraq as part of trading conditions in many business page articles, also devoted several articles in news pages to the contractual arrangements involving international corporations and the reconstruction of Iraq. Although the reports are not predominantly critical of these arrangements, their placing in news pages is notable, whereas other titles reserve them for the business pages only. Given the extent of the favourable impact of the end of the war on share prices in the UK, it is surprising that more was not said about it on the news pages. In June 2003, the economic impact is also reported in negative terms. The *Guardian* contains several reports by consumer and financial organisations, noting that the Baghdad bounce is absent in various sectors such as US consumer confidence and the UK housing market, while also noting reports that are more positive about other sectors.

## UK Politics

The Iraq crisis triggered resignations from the UK government, notably Robin Cook (former foreign secretary, then leader of the House of Commons), pre-invasion, and Clare Short, then international development secretary, post-invasion. The reporting of Clare Short's resignation was prefaced by a number of stories about her missing an important government meeting and vote. Although neither Minister resigned specifically over the issue of WMDs, in both cases their resignations preceded their speaking out on the issue as it grew in importance.

The newspapers also noted that the UK government lost many seats in the local government elections in early May, a result analysed in terms of the views about the Iraq war held by different groups of electors. The papers reported that the Labour vote fell dramatically in areas with large Muslim populations. Some titles linked this to a general questioning of whether the government had lost the trust of the population. This theme resurfaced in the reporting of the Brent East by-election, where a large Labour majority was over-turned by the Liberal Democrats.

However, the developing controversy over the Government's dossier about Iraq's possession of WMDs was overwhelmingly the most important domestic political event in relation to Iraq, starting in the last few days in May (see Chapter 9).

## What Really Happened?

To a large extent this question becomes entangled with the row about the (non) existence of WMDs. However, three other issues are given some treatment in the sampled newspapers: the media coverage of the war is analysed, especially in the context of a BBC documentary about al-Jazeera's war coverage; the conduct of Colonel Tim Collins comes under scrutiny; and the rescue of Jessica Lynch is re-evaluated.

One of the important factors in the situation in Iraq during and after the invasion has been the presence of reliable Arab language reporting of the situation in Iraq. The transnational Arab television channels reported the war in ways that diverged from western media, both by constantly denigrating the coalition invasion as aggression (Amin, 2003)[11] and by publishing material unwelcome in the West, such as the images of coalition dead and prisoners, and the damage done to Iraqi civilians. Here 'reliable' should be understood as the use of news gathering modelled on western norms: for example, lack of censorship, checking source information against other sources. Traditionally, Arab language media located in the Middle East have been dominated by media directly subordinate to the political system and by privately-owned 'loyalist' media, exercising self-censorship in the interests of the political system. These media tended to have an output dominated by 'protocol news', that came directly from the political system – typically, the Ministry of Information or the official national news agency. At the same time, some Arab nations had a more diverse, 'free' press system (Hafez, 2001: 5–8). The advent of transnational Arab language satellite broadcasting using western-inspired news gathering methods has fundamentally changed the pattern of media in the region. Channels such as al-Jazeera do not accept protocol news in the same way as the established Arab broadcasters. As a result, these new broadcasters are widely trusted in the Arab-speaking world (Amin, 2003).

More generally, Arab media interpretations of the Iraq war are seen to diverge from western ones (Amin, 2003). This perception is most dramatically represented in reactions to the decision by al-Jazeera to show footage of dead British soldiers during the fighting, which was attacked as contrary to the Geneva Convention and an assault upon human dignity. Both Iraqi actions in taking the photographs and al-Jazeera's editorial decision were widely attacked in the UK press. The station justified such footage on journalistic grounds, adding that in the Middle East the recent history of violence meant that such images were not sensational, but a 'mimetic' representation of the real world (quoted *Guardian*, 31.3.03). Fewer commentators pointed out that UK media had shown numerous pictures of dead and wounded Iraqi soldiers, and no complaints have been observed in UK media when the bodies of Saddam Hussein's two sons were publicly shown in August 2003. During the invasion, particularly during the period when they maintained good access inside Baghdad, Arab satellite stations gave prominence to civilian casualties inside Iraq, when coalition missiles or bombs hit civilian installations instead of military ones (see, for example, *Guardian*, 29.3.03). However, although al-Jazeera was blamed by coalition leaders for being too favourable to Baghdad, the Iraqi government nonetheless came close to expelling the station, enhancing its reputation for independence (*Guardian*, 3.4.03).

On 1 June, after the military campaign, the BBC showed a documentary about al-Jazeera's coverage, which included the controversial footage, albeit with the soldiers' faces disguised. The *Sun* launched a ferocious attack on the BBC for doing this (26–29.5.03), but the *Guardian* treated the documentary sympathetically; in a comment article the *Daily Mail* attacked the BBC (31.5.03: 15), but subsequently praised the programme for showing a view of the war that was likely to be more truthful than what UK viewers had seen during the invasion (2.6.03: 45).

On the evening before the first day of warfare, Colonel Tim Collins of the Royal Irish Regiment made a speech to the men under his command which was widely reported in the UK press (via an embedded correspondent of the *Daily Mail*). The speech was widely hailed in both the UK and US as inspirational. Subsequently, the Colonel was accused (reported 21.5.03), both by an Iraqi civilian and by an American army reserve officer, of unacceptable behaviour towards Iraqi civilians. This was shortly followed by the revelation that Collins was also under investigation over the suicide of a soldier under his command in Belfast.[12] During May and early June 2003, the accusations against him were prominently reported and commented upon in the UK press. The press coverage was divided in its approach. In summary, the right-wing press was supportive to the point of outrage that the accusations were being taken seriously, the *Daily Mirror* was ambiguous in its handling of the accusations, and the *Guardian* was scrupulously objective to the point of distance.

The *Sun* gave the story most prominence, devoting approximately twice as much space as any other sampled title. Its coverage is dominated by frequent references back to Collins' 'eve-of-battle' speech, by denigration of his Iraqi and American accusers, and by supportive statements by fellow soldiers. The *Sun* also quotes him as being 'stitched up' and 'hung out to dry'. The American reservist major who made accusations is called 'a slob' (24.5.03) and a US colleague of his is quoted as saying he is a 'whingeing loser' (26.5.03). The Iraqi that Collins is alleged to have beaten is reported as being a Ba'ath Party activist poorly regarded in his home town. The denigration of the Iraqi also appears in the *Daily Telegraph* (23.5.03: 4,

26.5.03: 5) and the *Daily Mail* (22.5.03: 1, 8, 23.5.03: 10, 24.5.03: 7). All three papers express editorial support for the Colonel, saying that the accusations are 'bizarre' (*Sun*, 27.5.03), 'idiotic' (*Daily Telegraph*, 29.5.03: 24) or unbelievable (*Daily Mail*, 22.5.03: 12). The *Daily Telegraph* also gives space to the allegations against him, and in discussing the evidence is balanced and objective (22.5.03: 1, 8, 24.5.03: 4), but is generally rather supportive. The *Guardian* reports the accusation against Collins in an objective manner, noting his high status in the media and also reporting that the Ministry of Defence was not as supportive as might be expected. The *Guardian* also reports that the *Sun* has obtained leaked material supportive of Colonel Collins. Indeed, the *Sun* regularly quotes sources close to the investigation, or other military sources, who say there is no evidence against him so far or that he is expected to be cleared (27.5.03, 26.6.03, 2.6.03), or who imply that they are forced to investigate him (22.5.03). The *Daily Mirror*, while opposing the war on political grounds – but in line with its sympathetic treatment of UK troops – treats Collins favourably, while also printing material supportive of his accusers (26.5.03: 11; 27.5.03: 4). All papers are more evenly balanced in the way they report the Belfast accusations against him than the manner in which they report the Iraq ones. However, the *Daily Mail* and the *Daily Telegraph* also link the Belfast accusation to the planned reduction of the Royal Irish Regiment, effectively accusing the government of using his case as a distraction or bargaining chip in the cuts (*Daily Mail*, 29.5.03: 12, *Daily Telegraph*, 29.5.03: 24). The fact that these two papers make the same accusation on the same day leads to the suspicion that the idea had derived from a common source. The *Guardian* had already noted that this link had been made by Northern Irish Unionist politicians (28.5.03: 6). After early June 2003, the story largely leaves the news pages. Presumably no new information about the army investigation was forthcoming, effectively depriving journalists of sources of information. However, since they had been readily forthcoming previously – at least to the *Sun* – one can only guess what happened to dry up the flow of information.

The events surrounding Colonel Collins are clearly interpreted in line with the newspaper titles' overall political sympathies and filtered through the line they have taken over the Iraq crisis. While the news reporting is 'factual', the choice of sources to quote is clearly presented to achieve the titles' editorial purposes. This is evident in an article in the *Daily Mail* (1.6.03: 29) in which the case against Colonel Collins is alleged to be linked to UK troops' discontent with the government's handling of the Iraq crisis. The unclear logic of the link reveals the editorial purpose. Whether the leaked material presented in the *Sun's* reporting was authorised or not cannot be directly established. However, there have been no reports of investigations or disciplinary proceedings linked to the leaks.

Jessica Lynch was a maintenance clerk in the US army in Iraq. She was captured in an ambush during the invasion, and was rescued by US forces from an Iraqi hospital on 1 April 2003. Both her capture and subsequent rescue have become controversial. At the time of both events, Lynch was hailed throughout the US media as an all-American heroine who had fought to the last bullet, had been shot and stabbed and had been heroically rescued. Accusations have since been made that the rescue was cynically exploited as a piece of 'feelgood' news after a bad week, in which even US generals had been negative about the progress of the war, and prices on the New York Stock Exchange fell (*Observer*, 6.4.03: 17). The BBC television programme 'Correspondent' broadcast on 18 May 2003 claimed that the events were largely mythical. It suggested that: her injuries were essentially road-accident-type injuries; she had been neither shot nor stabbed; and her rescue was specially staged for the cameras. The programme said that there were no Iraqi troops guarding the hospital and the doctor caring for her had tried to return her to the US forces but had been shot at as he approached.[13] The American organisation Project for Excellence in Journalism (PEJ) has analysed media coverage of the story, including its sourcing, and has concluded that it is riddled with inconsistencies (PEJ, 2003). The evidence of her involvement in a firefight has subsequently been dismissed, but more importantly it was publicly known shortly after her rescue that the hospital in Germany where she was being treated had denied she had gunshot or stab wounds (PEJ, 2003). In mid-April, two US newspapers published reports querying elements of the story but the 'mythical' version continued to dominate US media until the BBC programme was broadcast in May. Subsequently, the *Washington Post* refuted much of the earlier version, a report that was repeated on CNN later the same day (17.6.03). Whatever the truth of these events, it appears that the US media have largely accepted the 'mythical' version, whereas the UK media have largely accepted the BBC's version (for example, *Daily Telegraph*, 16.6.03; *Daily Mail*, 24.5.03): the rescue was 'a cynical piece of propaganda twisted (or even staged) . . .'.[14] According to the *Daily Telegraph* (18.6.03), the BBC's allegations about false information being fed to the media by the Pentagon are rejected in the US. The *Telegraph* story argues that transcripts of the Pentagon's briefings show that no false information was given out; however, journalists who chose to interpret the event in the most 'heroic' light were not corrected, and were 'perhaps encouraged to fill in' gaps in the official account. Indeed, the *Washington Post* noted that the Pentagon had 'not dispelled' the myth (quoted *Scotsman*, 24.6.03). However, the PEJ account shows that the original, 'mythical' version was sourced to 'unnamed' US officials, who of course would not appear on Pentagon transcripts of official briefings. Even in the UK, the *Sun* (21.6.03) refers to her as a heroine, gives details of how she was injured and says nothing about the controversy surrounding her rescue. It should be noted that the original video footage of her rescue was filmed by the US army's own camera crew, and was accepted by the media as valid reporting.

The level of civilian deaths in Iraq during the fighting is the final noteworthy issue because of the near-silence about it since the end of the invasion. General Tommy Franks, the US commander of the invasion forces, is quoted as saying 'we don't do body counts'. US/UK peace protesters have set up a body count and released the evidence on the

Internet. By the end of October 2003, they estimate that the minimum number of civilian dead was 7377 and the maximum was 9180. Differences derive from the uncertainty of certification of deaths, and the count is based on two authenticated sources for each death (see www.iraqbodycount.net; www.comw.org/pda/0305iraqcasualtydata.html). The civilian death count is occasionally reported in UK media, for example, the *Guardian* published a memorial page that recounted the lives of 100 Iraqi dead civilians on 16.5.03: 2 (see also *Daily Mirror*, 14.6.03). *Project on Defence Alternatives* gives a figure of between 3200 and 4300 civilians killed, and a total Iraqi death toll, including combatants, of between 10,000 and 15,000 (quoted *Guardian*, 29.10.03: 15).

## Conclusion

This chapter has sought to analyse the presence of the main themes found in the media reporting and absence of reporting of the post-invasion situation in Iraq. We found inter-title differences in treatment of particular events and themes. However, the analysis does not treat these differences in a systematic manner.

It is clear from coalition information management efforts to demonstrate that the war's purposes were being achieved that the media have played a central role in the course of post-invasion events. For example, the justification of publication of the photographs of Saddam Hussein's two sons shows the extent to which mediated information flows are central to the development of the situation itself: Donald Rumsfeld said that Iraqis 'deserved the certainty' that they were dead.

Shortly after the bombing of the UN headquarters in Baghdad (19.8.03), the US ambassador spoke of 'underlying improvements' in the situation (quoted *Guardian*, 26.8.03). The current (September 2003) list of press releases on the Coalition Provisional Authority's (CPA) website is a resolutely upbeat list of achievements (albeit tempered by announcements of murders of prominent Iraqis), for example: a reduction in curfew hours due to improved security, the first session of the new council of judges, the first battalion of the new Iraqi army graduates, (CPA, 2003). In a press conference in Baghdad (14.9.03) Colin Powell refers to:

> . . . people hard at work, rebuilding a nation, rebuilding a society. I saw people hard at work, knowing that the United States was going to support them in that work. And that work has a very simple, direct and clear purpose, and that is to help rebuild this country economically, its physical infrastructure, but most importantly, politically as well, so that we can move forward to the Governing Council with the appointment of cabinet ministers now. (www.defenselink.mil/news/cpa.html)

It is questionable to what extent this message has been reflected in media coverage of the post-war situation. Certainly, there is scant evidence of it in the UK press sample used here. The pressure group Fairpress has questioned the US media tendency to show a 'falsely bleak picture', when opinion polls in Iraq show optimism about the future (Fairpress, 2003).

The reporting of the continuing violence inside Iraq is clearly part of the pattern of attempts to influence public opinion about the extent to which war aims have been achieved. It is therefore crucial to see whether the violence is attributed to nothing more than a few 'rogue elements' of the former regime, or to a new popularly-based resistance. Both definitions can be found in media reporting, but in general as the summer wore on, the earlier coalition authority insistence on defining it as the remnants of the Saddam regime was decreasingly accepted. Indeed, by the end of October 2003, the CPA commonly refers simply to 'terrorists', for example, in Ambassador Bremer's mourning for the victims of the 12 October bombing (CPA, 2003).

This chapter opened with the question 'What range of definitions of the post-invasion situation has been given, and by whom?' Analysis of the coverage shows that there has been a tendency to move away from defining the violence only as a brief aftermath or as the remnants of the regime and towards seeing it as something more sustained, even if there is no certainty at all about the social forces that are driving the attacks on western personnel and installations. It also appears that the continued violence has attracted more media attention than have efforts at reconstruction or political development. The definition that prevails is a significant part of the development of the situation because it impacts upon various agencies' decisions about their degree of involvement in Iraq. Aid agencies may remove their personnel or scale down their commitment as the Red Cross and the UN did after the bombing of the latter's headquarters. No doubt it will also impact upon commercial organisations' willingness to invest in Iraq.

## Notes

1  For example, on 4.4.03 al-Jazeera showed a video tape of two women vowing to carry out a suicide attack on coalition forces; the following day, two women carried out such an attack on a US-manned checkpoint, according to the *Daily Telegraph* (5.5.03). Saddam was captured by US forces on 13 December 2003. Subsequently film of him undergoing medical examination was broadcast world-wide. This was clearly part of the coalition's strategy of demonstrating as publicly as possible that his regime was finished. The new local television service Iraq Media Network, set up by the occupying powers, is an integral part of this information policy. According to the Coalition Provisional Authority it is widely watched where access is possible, but where alternative access is available it is less preferred and trusted than the pan-Arab satellite channels (see www.cpa-iraq.org/audio/20031117_Nov-16-INR-media_habits_survey.html).

2  A UK journalist who had covered the war and post-war situation in Iraq, with whom we discussed this matter, said that whenever he checked out the two versions, the western account was more accurate.

3   And this despite coalition outrage at Arab channels showing pictures of coalition war dead and prisoners during the combat period. See Chapter 5 and also e.g., BBC News, 27.3.03 (http://news.bbc.co.uk/1/hi/world/middle_east/2889255.stm).

4   See bbc.co.uk/_39320811_iraw22_witchell_vi.

5   See the comments by Andy Oppenheimer of *Jane's Security and Terrorism Monitor* quoted in the *Guardian* (3.10.03: 5). The issue of WMDs is sufficiently important in the UK context to warrant a separate chapter; see Chapter 9.

6   By 'reliable' sources, we mean accredited organisational spokesmen or representatives of publicly known organisations, who have to take responsibility for their statements.

7   The paper continues to interpret economic policy in Iraq in this light: see 22.9.03: 22.

8   However, it turned out to be massively exaggerated, as the 'missing' items had in fact mostly been hidden in order to avoid damage. This was far less widely reported than the original supposition about massive losses.

9   bbc.co.uk/1/hi/world/middle_east/3001616.stm.

10  One possible explanation for its non-reporting was the fact that it was a key demand of al-Qaida. Whether the silence was the result of government silence or journalistic indifference has not been ascertained.

11  See also examples of al-Jazeera programming, discussed in Lamloum, 2003.

12  Colonel Collins was cleared of the charges relating to Iraq on 1 September, 2003. At the end of October 2003, the investigation concerning events in Belfast was not complete.

13  The programme transcript is available from the BBC website; it is previewed in detail by the reporter, John Kampfner, in the *Guardian*, 15.5.03.

14  See Justin Webb, the BBC's Washington correspondent, writing in the *Independent*, 24.6.03. The *Times* (21.6.03) says that US media have been slow to accept 'the truth' about her.

# PART III

## The Media Still at War

# 9

## WEAPONS OF MASS DESTRUCTION, THE HUTTON INQUIRY AND THE BBC

In the period before Gulf War II, there is no doubt that Iraq possessed chemical and biological weapons, and that the Saddam regime was making efforts to develop a nuclear capacity. On the basis of the use of poison gas against the Kurdish population of Halabja, it is clear that Saddam Hussein was prepared to use chemical weapons. After Gulf War I, during the period of UN-imposed sanctions against Iraq, a series of resolutions were passed which obliged Iraq to abandon such weapons, and to demonstrate to the UN, through an inspection and verification process, that they had in fact done so. Had the UN Security Council ordered an armed intervention in Iraq in 2003, it would have been on the basis of these resolutions. In theory, the Security Council could have ordered intervention not on the grounds that Saddam *possessed* such weapons, but on the grounds that he had failed to show that he had abandoned them. However, in most UK media reporting of the Iraq crisis, especially after the end of the UN phase, the question of whether Iraq complied with the demand to verify their non-possession of WMDs became indistinguishable from the substantive question of whether or not Saddam still possessed any, and whether his willingness to use them posed a threat to the rest of the world. In theory, these issues are analytically separable; however, the politics of the Iraq crisis blurred the edges of the distinctions, and in this respect the UK and US governments were distinctly complicit, as their 'dossiers' stressed the *actual* possession of WMDs and the threat that this posed.[1] Indeed, by the end of the summer of 2003, UK media were reporting the situation in terms of whether the UK government could justifiably claim that Iraq had posed a direct threat to the security of the UK – a claim that was manifestly absurd, since no-one had ever suggested that Iraq was capable of attacking this country directly, let alone had the intention to do so. This error was the result of a fudge by the UK government: in evidence to the Hutton Inquiry (see below), the UK Secretary of State for Defence, Geoff Hoon, admitted that he had not bothered to try to correct media misinterpretations of the dossier that gave the impression that Iraq possessed strategic weapons of mass destruction, as opposed to battlefield weapons (Hoon, 2003b: 81–4).

## The Casus Belli

Because the UN resolutions about Iraq were framed in terms of these weapons, they became central to arguments about the justifiability of armed intervention. No doubt they were more important in this respect in the UK than in the US, since the British government had arguably made the role of the UN in the crisis more central to its policy than had the Bush administration; nonetheless, the weapons featured prominently in the presentation to the Security Council made by Colin Powell, US secretary of state, in February 2003. As we show in the analysis of the media coverage of the pre-military phase of the crisis, UK media – and, as it later turned out, the UK public – placed more emphasis on the weapons as the reason for going to war than did the American administration and public, for whom the intervention in Iraq was more intimately linked to the 'war on terrorism' and specifically the attacks of 11 September 2001. UK public support was shown to be heavily dependent on the existence of the weapons and on UN approval of intervention; although disapproval of UK involvement in armed intervention dwindled within days of the beginning of the invasion, it grew again in the aftermath of the invasion phase.[2]

## Media Coverage of the WMDs

During the protracted negotiations in and around the Security Council in the winter of 2002–3, UK media noted that the government's justification for advocating armed intervention in Iraq was subtly shifting ground: from an overwhelming emphasis on WMDs and the UN resolutions, to a focus on the human rights abuses of the Saddam regime, and the justifiability of seeking regime change (for example, *Guardian*, 15.2.03). However, the public record was clear: both the US and UK governments had insisted that Saddam possessed and continued to develop weapons of mass destruction, and made the case for intervention on this basis. As the row over WMDs developed after the military phase of the crisis, this record was quoted in the media to demonstrate the continued importance of the issue (for example, *Guardian*, 30.5.03; *Daily Telegraph*, 15.5.03: 16; BBC News 29.5.03).[3]

During the invasion phase, 'fear' of WMDs was evident in reports of troops wearing chemical protection suits, and of commanders issuing warnings about the risks involved. For example, in the first days of combat both the BBC and ITN repeatedly showed soldiers and reporters wearing anti-chemical suits as missiles were fired over the border. For Richard Bilton, based with the military (BBC1, 20 March), chemical attacks were 'a very real threat'; Sue Saville (ITV1, 20 March) interviewed a soldier who stressed 'the importance of having your kit on you', while Martin Geister's interviewee (ITV1, 20 March) argued that 'some sort of chemical attack is likely to come'. On 28.3.03, the US Command Centre in Qatar said that they had had warnings that at a certain point the Iraqis would use chemical weapons. There were numerous reports during the war of finds of chemical protection suits in Iraqi military buildings, and of reports from Iraqi prisoners that they possessed evidence of chemical weapons being moved onto the battlefield (for example, *Guardian*, 29.3.03). A French reporter, unofficially embedded with the US 3rd Infantry Division, found that the troops he was with seriously believed that Saddam possessed chemical weapons and would use them on the battlefield (Eudes, 2003). In the event, as far as we know, no such weapons were used.

When pressed by a PBS reporter at a speech in New York in late May about why these warnings were given, and yet these weapons were not used, Secretary of Defense Donald Rumsfeld said no-one knew why they had not been used, but that the intelligence warnings were enough to warrant precautions.[4] Subsequently, it was admitted by Lieutenant General James Conway that these fears and warnings were the result of faulty intelligence and that the battlefield risks were less than claimed or even non-existent. These admissions were noted in the UK press (*Guardian* and *Daily Mirror*, 31.5.03). However, a later briefing by the Iraq Survey Group, published in the *Boston Globe* and broadcast on Fox News, said that they had found evidence that Iraqi troops did have orders to use chemical battlefield weapons (*Daily Telegraph*, 13.8.03: 10).[5]

The post-invasion row over WMDs as it appeared in UK media had three elements, essentially:

- the failure to find any physical evidence of their current or recent existence in Iraq (despite documentary evidence of development programmes);
- admissions from inside US governing circles that their current existence was questionable; and
- political developments, as opponents of the governments sought to emphasise the significance of the physical absence of these weapons.

During the period 1 May to 1 October, evidence about the presence or absence of WMDs inside Iraq appears to have been largely lacking: we infer this from the mixture of near-silence and ambiguous reports in the media on the subject. While discoveries of things that might have been parts of WMD development or deployment were trumpeted by the US administration, acceptance that they did not amount to much was significantly less publicised (*New York Times*, quoted *Daily Telegraph* 5.5.03: 16; *Daily Mail*, 26.6.03).[6]

In the immediate aftermath of the invasion, inspection teams were deployed in Iraq to search for the weapons. It rapidly became apparent that they were finding nothing: in the memorable phrase of a US officer, 'we came to bear country, we came loaded for bear, but we found out the bear wasn't here' (*Daily Telegraph*, 12.5.03). The failures had already been noted in the *Washington Post* in late March, but this was little noticed in UK media (*Guardian*, 30.5.03). In May 2003, all sampled UK titles reported on the progress of these searches, with the majority of mentions falling between 7 and 22 May. This burst of interest was sparked by two things: firstly, by the US claim to have found a mobile chemical warfare laboratory (announced on 7 May)[7]; secondly, by the announcement that the US military team responsible for the searches was being sent home as there was nothing left for it to do (*Daily Mirror, Guardian,* 12.5.03). UK national newspapers vary in their acceptance of, or scepticism towards, the reported find and the likelihood of further finds. It was later stated by a 'former UN weapons inspector' that this 'laboratory' – in reality an open truck – bore no traces of any biological agents (reported *Daily Mirror,* 30.5.03). From 23 May onwards, the story shifted focus and mentions of the searches tended to be retrospective, used as evidence in the context of new developments.

On 23 May, the *Guardian* and the *Daily Telegraph* both noted that the CIA was conducting a review of its pre-war intelligence about Iraq, and that this cast doubt on the reliability of allegations about WMDs; despite denials from US Secretary of Defense Donald Rumsfeld (on 27 May), this interpretation was not retracted. Previously, on 9 May, Deputy Secretary of Defense Paul Wolfowitz had given an interview to *Vanity Fair* in which he said that the decision to focus on WMDs in the confrontation with Iraq was taken for reasons of bureaucratic convenience. The interview was published on 30 May, but advance publicity about his remarks was picked up by the *Washington Post*, who interviewed Wolfowitz about this point, and published it on 28 May. Wolfowitz' comment was widely reported in the UK press, but despite a 'correction' from the Pentagon following the *Vanity Fair* publication, Wolfowitz' remarks continued to be interpreted in the UK press as a revelation of previous dissembling. The BBC reported it without stressing any negative evaluation.[8] Previously, on 27 May, Rumsfeld had said in a speech to the Council on Foreign Relations in New York that it was possible Saddam had destroyed the weapons before the war. This was reported in US media and the BBC news the following day, and in the UK press on 29 May.[9]

These two sets of comments, coming close to each other, and in conjunction with the CIA review, were sufficient to spark a storm in the UK media on 28 and 29 May. Robin Cook, former UK foreign secretary and leader of the House of Commons, who resigned from the government over the decision to go to war with Iraq, speaking on Channel 4 News on 28 May, called the Rumsfeld comments 'breathtaking', claiming they blew a 'gaping hole' in the arguments for war, proving that Saddam did not present a threat to the world. UK government officials denied that Rumsfeld's remarks contradicted UK policy, insisting the issue was about compliance with UN resolutions, obliging Saddam to prove he had abandoned the weapons (cited in the *Guardian,* 29.5.03). However, what dominated reporting of the event was Cook's analysis, supported by similar comments by other left-wing Labour figures. All sampled papers reproduced Cook's quotes. On 29 May, the *Daily Mirror* amplified them in a series of articles spread over two pages, the *Mail* called Rumsfeld's remarks a 'stunning admission', recalling Wolfowitz' comments in the same report, and the *Daily Telegraph* referred to embarrassing divisions between the US and the UK on this issue, stating that there 'will be scepticism' as a result. Across the divides of both political alignment and media sector, the UK press were unanimous in its assessment of the meaning of these comments by US administration figures. While the statements by Rumsfeld and Wolfowitz were the main elements in the development of the storm in the UK, they also correlated with previous reports in the UK broadsheet press noting that, even before the military phase of the crisis, the UK intelligence services were uneasy about the political use of intelligence in the justification of war.[10]

It is into this fertile ground that the seed of a report on BBC Radio 4's 'Today' programme fell on the morning of 29 May 2003. The broadcast item stated that a defence expert relayed to the reporter, Andrew Gilligan, that Alastair Campbell, the Prime Minister's Director of Communications and Strategy, had pressured the UK intelligence services to provide a more dramatic presentation of the facts about Saddam's WMDs. In the BBC's words, the dossier was 're-written to make it "sexier"'.[11] It is this report that caused the explosion of controversy which led, ultimately, to the suicide of weapons expert Dr David Kelly – the source of the quote in question – and to the setting up, by Tony Blair, of an inquiry, under the chairmanship of Lord Hutton, into the circumstances surrounding Kelly's death.

In May 2003, articles about WMDs account for a minority of reports (with Iraq as the main theme) in the sampled UK press titles, as shown in Table 9.1.

**TABLE 9.1**   Percentage of reports (with Iraq as the main theme) devoted to WMDs

| Daily Mail | Daily Telegraph | Guardian | Daily Mirror |
|---|---|---|---|
| 8% (n = 9) | 7% (n = 14) | 10% (n = 26) | 12% (n = 19) |

The *Guardian* and *Mirror* (left-wing titles) gave more attention to this topic than the right-wing titles (*Mail/Telegraph*), whether measured by number of articles or by the percentage of articles on this topic. In June 2003, the number and percentage of articles rose rapidly: in the two tabloid titles (*Mail/Mirror*) they occupy between one-third and half of all reports on Iraq. It is approximately at this time that government rhetoric about WMDs started to shift ground. In the dossiers published to justify the invasion, Iraq's actual possession of WMDs was stressed. However, under pressure of revelations about ambiguities in the intelligence assessments of the situation, the government started to speak of programmes for the development of such weapons, rather than their actual possession. This was duly noted in the press (see, for example, *Guardian*, 4.6.03: 22).

At this stage, in early June, the identity of the BBC's source was unknown and the government denied the allegation that the substance of the dossier changed after it was prepared by the intelligence services. The allegation broadcast was that in making the presentation of the facts more dramatic, the government had exaggerated some details, notably the claim that the WMDs could be ready for operational use in 45 minutes. Crucially, other allegations suggested that intelligence service personnel were unhappy with the way in which the government used their material, and that the government knew one of the details to be false (this last allegation turned out to be false, and was admitted by the BBC to be such at the Hutton Inquiry – see below). At the end of May and in early June 2003, these allegations were *interpreted* in the press in this light: that is, whatever the scope of the changes made by Downing Street to the Intelligence Services material, it amounted to changing the facts in order to justify the war. Clare Short, former secretary for international development who resigned in mid-May, publicly accused the Prime Minister of lying about this matter (widely reported in the UK press 2.6.03) and General Sir Peter de la Billiere (who commanded UK troops in Gulf War I) said that *if* the Prime Minister had lied, he should resign (Billiere, 2003). Three articles in the *Daily Mirror* on 2 June argued that the changes that the government made to the dossier amounted to lies. While the language used in the broadsheets is more circumspect, referring to charges by others rather than making the allegations themselves, they leave no doubt that the charges are serious. The BBC news reports are similarly circumspect, quoting allegations made by others (for example, BBC News, 3.6.03). However, regardless of how the allegations were made, it is clear that the accumulation of pressure produced political results: the Parliamentary Foreign Affairs Select Committee decided that it would hold public hearings into the matter (announced 3.6.03) after 'calls for a probe have grown' according to the BBC News.[12] Articles about WMDs (most of them about these allegations and their results) accounted for roughly one-third of articles about Iraq in the tabloid titles we looked at in June; although we have not attempted to count the articles in the broadsheet press during this period, the volume was high, more or less on a daily basis. The media's role as a relay of these calls was clearly central.

It is in this context that the tortuous process through which evidence was produced and the name of the BBC's source eventually revealed should be understood. Determining the exact nature of the chain of events was a central element in the Hutton Inquiry. What seems uncontroversial is that allegations prominently repeated in the media, in combination with the doubts already expressed in the US, created a climate in which the pressure for public evidence in some form was difficult to resist. Given the conflict between the BBC's allegations and the government's defence of its statements, and the strength of feeling involved, the identity of the BBC's source became a crucial element in the profile of the event. Eventually, Dr Kelly's name as the source emerged and he was summoned to give evidence to the UK Parliament's Foreign Affairs Select Committee. In parallel, the Intelligence Committee considered these allegations, but it meets in secret and reports only to the Prime Minister. With only these two committees as the superintending bodies, the government was still largely in control of the process. However, Dr Kelly's death changed the situation, and the government was obliged to set up a public inquiry that was independent of the parliamentary political process.

## Subsequent Developments (1): The Media Reception of the Iraq Survey Group Report

On 2 October 2003, the Iraq Survey Group – the US inspection team in Iraq led by David Kay – presented its interim report to the US Congress.[13] The information it presented, and especially facts about the relationship between the physical and the documentary evidence, was sufficiently ambiguous that both proponents and opponents of the war were able to use it to support their case.[14]

The group reported no finds of actual weapons, but did show documentary evidence of a weapons development programme and one piece of physical evidence (a vial of botulinum). According to the *Times* (3.10.03: 1) the report provided evidence to both proponents and opponents; however, the *Guardian* (3.10.03: 1) reported it as clear evidence that the opponents of the war were right all along.

The American media reported this in significantly different ways. For example, the right-wing *National Review* stated:

> Of course, Saddam knows better than the media – as does David Kay. Far from being a failure, Kay's interim report is an important breakthrough. Kay has validated the reason for going to war: Saddam's regime was not in compliance with its UN obligations.
>
> Kay has actually done more than simply justify the war to oust Saddam by demonstrating a past history of Iraqi violations. Kay has shown that Iraq never had any intention of complying with the demands of the UN inspectors. (http://www.nationalreview.com/comment/apostolou200310031526.asp)

This interpretation was reproduced on Fox News (5.10.03) and the online Townhall.com.[15]

Other US titles headlined the report thus on 3.10.03:

*New York Times*: No Illicit Arms Found in Iraq, US Inspector Tells Congress
*Washington Post*: Search in Iraq Finds No Banned Weapons
*Los Angeles Times*: Inspectors Find Aims, Not Arms
*Boston Globe*: US Report Finds No Illicit Arms
*New York Post*: Dubya: Iraq Was Close To WMD

US broadcast media interpreted it thus:

CNN, 2.10.03: No 'Smoking Gun' Expected

WASHINGTON – Two months after the head of the CIA's search for Iraq's suspected weapons of mass destruction said 'solid progress' was being made, officials say he will tell members of Congress on Thursday that his team has not found any banned weapons.

David Kay, a former UN weapons inspector, is expected to report that Iraq had civilian technology that could have been converted to weapons programs on short notice, and an extensive effort to conceal that capability, the officials say.
(www.fox11az.com/news/other/stories/KMSB_local_wmd_100203.535703f5.html)[16]

CBS, 3.10.03

It was one of the main reasons cited for the war against Iraq: to find and destroy abundant anthrax, mustard gas and missiles that Saddam Hussein was said to have stashed. In an interim statement to Congress in October 2003, chief US weapons inspector David Kay said the search had come up empty so far, but that he needed six to nine months more before he would feel confident enough to issue any conclusions about Iraq's weapons program.

PBS 'NewsHour', 2.10.03

JIM LEHRER: So, as of now at least, you have found no weapons of mass destruction, correct?
DAVID KAY: That is correct. We have found no actual weapons at this stage, although we're not foreclosing any files or any possibilities. We're still at work.
JIM LEHRER: At this point, where does the preponderance of the evidence lean? . . .
(www.pbs.org/newshour/bb/middle_east/july-dec03/kay_10-02.html)

On the following days, all sampled US media focused on the fact that the report had indeed given rise to conflicting interpretations within Washington. According to a report in the *Guardian* (4.10.03: 17), the dominant interpretation of the report in US media focused on the absence of the weapons rather than the evidence for a weapons programme, whereas the White House insisted on the evidence of weapons development.

The mainstream US media saw the main importance of the report lying in the absence of weapons themselves, but they also conceded that the report could and did give rise to conflicting interpretations. However, over the following days, the controversy continued, as Kay went on American television to stress that in his opinion the media insistence on the absence of weapons was a misinterpretation of his report. This followed the line taken by Bush in comments to the media on 4 and 5 October.[17] However, other media stressed that the report's main importance was the absence of weapons (for example, *San Jose Mercury*, 4.10.03; *Guardian*, 7.10.03: 1).

## Subsequent Developments (2): Some Implications of the Hutton Inquiry

In the immediate aftermath of the Gilligan/'Today' broadcast, the BBC robustly defended the claims it had made, complaining bitterly about 'intolerable pressure' put on it by the No. 10 press office throughout the Iraq crisis: on 26 June Richard Sambrook, director of news at the BBC, responded to a leaked letter from the Prime Minister's Director of Communications and Strategy, Alastair Campbell, with a statement in which he referred to 'an unprecedented level of pressure on the BBC from Downing Street'[18] and in a published reply to Campbell accused him of 'a personal vendetta against a particular journalist whose reports on a number of occasions have caused you discomfort' (posted on the *Guardian* website, Friday, 27 June 2003, 5.00 p.m.). Another *Guardian* journalist said that it was 'an open secret' that Campbell was in the habit of leaning heavily on those responsible for reports which displeased him.[19] The publication of these documents, itself close to unprecedented, is an indication of the fraught nature of the circumstances, and the extent to which the exact nature of information flows through the public domain is itself an integral part of the events in question.

Subsequently, the BBC admitted that an important allegation made in the broadcast was incorrect, namely the allegation that Dr Kelly had said that the claim that Iraq's WMDs could be ready for use in 45 minutes was inserted by Government knowing that it was false (Hutton, 2003: 46: 101, ll.3–8).[20]

But they continued to contend, to the end of the Hutton Inquiry, that the overall import of Gilligan's broadcast had been correct: that there was indeed disquiet among intelligence officers and other government personnel about the claims in the dossier, that the Prime Minister's staff were indeed directly involved in the drafting of the dossier, and that this process strengthened the claims made in it.[21] Ultimately, the BBC modified its position, claiming that it was in the public interest that their source's interpretation of the weapons dossier should be made public *even if his interpretation was questionable* (Hutton, 2003: 46: 96, ll.5–17).

Given the lack of evidence about the actual existence of WMDs in Iraq, it is difficult to argue that any of the material about Iraq's possession of WMDs can be shown to be true in the fullest sense of the word.[22] However, the argument as defined in the confrontation between No. 10 and the BBC in June and as rehearsed in the Hutton Inquiry is not about this: it is about who knew (or believed) what, when, and whether they were justified in speaking about it in public. It is not our place to pronounce on this matter, especially since at the time of writing Lord Hutton's conclusions are not published. However, various elements of this row go to the heart of the role of the mass media in a democracy: the question of objectivity in journalism, the role of naming sources as a strategic move, whether the row about the details of the BBC Radio 4 'Today' report was a diversionary tactic on the part of the government worried about public opinion, and the role of the BBC and public service broadcasting. These are all central to the democratic role of the mass media because they intimately involve the reliability and credibility of information as it passes through the public domain.

The public interest definition of journalism depends in part upon freedom of expression of opinion, and upon the importance of the availability of reliable information in the public domain about matters of public importance and interest. The latter is our focus here, and is especially important in the case of broadcast journalism because of the statutory obligations placed upon it. If an important event occurs, it is appropriate that journalists record what happened, including interpretations of the event made by relevant participants and witnesses. Here, the role of the journalist is to select the events that are appropriate and the range of individuals relevant to canvass, and to give a clear, accurate and timely account of what has happened or is said to have happened by relevant people. Crucially, the journalist does not necessarily assert that what is said is the truth because journalistic objectivity consists of the statement 'x (who ought to know) says that this happened'. Specifically, when someone who is the accredited representative of an organisation speaks on the record, the statement has a high status:

> ... when the spokesperson is speaking within the competence of his institutionally determined role an accurate account of this is normally accepted as true for all practical purposes. (Murphy, 1991: 12)[23]

On this definition, journalistic objectivity does not consist in – or warrant – the assertion that what the person quoted says is true in the full, quasi-scientific sense of the term. Moreover, substantial elements of interpretation are involved in this definition of objectivity, notably the selection of what is considered important and relevant. The interim report of the Iraq Survey Group gave rise to exactly this sort of controversy in the US.

Objectivity, as the concept underpinning professional journalism as well as the expectations of the public, is in itself inherently ambiguous. As the major signifier associated with the occupation of journalism, 'objectivity' is associated and often confused with ideas of 'truth', 'impartiality', 'balance' and 'neutrality'. For example, a journalist's aim may be to reach the truth (and in order to approach the truth they may need to be impartial), but that does not necessarily imply that the means used or the means that could be used are objective (Frost, 2000: 35–8). Similarly, balance refers to the equal amount of space and time provided for conflicting sides. It does not follow, however, that this makes reporting either 'objective' or 'true'. Finally, neutrality may be problematic when one considers moral imperatives as part of the function of journalism (Seib, 2002: 85). We have already seen that both the government and the BBC refused to countenance any 'moral equivalence' between a democratic government and the Saddam regime.

The confusion arising from the signifying processes associated with objectivity leads to further ambiguities when examining the value of objectivity itself. From the 1920s onward, different disciplines within the humanities and social sciences have convincingly demonstrated that social reality itself, and the knowledge about this reality, are both socially constructed (Schudson, 1978). It can be helpful, therefore, to treat 'objectivity' in two distinct ways: as a theoretical imperative underpinning reporting and as a strategic ritual enabling the defence of the practice as a profession (Tuchman, 1972). In the first instance, objectivity is conceptualised as an impossible goal. However, 'objective reporting' is associated with ways of gathering news (knowledge about places, people, events) and conveying them in a detached, impersonal way, free of value judgments. Nevertheless, the act of reporting itself places limitations (such as space, time, pertinence) on the ability to report the whole known truth (Tumber and Prentoulis, 2003). It follows, therefore, that the necessity of selection and the hierarchical organisation of a story suggest more of a subjective rather than objective outcome (Bovee, 1999: 114–16, 121; Bourdieu, 1996: 21). We have seen many examples of such a process in the earlier chapters of this book. In addition, the structural environment of the institutions of reporting is also restricted by economic and political factors that lead to a subjective outcome (Schudson, 1978). Furthermore, the desirability of such a reporting is becoming increasingly questioned (see Seib, 2002: 85; McLaughlin, 2002: 153–63; Bovee, 1999: 121, 124, 128).

In contrast, objectivity used as a strategic ritual, allowing for the defence of the profession (Tuchman, 1972; Bovee, 1999: 123–4), becomes a convincing argument if one compares journalism with social sciences. The latter demands a 'reflexive epistemological examination', which the former does not and cannot engage with while processing information (Tuchman, 1972: 662). The procedures of the verification of facts, the separating of 'facts' from 'analysis', the presenting of conflicting possibilities and supporting evidence, the judicious use of quotation marks, the structuring of information in an appropriate sequence and the criterion of common sense in assessing news content, whilst enabling the claim to objectivity (which functions as a shield from criticism), do not guarantee objectivity. Instead, they only allow an operational view of objectivity (Tuchman, 1972: 662–79, see also Tumber and Prentoulis, 2003).

Journalistic objectivity was the ultimate line of defence taken by the BBC in the row about the Gilligan broadcast, and repeated before the Hutton Inquiry by Andrew Caldecott (the QC for the BBC at the Inquiry): even if what Gilligan stated that Kelly had said turned out not to be entirely true, it was nonetheless in the public interest that the views of a relevant expert on the topic should be made known. If the intelligence services were dubious about the quality of information used in the government's dossier, this was important even if the people in question were themselves wrong. The journalists' judgment was that the interpretation was important because of the identity of the speaker in relation to the topic in question:

> Each of these three experienced journalists independently judged that Dr Kelly's criticisms should be heard by the public. They did not know them to be true. How could they? The intelligence world is closed and the BBC did not have a key. They therefore did not present them as true, but they did present them as credible. That broad judgment the BBC defends as entirely right. I have already referred to the obvious public interest in the subject matter of Dr Kelly's concerns, but there were other factors in play. He combined two crucial areas of expertise. (Hutton, 2003: 46: 96, ll.5–17)

In other words, the journalism would only be wrong if either they had chosen an inappropriate person as a source, or had given an inaccurate account of what he said. However, this distinction should not go without critical analysis. Shortly after this argument by Caldecott, Lord Hutton made the point that since objectivity in the journalistic sense was not necessarily the same as truth, it might not be a good defence of what had happened:

> I recognise, Mr Caldecott, that there is a distinction between the BBC making a direct charge and the BBC reporting a criticism made by a source, but there is the point that can be made against that view that as regards the person who is the object of the criticism it matters little to him, whether he be a person or whether it be the government, that the report does not directly allege the misconduct on his or its part. (Hutton, 2003: 46: 108, ll.4–12)

Caldecott's answer deserves attention:

> First of all, I think I accept the broad premise put to me that to the person criticised it will still remain a serious charge even if it is not adopted as true. And it is for that reason that the law of defamation has a doctrine called the repetition rule, that the mere fact you have quoted someone as saying something does not provide a defence. You have to show that the underlying charge was true. . . . But that is to look at it entirely from the perspective of the individual criticised. In the context of public interest issues there is a quite separate consideration as to the value of the material in the public interest. In that context it is very important that publishers make clear whether it is their conclusion after thorough investigation or whether it is merely the conclusion of the source which they are reporting. (Hutton, 2003: 46: 108, ll.15–22; 109, ll.1–9)

Caldecott distinguishes between defamation, which he says is ultimately a private matter, and matters of public interest, and asserts that the relationship between truth and credibility is somewhat different in the public context. If a source who is credible – who has knowledge of the topic and/or is involved in it – offers information to the media, then publication is legitimate, even if the assertions involved are later found not to be true. In other words, he rejects Lord Hutton's point by distinguishing between private and public matters, not by reference to the truth of the case.

It has often been said that journalists' acceptance of the status of sources is the breeding ground of untruth in the public domain – although usually this accusation is made about the influence of government and corporate influence over the media, not the influence of opponents of those in power. The point is made at length by Daniel Hallin in his analysis of the American media and the Vietnam war: he shows that US media did, for the majority of the duration of the war, accept the interpretations of events given to them by official representatives of the US government and armed forces. The classic example of untruth produced in this way is the Gulf of Tonkin incident, in which publicity about a non-existent attack by the North Vietnamese navy on US warships was used as a justification for pre-arranged military escalation (Hallin, 1986: 15–19). Indeed, it was *because of* that acceptance – not despite it – that criticism of the war grew, for these sources were regularly in disagreement with each other and therefore gave conflicting information to journalists (1986: 67–79, 87–8, 159–67). It was thus the objective method in journalism that faithfully reproduced government accounts of the war, even when they were in conflict with each other.[24] Murphy's analysis of the Stalker affair – from which the earlier quotation is taken – follows essentially the same line of argument as Hallin, but develops it by distinguishing between 'routine' journalism and the 'investigative' journalism which comes into play when journalists' suspicions are aroused, for example by inconsistencies in what they are told. Similarly, the media coverage of the confrontation between Shell and Greenpeace around the Brent Spar storage tank in 1995 included publicity given to a claim by Greenpeace regarding the contents of the tank which later turned out to be false, and was admitted to be the result of a mistake by Greenpeace.[25] It is clear from contemporary media coverage of the Brent Spar affair that Greenpeace was regarded at the time as a credible (and productive) source by journalists, and reproducing their claim about the contents was thus in accordance with the objective method (Palmer, 2000: Ch. 6). The point is also made in a more general way in Willis (1991), who argues at length that reporters regularly fail to distinguish between 'accuracy' – which he defines in terms identical to Murphy's words above – and 'truth', in other words what emerges when a source's interpretation is checked against alternative information sources (1991: 2–5). Sabato argues that media competition now exercises such pressure on journalists that even a rumour launched by an unscrupulous person will be reproduced by mainstream news media simply on the grounds that it is now in the public domain (1993: 222–5).

Lord Hutton has thus questioned the viability of a distinction that goes to the heart of contemporary journalistic practice. Even if the grounds on which he chose to base his query were the confined grounds of the law of defamation – as Caldecott implies in his response – the query points in the same direction as the criticisms of journalism made by academic commentators. No sooner had the Hutton Inquiry finished its evidence-taking stage than Mark Thompson, Chief Executive of Channel 4, picked up on the implied threat in Lord Hutton's query:

> Some of Lord Hutton's questioning of the BBC could suggest a rather narrow perspective on at least one of these questions – that of reporting a claim. It is to be hoped that in his conclusions, Hutton recognises that, in covering public affairs, the fact that A believes that B did something can be an important fact in itself which it is in the public interest to report, even if there is insufficient evidence that B did the thing in question. It would wrong to treat all such reporting as if it were nothing more than 'publishing a libel'. (Thompson, 2003)

As we have seen, the government sought to discredit the BBC report by accusing it of being incorrect, by publishing a list of objections to it, by putting pressure on the corporation to retract it. The BBC refused and stuck by the accuracy of the report – even if it was later forced to admit some inaccuracy in it. At this stage, the government did not know who the journalist's source was. Subsequently, the source became known to the government when Dr Kelly volunteered the information to his immediate employers that he had had conversations with Gilligan and possibly was the source. Armed with this knowledge, the government sought to discredit the story by casting doubts on his viability as a source: it sought to use the revelation of his name as a tactic. It queried whether the broadcast description of his status in the intelligence apparatus was correct and it questioned his character.[26] These tactics failed to produce any of the desired results, as the differences in the ascription of his status were minimal and the personal slurs were rapidly retracted; however, as is now well-known, they did lead to the least desired result, namely Dr Kelly's suicide. The fact that these elements of the strategy failed should not blind us to the significance of the attempt.

The credibility of sources depends upon the recognition of their authority. If the source speaks on the record, clearly readers can make their own minds up on the subject. However, a substantial part of news output – and often the most dramatic, controversial and interesting part – consists of information derived from unnamed sources. Under these circumstances, it is the journalist's judgment which serves as a warrant for the credibility of the source, usually revealed in one of the coded phrases used under these circumstances, such as the classic (and now dated) 'usually reliable sources'. UK politicians have colluded in this device by making many briefings to journalists completely unattributable, and especially, until recently, the lobby briefings which were the basis of the flow of political information to the mass media (Hennessy and Walker, 1989); similar devices are commonplace in other nations too (Lemieux, 2000: 176–8; Sigal, 1973: 112–15). However, we should also accept that anonymity protects sources who act against the interests of those in power and journalists' insistence on maintaining confidentiality has a powerful public interest defence. Unattributable information is thus a two-edged sword: its defenders claim that it enables information that would otherwise be hidden to reach the public domain; its critics maintain that it produces unreliable information and operates predominantly to the benefit of the powerful by reinforcing secrecy. From the point of view of those in power, it is also a two-edged sword: it protects those who undermine public authority by allegations of wrong-doing, and may be used to manipulate situations for self-interest. Confidentiality agreements between employers and employees are a partial protection (from this point of view, official secrets legislation is just one such agreement), but are undermined by journalists' refusal to break confidence. Legal action against employees, including state employees, for breach of secrecy or confidentiality, is rare: it is largely the threat of possible legal action that operates to secure secrecy (Downing, 1986; Champagne, 1988).

What was the motive of No. 10 Downing Street in trying to expose the identity of Gilligan's source? Cynically interpreted, it might seem to have been merely an attempt to 'encourage the others' to keep their mouths shut. However, Alastair Campbell's diary, produced in evidence at the Hutton Inquiry, suggests otherwise.[27] It records that the Defence Secretary Geoff Hoon wanted to 'throw the book' at him, but was dissuaded – partly on humanitarian grounds, partly on tactical ones: a 'plea bargain' seemed more useful politically. Leaving tactics aside, the diary is clear that the purpose of getting the source's name into the public domain was to discredit the Gilligan report:

> [Hoon] says that [Kelly had] come forward and he was saying yes to speak to [Gilligan], yes he said intel. went in late, but he never said the other stuff. It was double-edged but [Hoon] and I agreed it would fuck Gilligan if that was his source. He said he was an expert rather than a spy or full-time MoD official. (Campbell, 2003: 4 July)[28]

In other words, revelation would tend to undermine the credibility of the report: the source was falsely identified as a member of the intelligence services; and at this stage, Kelly's words to his employers suggested that he had been mis-reported by the BBC. Interestingly, little mention is made of the motives that Dr Kelly may have had for speaking to Gilligan: the only report that we have found that comments on this question is this aside in the *Daily Telegraph* (30.5.03), which describes the information as 'a leak with all the marks of a pre-emptive strike' in a 'game' of blame attribution in the context of the Wolfowitz and Rumsfeld statements about WMDs, as interpreted in UK media. While it is unsurprising that nothing should be said about this in the aftermath of Dr Kelly's death, it is clear that his leak of information to Gilligan must indeed have had a motive, and it is a part of the structure of the information flows that constituted this element of the Iraq crisis.[29]

Clearly, the role of unattributable sourcing was ultimately the ground in which this confrontation grew. Of course, the practice is so widely accepted that it is practically invisible in the public debates, overshadowed by argument over the extent to which Gilligan's report accurately represented what Kelly had said, by the fact that Gilligan had used a single uncorroborated source and by the disagreement about whether the substance of the accusations was correct or not. No doubt these are politically the most important issues. However, they only come to the fore in the way that they do because of the role of unattributable sourcing. It is also likely that increased media competition is ultimately responsible for the ever-growing use of partly substantiated information in news, as this analysis of the editorial policy of Radio 4's 'Today' programme suggests:

> Critics believe that the flagship news programme's mission to make the headlines, rather than just follow them up, has exploded in its face.
>
> 'When Rod Liddle, the former editor, joined 'Today', the emphasis was on breaking our own stories,' said the radio reporter. 'It was all more off-the-agenda, not just the big political interviews of the day. Liddle got Gilligan in to cover defence and Roger Harrabin to cover the environment. He gave their stories a high profile in the programme. There was some very good stuff and also some stuff that didn't deserve the profile it was given. Reporters had a lot more freedom too. They could go off and do features'.
>
> The arrival of Kevin Marsh as editor once Liddle opted for a career as a pundit has changed the climate. There are grumbles about increased shift work, and some of the more quirky stories are not given as much airtime, but Marsh still wants big, exclusive stories and has a penchant for investigative work with a strong political angle. His news approach, described by one colleague as 'forensic', is just the kind to sanction the revisiting of a story like the September dossier and its '45-minute' warning. (Thorpe, 2003)

Lastly, the accusation was made that Alastair Campbell cynically exploited media interest in the row between No. 10 and the BBC in order to create a diversionary tactic which would deflect attention from the 'real' issue, that is, whether there ever were any WMDs in Iraq. If that was the intention, it was singularly unsuccessful, since it ensured that the issue of WMDs continued to dominate the news media for months afterwards. Alastair Campbell is regularly said to be a skilled practitioner of the art of news management, and although he could not predict the tragic outcome of his intervention and its impact upon the overall process, it seems unlikely that someone with his record of achievement in this respect would make such an error of judgment. As Roy Greenslade pointed out in an article in the *Guardian* (12.7.03), the accusation was made by people who had no knowledge of the private, ongoing recrimination between No. 10 and the BBC over the whole tone of the corporation's coverage of the war, which was only revealed in the public exchange of letters between Sambrook and Campbell in the aftermath of the 'Today' broadcast.

Indications of a developing row were evident at the end of March 2003 when John Reid, the Labour party chairman, was reported to have accused the BBC of acting like a 'friend of Baghdad' in its coverage of the war (Brown and Elliott, 2003). In April 2003, Tony Blair's office and the Ministry of Defence criticised BBC reports from Baghdad which claimed that Iraqis are living in 'more fear than they have ever known', as chaos succeeded dictatorship. No. 10 criticised Gilligan's report at its daily briefing and Adam Ingram, Geoff Hoon's deputy, speaking at a defence ministry briefing, accused the BBC of 'trying to make the news rather than report the news' (White and Hall, 2003). Further complaints arose at the beginning of June 2003 over the broadcasting of a BBC documentary which showed footage of the bodies of two British soldiers killed in Iraq. Tony Blair and Geoff Hoon joined the families in trying to persuade the BBC to pull the film and then joined them in condemning it (see Deans, 2003d). The *Sun* joined in, accusing the BBC of arrogance in refusing to withdraw the offending bits of film and condemning the corporation as 'bloated, biased and disloyal with its "compulsory" license fee' (Bennett, 2003).

In their coverage of the Hutton Inquiry, the national press divided along predictable lines, although equivocation was evident for some in the choice between the government and the BBC. The *Mirror* used its anti-war stance to criticise Blair and Campbell; the *Mail* and *Telegraph*, both no lovers of the BBC or the Blair government, took their venom out on Alistair Campbell. The *Mail*, in fact, wrote a number of editorials praising the BBC, whilst the Murdock press (*Sun* and *Times*) lost little time in attacking the BBC (see Greenslade, 2003c, 2003d).

Right-wing commentators were also out in force, lining up to criticise the BBC. Richard Littlejohn wrote in the *Sun*:

> I'm not arguing that the BBC should be the broadcast arm of the Brtish government. But it has a duty to be fair and balanced. While plenty of individual editors and correspondents have done just that, the overall tone of the BBC's coverage since before a shot was fired has been carping, anti-war, anti-British, anti-American. They must have a sign in the BBC newsroom reading: Accentuate The Negative. (Littlejohn, 2003)

Janet Daley, writing in the *Telegraph*, accused the BBC of playing at power games by refusing promptly to detract its earlier version of the Gilligan story and of using government requests for a correction of the story as a spurious and puerile reason for standing up to government pressure (Daley, 2003: 22).

And in an article in the *Sunday Telegraph*, Max Hastings, former war correspondent and newspaper editor, laid the blame at the feet of Greg Dyke, the director general of the BBC, for not sorting out the Gilligan affair inside the corporation (Hastings, 2003: 23).

These incidents are examples of much wider and far-reaching criticisms of the BBC throughout and subsequent to the invasion, and these attacks need to be viewed as part of a wider debate surrounding the future of public service broadcasting and of the BBC in particular.

Most conflicts involve a battle for information management and Gulf War II was no different in this respect. All governments attempt to control the flow of information reaching the public and will criticise news organisations for any sign of an 'unpatriotic stance'. In Britain, the BBC comes in for special scrutiny because of its unique position in the history of broadcasting. In times of crisis, it is expected to conform to the 'national interest' and when it is perceived as failing in its patriotic duty, threats are made to its structure, financing and future. For example, over the last 50 years the BBC has been criticised by the government for its coverage during the Suez crisis (1956), the Falklands conflict (1982), the bombing of Libya (1986), and Ireland (1979–97). During Gulf War II and the subsequent Hutton Inquiry, a combination of the government, Murdock- owned media and right-wing columnists have taken the opportunity to launch a series of attacks on the integrity of BBC journalism and to question the future of the corporation at a time when its charter is up for renewal.

Apart from the attacks made by the Murdock press on BBC journalism, specifically over its role in the Kelly affair, other parts of the Murdock empire have weighed in on the BBC's future. For instance, in delivering the James MacTaggart lecture at the Edinburgh festival in 2003, Tony Ball, the then chief executive of BSkyB, argued that a majority of people were dissatisfied with the licence fee and the BBC's growth was unjustifiable. He suggested that the BBC should be banned from importing foreign programmes and films, that every BBC channel should be subject to certain criticisms and that it should be forced to sell off its most popular programmes every year (see Wells, 2003: 2). Conrad Black, owner of the *Daily Telegraph* and the other Hollinger group titles, attacked the BBC for accusing Britain and the US of lying (ABC Online, 11 June 2003).

It has been suggested that the row about WMDs and the Gilligan report has caused the BBC to be excessively careful (*Guardian*, 21.10.03: Leader). By the end of October 2003, the BBC had twice been accused of losing its nerve in reporting current events. The investigative journalist Michael Crick obtained material which alleged that the then leader of the Conservative Party, Iain Duncan Smith, had misused taxpayers' money in his Party office; and in an interview with the Archbishop of Canterbury, the BBC Radio 4 'Today' presenter John Humphrys asked an unscheduled question about the archbishop's attitude towards the morality of the Iraq conflict. In both cases, the BBC withdrew the material in question before broadcast. In the case of Mr Duncan Smith, it was widely supposed that it was fear of libel that caused the decision,[30] and in the case of the Archbishop of Canterbury a complaint was made about the fact that the question had not been agreed in advance.

In the lead up to the renewal of the BBC charter, the attacks are likely to increase. The Blair government was seen, pre-Iraq, as a friend of the BBC. Both Greg Dyke, the director general, and the chairman Gavyn Davies, are known New Labour supporters. The Kelly affair has undoubtedly soured relations, but a Labour government knows that it needs the BBC because it cannot rely on much political support from the national press.

Since New Labour came to power in 1997, there have been a number of reports and reviews into various aspects of the BBC[31]. In December 2003, Tessa Jowell, the secretary of state for culture, media and sport, announced a public debate on the future of the BBC.[32] Although previous Labour governments have been involved in rows with the BBC, the major source of antagonism over the years for the corporation were Conservative governments. Sections of the Conservative Party have long dismissed the social benefit of the BBC in economic terms and have also laid into the liberal values associated with the BBC. It is too early to say how far New Labour, post-Hutton, will be prepared to defend the cultural values inherent in public service and independent broadcasting.

## Notes

1   There is an outline of the UK government's case, stressing the existence of WMDs, in the Prime Minister's press briefings at www.number-10.gov.uk/output/page2485.asp. The text of Colin Powell's address to the UN Security Council, which uses the same material as the UK intelligence document, is to be found at www.usatoday.com/news/world/iraq/2003-02-05-powell-transcript_x.htm.

2   YouGov poll, reported *Daily Telegraph*, 30.5.03; Lewis, 2003b.

3   http://news.bbc.co.uk/1/hi/world/middle_east/2948068.stm.

4   The full transcript of his speech, questions and answers is at: www.defenselink.mil/speeches/2003/sp20030527-secdef0245.html.

5   This is a 'trail' of the report presented to Congress in early October, and analysed in more detail below.

6   See also the list of claims later shown to be false made on Fox News and not retracted, or only partially retracted, in Steinrich, 2003.

7   Reported *Daily Telegraph*, *Guardian*, *Daily Mirror*, 8.5.03.

8   http://news.bbc.co.uk/1/hi/world/middle_east/2945750.stm. The correction essentially turns on the context in which Wolfowitz referred to bureaucratic convenience. The full transcript of the interview is available at www.defenselink.mil/transcripts/2003/tr20030509-depsecdef0223.html. The text of the Pentagon's correction is on the CNN news website, dated 30.5.03.

9   http://news.bbc.co.uk/1/hi/world/middle_east/2942978.stm. This is the same speech as referred to in note 4.

10   Peter Beaumont and Gaby Hinsliff (*Observer*, 24.2.03); Raymond Whittaker (*Independent on Sunday*, 27.4.03). See also Richard Sambrook's reply to Alastair Campbell's letter demanding an answer to a series of questions about the broadcast. The same articles are referenced again in the summary of the BBC's case in the Hutton inquiry by their QC, Andrew Caldecott; see http://www.the-hutton-inquiry.org.uk/content/transcripts/hearing-trans46.htm. The extent to which they were responsible for the BBC's attention to this matter is unclear, however, Sambrook and Caldecott quote them as *justification* of the attention.

11   http://news.bbc.co.uk/1/hi/uk_politics/2945996.stm.

12   http://news.bbc.co.uk/1/hi/uk_politics/2958160.stm.

13   It was trailed in a public statement at the end of July (*Daily Telegraph*, 1.8.03).

14   At the time of writing, the situation in the US has been less politically explosive than in the UK, but poll evidence during the late summer shows declining support for the administration's policy towards Iraq. In April 2003, answers to

the question 'Is the US in control in Iraq?' got 71% agreement; by September, 2003, the percentage agreeing had reduced to 47% (quoted *Daily Mail*, 5.9.03: 12).

15   Frontpagemag.com/Articles/ReadArticle.asp?ID=10165 reproduces the Fox News item; see also townhall.com/columnists/frankjgaffneyjr/fg20031007. shtml. In the UK, the *Sun* reproduces this argument: see http://209.157.64.200/focus/f-news/994155/posts, which quotes an article by Richard Kavanagh, political editor of the *Sun*, dated 2.10.03.

16   We have failed to find the original CNN story; it is quoted on the Fox website as referenced.

17   See usatoday.com/world/iraq/2003-10-5-kay-iraq_x.htm; CNN (5.10.03).

18   http://news.bbc.co.uk/1/hi/uk_politics/3024670.stm. The text of the BBC's statement in reply to the Campbell accusations is at http://news.bbc.co.uk/1/hi/uk_politics/3021044.stm.

19   'Any correspondent who files reports for the BBC which are off-message knows what to expect; either an abusive tirade from Campbell in person or a multipaged letter complaining to their boss of their lack of journalistic rigour, or sometimes both' (Emily Bell, *Guardian*, 21.7.03).

20   http://www.the-hutton-inquiry.org.uk/content/transcripts/hearing-trans46.htm.

21   See the summary of the BBC's case to the Hutton inquiry by A. Caldecott, QC, on the Hutton inquiry website: http://www.the-hutton-inquiry.org.uk/content/transcripts/hearing-trans46.htm.

22   This is not the place for an epistemological argument about the nature of truth. We are arguing on the assumption that there are broadly speaking two definitions of truth: (1) a quasi-scientific definition, in which truth consists of a concordance between a statement and a set of verifiable observations about the real world – here, statements are objectively true or false, regardless of the speaker's motive, and the opposite of truth is 'non-correctness', 'mistake', etc.; (2) a quasi-legal definition, in which truth consists of a concordance between what the speaker honestly believes to be the case and what he or she says; here motive is paramount, and the opposite of truth is perjury or lies. When we say 'truth in the fullest sense', we mean the quasi-scientific sense of the word, where motive is only marginally relevant.

23   For a theoretical discussion of the role of primary definers and source-media relations, see Schlesinger and Tumber (1994: Ch. 1) and Palmer (2000: Part 3).

24   In particular, Hallin analyses the role of relatively junior field commanders in Vietnam whose relatively pessimistic accounts of the conduct of the war conflicted directly with optimistic accounts given at US headquarters in Saigon and in Washington (1986: 38–43).

25   'Unfortunately Greenpeace made a mistake in its oil sampling which led to an overestimate of the amount of oil on board. . . . When this error was discovered, Greenpeace apologised for the error to Shell by letter'. http://archive.greenpeace.org/comms/toxics/dumping/jun20.html.

26   It did so through a convoluted process which is examined in detail through a number of witnesses in the Hutton hearings. The details are of marginal relevance here.

27   See http://www.the-hutton-inquiry.org.uk/content/cab/cab_39_0001to0002.pdf.

28   http://www.the-hutton-inquiry.org.uk/content/cab/cab_39_0001to0002.pdf.

29   Jeremy Gompertz, QC, representing the Kelly family at the Hutton inquiry

suggested that Kelly had been deliberately used as a political pawn in the government's battle with the BBC. Gilligan was said by the family to be unreliable; see http://www.the-hutton-inquiry.org.uk/content/transcripts/hearing-trans45.htm.

30   The case was subsequently referred to the Parliamentary Ombudsman.

31   These include: Independent Review of the Transparency of the BBC's Financial Reporting; Review of the BBC's Fair Trading Commitment and Commercial Policy Guidelines; The Future Funding of the BBC; Collecting the Television Licence Fee. For all these details see http://www.culture.gov.uk/default.htm

32   The public consultation is intended to give people the chance to put their views directly to Ministers at meetings across the UK and is the first stage in the review of the BBC's Royal Charter which is up for review by 1 January 2007. The second stage of the review, expected to begin around the end of 2004, will bring together the results of the consultation and the conclusions of other reviews – including Ofcom's (the newly established regulator – Office of Communications) review of public service television, the review of BBC online and forthcoming review of the BBC's new services – into a Green Paper. This will be published for further consultation. A White Paper will follow, with another round of consultation. The document *The Review of the BBC's Royal Charter* and further information on the BBC and Charter Review can be assessed at www.bbccharterreview.org.uk

# 10

# CONCLUSION

This book is about news gathering and reporting in war. It is also a story, like all war and conflict reporting, about a battle for information and the winning of hearts and minds. As governments attempt to use all means possible to control the flow and content of information – whether through 'old fashioned' methods of censorship and psychological operations or more sophisticated new ways of ensuring media co-operation – the degree of their success depends on the ingenuity and determination of journalists and news organisations to resist these pressures.

This study has deliberately considered the reporting of the war in the Gulf in three stages: pre-invasion, invasion and post-invasion. Certainly, there are good reasons for making the reporting of the major combat period the main focus of investigation – after all, studies of war reporting and political opinion have for many years been based in the established knowledge that US media reporting of the Vietnam War was a crucial element in the development of public opinion about that war. However, public consent to the reasons for fighting is at least equally important.[1] The nature of the outcomes of a conflict can also be important in the process of consent, depending upon the circumstances. The extent to which the outcomes of a war are crucial in maintaining consent for the policy largely depends on whether there is any ongoing domestic cost incurred by the policy (and, of course, on levels of public attention to it).

Moreover, it is widely agreed that for US public opinion, the casualty rate among US forces is closely linked to the maintenance of consent: what is colloquially known as 'the Dover test' has been a crucial element in it. The Dover test is the number of military dead returning to the US military mortuary at Dover, Delaware, where there is currently a ban on filming the returning coffins. The resultant lack of publicity may reduce public awareness inside the US about the level of casualties (see Younge, 2003; cf. Reuters, 2003). However, as long as the policy upon which war is fought is accepted as correct, news reports or pictures, whilst disturbing, will not necessarily weaken support for the war or possess the power of social disruption. 'It is only if genuine questioning of policy is taking place, sufficient to enquire over the legitimacy of the exercise, that news, indeed all news, even battle victories, becomes bad news. News can become an articulator of concern when the images presented interact with other information that questions the validity of policy' (Morrison and Tumber, 1988: 349). As the number of British and US military casualties in Iraq increases alongside continuing public questioning over the original policy goals of going to war and subsequent reconstruction, the definitional power of mass-mediated information about these matters is likely to become increasingly central to the maintenance of consent for policy.

Our study has therefore focused on the overall development of the crisis, not just on the invasion phase. When we consider the reporting of the war in this wider frame, differences between the 2003 Iraq crisis and previous events are clear. First, the question of access. The last two wars preceding Gulf War II (Kosovo and Afghanistan) were characterised by a relatively low level of access to the battlefield, whereas Gulf War II was the exact opposite, with unprecedented access given to journalists and news organisations.

Gulf War II was the most covered war ever, with more than 3000 journalists assigned to the region. The cost to news organisations of mounting their operations was very expensive and subsequent economies will inevitably lead to cuts in other news gathering operations. Our analysis of the news gathering process has shown the degree of planning undertaken by the Pentagon of the process of embedding journalists with military units. For news organisations, starved of access in previous conflicts, the opportunities presented by this access led them to be willing partners in the process. Many of the embedded journalists saw very little action, whilst some of those that did were able to send back live reports direct from the theatre of war to homes around the world. Audiences were able to see live pictures of tanks moving across the desert, fighting in cities and the capture of prisoners. The degree of live action was unprecedented. But, as our study shows, embedded journalists only provide a small and narrow part of the big picture (paradoxically, a point made during the conflict by both US and UK officials – at stages when the narrowness in question did not suit their purposes). For the embedded journalists, living alongside the troops and relying on them for protection, the process of identification is all too possible. The participant journalist, as opposed to the observer, can become a very unstable operator in this closed environment. The large news organisations, as our study indicates, could mitigate for these dangers because they had non-embedded journalists operating in other areas of the region. But the dangers for these journalists was all too evident, from operating and censorship restrictions in Baghdad, to death and injury from 'enemy' and 'friendly fire'.[2] Whilst journalists and news organisations enjoyed the access afforded them by the embedding process, elsewhere obfuscation and misinformation were as familiar as in previous conflicts. At the Central Command headquarters in Doha, Qatar, and in Washington and London, journalists trying to obtain information and confirmation about reported incidents faced either silence or delay. The military and defence officials were unable or unwilling to respond to the speed of communications demanded by journalists in the field. In comparison, military personnel on the battlefield were often much more co-operative.

Our study of the media coverage of the war shows that in the reporting of the pre-invasion phase in the UK press there was a high degree of scepticism about the process, which was partly, but not exclusively, aligned with the long-term allegiance of press titles. This was accompanied by poll data that showed consistently high levels of opposition to war, or to war without UN approval. Although we carried out no systematic analysis of television news output during the pre-invasion phase of the crisis, it is clear from the remarks about it quoted in Chapter 6 that the BBC was sensitive – at this phase of the crisis – to the need to reflect opposition to US policy as well as support for it. The scepticism took the form both of reporting opposition to the policy and of sceptical analysis of the process of policy formation and implementation. Active campaigning against the policy was also prominent in left-wing press titles. In summary: there was no consensus in UK media about the reasons for going to war.

The reporting of the post-invasion phase has also been predominantly sceptical. This takes the form of a dominant focus on bad news regarding the situation inside Iraq and of an intensely sceptical – not to say aggressive – reporting of the UK government's justification for going to war, no doubt due to the lack of consensus manifest pre-invasion. The *casus belli* was Iraq's possession of WMDs, even if coalition leaders' rhetoric also insisted on other reasons for fighting, in particular the alleged links between the Saddam regime and Islamic terrorism and Saddam's human rights record. Had the invasion produced a smooth transition of power from the Saddam regime to another Iraqi government, it is possible to speculate that the motives might have ceased to be controversial. Whatever the nature of the reporting of the actual invasion itself, the reporting of the scenario after the fall of Baghdad returned to, at least the same level of scepticism in the coverage pre-invasion. In some measure, the level of scepticism in the UK press increased post-invasion, as titles that supported the war and found positive elements in the post-war situation inside Iraq were largely negative on the subject of WMDs.

Previous analyses of war reporting provide a framework for understanding the reporting (in its three phases) of Gulf War II, particularly in the UK. In his study of the US media and the Vietnam War, Hallin (1986) argued that the way the media report events is closely tied to the degree of consensus among the political elite, the 'sphere of consensus' as he labels it. Hallin's view contrasts with the conservative analysis of the media at that time as 'anti-establishment' institutions which were 'undermining the authority of governing institutions' (Hallin, 1994: 11). The explanation for the media's 'volte-face' in their support for/rejection of the war was grounded in 'commitment to the ideology and the routines of objective journalism' (1986: 63–9). Up to 1967, there was relatively little disagreement among the policy elite and reflecting this official viewpoint did not 'seem to violate the norms of objective journalism' (1994: 52–3). However, during the period 1963–67, reporters in Vietnam itself were being given accounts of the war by serving officers in the US military which were not compatible with the largely optimistic accounts coming out of Washington; during this time, both versions of how the war was going were reported (1986: 38–9).

The gradual breaking down of the national security consensus and the Cold War ideology amongst the political elite, together with the concern over the conduct of the war, was reflected in the coverage by the news media. The media were able to respond to the growing strains and divisions within the foreign policy elite by producing far higher amounts of critical news coverage without abandoning objective journalism for some activist and anti-establishment conception of their role. As opposition to the war moved into the mainstream, the news media reflected this movement of debate into 'the sphere of legitimate controversy'. The media reflect the prevailing pattern of political debate: 'when consensus is strong, they tend to stay within the limits of the political discussion it defines; when it begins to break down, coverage becomes increasingly critical and diverse in the viewpoints it represents, and increasingly difficult for officials to control' (Hallin, 1994: 53–5).

It is evident that as policy debate moves from the 'sphere of consensus' to the 'sphere of legitimate controversy', governments and administrations become concerned at the possible loss of control over the news agenda. Censorship and flak consequently become prominent features of their response to the increase in media activity as journalists begin to question government statements and become more sensitive to other official and non-official viewpoints (Hallin, 1994: 71; see also Morrison and Tumber, 1988: 228).

A similar formulation of source behaviour to account for media–government relations is Bennett's (1990) 'indexing hypothesis': 'Mass media news professionals, from the boardroom to the beat, tend to "index" the range of voices and viewpoints in both news and editorials according to the range of views expressed in mainstream government debate about a given topic' (1990: 106). According to the hypothesis, non-official sources only appear in news stories when their opinions are 'already emerging in official circles'. The possibility of contention between official sources is acknowledged and this is sometimes reflected in the news media, but when that institutional opposition collapses, even if public opinion is opposed to a particular policy, the volume of opposition in news and editorials is indexed accordingly. In effect, the news media revert to the established line at the expense of the democratic ideal (1990: 113).

In exploring the coverage of three military interventions that won bipartisan support in Washington, Mermin (1996) concurs with the indexing hypothesis but adds an amendment to the effect that the major media are doing something to maintain the illusion of fulfilling the journalistic ideals of balance and objectivity. What the news media present as subject to question and debate 'is the *ability of the government to achieve the goals it has set*. When there is no policy debate in Washington, reporters may offer critical analysis *inside the terms of the apparently settled policy debate*, finding a critical angle in the possibility that existing policy on its own terms might not work' (1996: 182, italics in original).

Focusing on this 'critical angle' helps to explain the perception among politicians and business leaders that journalists are overly independent and critical of government, and to illustrate that there is a significant element of present-day conflict in the news. Some journalism can find conflicting possibilities in the effectiveness of the government in achieving its own goals, while still not presenting 'the policy decision that set those goals in the first place as open to critical analysis and debate' (Mermin, 1996: 182).

To fulfil the idea of independent, balanced coverage when official sources are united behind a particular policy, journalists attempt to fill the void 'by finding conflicting possibilities in the efforts of officials to achieve the goals they have set' (Mermin, 1996: 191). In cases concerning the effectiveness of government policy, the reader-viewer is a spectator to the 'political game' with the tools to predict whether or not the leadership is likely to win or lose, whereas the focus of policy formulation views the reader-viewer as a citizen with the tools to deliberate on the soundness of the President's decision (1996: 191). Therefore, when there is consensus in the policy formulation, the vigilant reporting may rest solely on the effectiveness and politics of the policy's execution. Mermin does not see his argument as contradicting the indexing hypothesis. Rather, 'seeing the critical angle that is covered may help to account for the conviction of journalists that they offer independent, balanced reporting, and the view of politicians that the media are highly critical, perceptions the indexing hypothesis does not convincingly explain' (1996: 189).[3]

A similar argument is that a focus on bad news that is part of a generalised critique of the 'deliverability' of policy is part of an overall process which potentially results in public cynicism. For example, a study of the framing of elections in terms of electoral strategy rather than political issues – a focus on winners and losers, opinion poll evidence, the assessment of candidate's performance, all couched in the language of games or war – concludes that such framing of political issues produces voter cynicism (see Cappella and Jamieson, 1996). While 'horse-race' reporting of elections is not the same as a focus on the deliverability of policy, the two ways of framing events have the common element of a focus on strategy, rather than on principle.

Looking at the coverage of Gulf War II, it is clear that reporting of the pre-invasion phase largely eschewed a period of consensus compared with Hallin's sphere of consensus period during the Vietnam War. Unlike the anti-Vietnam protests, which were largely marginalised and dismissed by the US media as predominantly the preoccupation of student activists, the anti-war protest over Gulf War II, consisting of a politically and socially diverse coalition,[4] was given space and prominence in the media. The anti-war position of European allies, particularly France and Germany, and the scepticism surrounding the UK government's dossier setting out the reasons for war, added to the criticisms ('sphere of legitimate controversy') present in the media during the pre-invasion phase of the conflict. Moreover, a substantial proportion of broadsheet press coverage of the pre-invasion phase of the crisis was given over to analysis of the implementation and/or outcomes of policy. This coverage was evenly balanced between negative and positive mentions. Tabloid coverage of this matter was briefer, but overwhelmingly negative (see Chapter 6: Tables 3-4, 14). During the invasion phase, the media generally moved back to the 'sphere of consensus' (although some newspapers maintained their anti-war stance) and then returned to a 'sphere of legitimate controversy' after the fall of Baghdad (the post-invasion phase) because the reasons for going to war were still being questioned and gained particular prominence during the Hutton Inquiry. Evidence of the validity of Mermin's formulation can be seen during the invasion phase in the way that the coalition's policy goals and military implementation of it were questioned. After only a few days of the campaign, the media raised doubts about the ability of the coalition to win the war quickly, as events did not go as smoothly as the media had been led to expect. This formulation is evident in the post-invasion phase where the media have given space to the questioning of the implementation of policy in Iraq even by those supporting the original policy of war without UN approval.

Finally, in writing this study we have been led to consider the nature and role of journalistic objectivity. This matter is raised in examining journalistic practices of embedded reporters, and in looking at the pressures put on journalists by governments. We have also seen that this matter was raised at the Hutton Inquiry hearings, in the form of fundamental questioning of the relationship between journalists and their sources.

During warfare, objectivity in the sense of giving as much credibility to the enemy as to the spokespersons of one's own nation is close to impossible in mainstream media. When the BBC appeared to be doing this during the Falklands War, they were stridently criticised in Parliament. Peter Arnett, the CNN correspondent who covered Gulf War I from Baghdad, was accused of lying when he reported that smart bombs sometimes hit the wrong target, and was criticised for acting as a conduit for enemy misinformation. In neither case was the media organisation, or the reporter in question, actually taking the side of the enemy. The mere fact of reporting what happened was sufficient to attract such venom. The UK government made similar criticisms of the BBC during Gulf War II and this attack has since been used by a coalition of other newspapers and media organisations to make more general assaults on the BBC. Yet at the same time, the poll evidence about public views of the media coverage of the war suggest that the public place a high value upon such objectivity, even under wartime conditions, especially since the circumstances in question (war) make objectivity a fraught exercise. It seems likely that this element of journalistic professional practice and media ethics will be subject to critical scrutiny in the future. The remarks made at the Hutton Inquiry focus on a central element of the public supervision of the policy formation process. By the same token, the limits to objectivity seen in some embedded journalistic practice and in government pressure indicate how central is the relationship between this element of media ethics and the formation of public consent. This triangular relationship – policy formation, media ethics and public opinion – has certainly been at the centre of academic debates for many years, including scrutiny under wartime conditions. Now perhaps the debate will be conducted, and forcefully, in a more public arena.

## Notes

1  As Hallin shows, in the case of Vietnam, the reasons were deeply embedded in the Cold War ideology that dominated US thinking about foreign policy during the 1950s and 1960s (1986: 48–52).
2  See also News Safety Institute (2003).
3  For discussion of this, see Tumber (2002b).
4  The 'Stop the War Coalition' included the Liberal Party, Labour politicians, CND, the Muslim Association of Britain, celebrities, the Mirror Group of newspapers and the *Daily Mail*, amongst others.

# POSTSCRIPT: THE PUBLICATION OF THE HUTTON REPORT[1]

The publication of Lord Hutton's Report was a media event in its own right, with the launch covered live on television and radio. Copies of the Report were delivered 24 hours in advance to the major interested parties (the government, Dr Kelly's family, and the BBC)[2] on the condition that they signed confidentiality agreements binding them to public silence until the moment of publication. Lord Hutton made his presentation in the Royal Courts of Justice on Wednesday, 28 January 2004. His presentation was broadcast on two BBC television channels and on Sky News. However, the *Sun* newspaper had succeeded in penetrating the barrier of confidentiality and published a summary of the Report's main conclusions on the morning of the Report's launch.[3] The BBC broadcast a summary of the *Sun*'s material in its evening news bulletin of the previous day.[4]

The BBC's live coverage of Hutton's conclusions was part of a special three-hour programme. It included Prime Minister's Question Time live from Parliament in the half hour before Lord Hutton's oral presentation, and the Prime Minister's statement to the House of Commons in response to the Report, also broadcast live. This was followed by extended commentary in the studio. Sky News provided 'non-stop live coverage' of the event.[5]

Lord Hutton's terms of reference were to examine the circumstances surrounding the death of Dr David Kelly.[6] In his Report he addressed three principal issues:

- The creation of the government's dossiers on weapons of mass destruction (since it was Dr Kelly's briefing to Andrew Gilligan on this subject which was the start of the process leading to his death);
- The role and nature of the BBC's report based on this briefing and the subsequent government complaints about it;
- The process by which Dr Kelly's name was made known as Gilligan's source and its role in his death.[7]

On the first point, Hutton exonerated the government of the main charges of distortion of intelligence material ('sexing up' the document), arguing that the changes made at the government's behest were largely cosmetic, and that the relevant authority (the Joint Intelligence Committee) had ensured that the contents of the dossier were compatible with available intelligence.

On the second point, Hutton severely criticised Gilligan's broadcast, not only stating that the element of it already admitted to be wrong (see above,

p. 147) was 'unfounded', but that other elements were too. Hutton also severely criticised the BBC's editorial and management processes, which had allowed the news report to be broadcast unchecked and resulted in senior BBC personnel not having an adequate subsequent overview of the issues involved in the government's complaint. The criticisms of the BBC were sufficiently severe that the chairman of the BBC Board of Governors (Gavyn Davies), the director general (Greg Dyke) and reporter Andrew Gilligan were obliged to resign.[8]

On the third point, Hutton argued that although the Ministry of Defence (MOD) could have done more to protect Dr Kelly from the consequences of his interview with Gilligan, he exonerated the government from any causal role in his suicide, and accepted the government's explanation that the process by which Dr Kelly's name became publicly known was justified by circumstances. Once Dr Kelly had told his employers that he was likely to be the source in question, and given that the Parliamentary Foreign Affairs Committee were investigating the circumstances in question, it was necessary for the MOD to say enough to avoid the charge of covering up activities by a government employee. Specifically, Hutton exonerated the Prime Minster from responsibility for the elements of the MOD's actions which directly resulted in Dr Kelly's name being made public.

On the day of the Report's launch, most media analysis and commentary consisted of summaries of the Report, of responses (or summaries of responses) by the leading players (the government, opposition, the BBC and the Kelly family), and brief comments about the relationship between the main thrust of the Report and previous expectations about its contents. In the latter case, the main divergence between the Report and expectations of it was that the government was found to be blameless, and the BBC found to be strongly at fault, whereas expectation was that blame would be more evenly apportioned.

On the day following publication (29 January 2004), results and reactions to the Hutton Report were the main story in the national daily newspapers. All national papers covered either the report itself, or its immediate impact, on the front pages, and approximately half of them dedicated special sections to it. With the exception of the red-top tabloids (and the *Financial Times*), all papers devoted more than ten pages to the story. The report was also front-page news in some American broadsheets and in major European titles such as *Le Monde*, *Die Welt* and the *Frankfurter Allgemeine Zeitung*.

The common themes in UK press treatment of the report were:

- Surprise at Lord Hutton's exoneration of the government in respect of all the accusations that had been made. This was close to universal: only the *Sun* and the *Times* did not express surprise, or recognise the surprise that other titles observed among the political class (the *Sun* had leaked the conclusion of the Report the day before).
- Recognition that Lord Hutton's comments on the BBC's editorial and managerial processes had created a crisis for the Corporation.[9]

- Recognition that the Kelly family would get little satisfaction from Lord Hutton's analysis of the process which led to the scientist's death.

However, the presence of common features of coverage hides significant variations in the treatment of these themes. First, surprise at the extent of the Report's exoneration of the government was expressed in the form of shock at a 'whitewash': the *Independent*, the *Guardian*, the *Daily Mirror* and the *Daily Express* all used this term and the *Daily Mail* used other forms of words to convey the same idea. Other titles, whilst maintaining a more objective tone, quoted the words of the outgoing chairman of the BBC Governors, Gavyn Davies, expressing incredulity at the lack of balance in Lord Hutton's judgments of the BBC and the government. The *Times* and the *Sun* concentrated more of their coverage on the blameworthiness of the BBC, a line fitting with News International's long-term agenda of attacking the Corporation (see above, pp. 155–6). Secondly, many titles included overt attacks upon the Hutton Report, blaming it for partiality and naiveté. For example, the *Daily Mail* called him 'indulgent' and 'understanding' towards Alastair Campbell (p. 10), and said his report 'does a great disservice to the British people' (p. 19); according to the *Daily Mirror*, he was 'exceedingly generous' in his judgment of the government (p. 8). However, not all titles adopted this line: the *Daily Telegraph*'s coverage is mainly neutral, with the only overt attack upon the Report coming in an opinion column by the Conservative MP and *Spectator* editor Boris Johnson (p. 23).

Other newspapers concentrated on the fact that Lord Hutton's terms of reference prevented him (in his analysis) from asking certain questions that journalists judged pertinent, and most notably the question of the absent weapons of mass destruction. The Hutton Report focused on the honesty of the use of intelligence by the government, not on the reliability of the intelligence, and this was a theme frequently picked up in the coverage of the Report (*Daily Express*, p. 12; *Daily Mirror*, pp. 1 and 8; *Daily Mail*, pp. 18–19; *Independent*, pp. 1–2, 5, 6–7, 23; *Guardian*, p. 15; *Daily Telegraph*, pp. 7 and 23; *Financial Times*, p. 2).

One theme is clearly shared across the national press: the Conservative Party's attack on Tony Blair was a failure. The Conservative Party leader, Michael Howard, concentrated his attention on whether the Prime Minister had lied about his role in the process by which Dr Kelly's name became public. The national press either said nothing about Howard's tactics in the House of Commons, or commented that they were a failure; the most complementary note came in an anonymous quote to the effect that he 'had done his best' (*Times*, p. 46). It was subsequently noted in the press that Howard had cancelled pre-scheduled media interviews on 28 January, in recognition of his failure (*Observer*, 2.2.04: 17).

Two important media issues have emerged following the publication of the Hutton Report. The first concerns the question of journalistic procedure and the second the future governance of the BBC.

Lord Hutton said in his Report that:

The communication by the media of information (including information obtained by investigative reporters) on matters of public interest and importance is a vital part of life in a democratic society. However the right to communicate such information is subject to the qualification (which itself exists for the benefit of a democratic society) that false accusations of fact impugning the integrity of others, including politicians, should not be made by the media. Where a reporter is intending to broadcast or publish information impugning the integrity of others, the management of his broadcasting company or newspaper should ensure that a system is in place whereby his editor or editors give careful consideration to the wording of the report and to whether it is right in all the circumstances to broadcast or publish it. (*Report*, para. 291, also in para. 53 (2) of the oral presentation, at www.the-hutton-inquiry.org.uk/content/rulings/statement280104.htm)

This element in Lord Hutton's report was widely commented on in the media in the days following the Report's publication (for example, Channel 4 News, 7.00 pm, 28.1.04; *Observer*, 1.2.04: 1, 21). All three BBC 'casualties' of the Report argued that Hutton was wrong in this respect. Gavyn Davies asked: 'are his conclusions on restricting the use of unverifiable sources in British journalism based on sound law and, if applied, would they constitute a threat to the freedom of the press?', a theme echoed in Greg Dyke's accusation – based on consultation with the BBC's lawyers – that Hutton was wrong in law in this respect and that the implications could be damaging for the media, preventing newspapers and broadcasters from reporting the concerns of whistleblowers or the comments of government insiders unless there was proof that what they were saying was true. Andrew Gilligan made the same point in his resignation statement.[10] The issue was clearly stated in the *Guardian* (29.1.04):

The current law of defamation acknowledges the possibility of the right to be wrong and it is important that the civil courts take a view over whether a story was in the public interest, the nature of the sources of the information, and journalistic and news organisation checks. (www.media.guardian.co.uk/huttoninquiry/story/0,13812,1133968,00.html)

The *Guardian* quoted Lord Lester QC to support this position:

I very much hope Lord Hutton's report will not be misinterpreted as a signal for greater self-censorship or government interference. The BBC, like the rest of the media, must be free to publish opinions honestly believed to be true from apparently reputable and senior sources on matters of legitimate public interest or comment. (www.guardian.co.uk/guardianpolitics/story/0,3605,1133734,00.html).

Before the publication of the Hutton Report (and no doubt in anticipation of criticisms to emerge) the BBC made two main changes to their journalism procedures: single-source stories were to be more rigorously checked; the 'Today' programme's 'two-ways'[11] were to be more strictly policed. They also added three elements to their accountability mechanisms: BBC journalists were no longer to be allowed to write for newspapers;[12] a deputy director general, Mark Byford,[13] was appointed to oversee a strengthened complaints unit; and the Governors were to be provided with a dedicated support unit making them less reliant on management for information.

Following his appointment as acting director general of the BBC, Mark Byford announced that there would be an internal inquiry at the Corporation into what went wrong over the Andrew Gilligan affair. It would examine how the BBC could avoid making similar mistakes in the future and how the Corporation could work to rebuild trust.

Only the *Guardian* newspaper (so far) has issued new guidelines, which includes a section on the use of sources which says journalists should use anonymous sources sparingly and that, except in exceptional circumstances, they should avoid any use of anonymous pejorative quotes. The guidelines also tell staff to avoid 'flamming' or 'sexing up' stories, and to put allegations to the people about whom they are writing in good time.[14]

In his resignation statement, Gavyn Davies also issued a warning against future attempts to change the regulatory system of the BBC:

> He (Hutton) has not suggested that the governance of the BBC has systemic defects which need to be remedied. Critics of the system should take careful note of this. But he has concluded that in the highly unusual circumstances of last summer, the governors should have conducted their own investigation of Mr Campbell's complaints.

For the BBC itself, the current structure of having the director general as editor in chief is untenable. What was suitable 80 years ago when the BBC was in its infancy is unworkable in an age of 24/7 news broadcasting on multiple television and radio channels when the BBC is producing 40 hours of news a day. It is conceivable that had Greg Dyke not been editor in chief it would probably have been Richard Sambrook, head of news, who would have had to resign.

It is fortunate for the BBC that the Hutton episode had not fully unravelled before the passing of the Communications Act (2003) which set up a new independent industry regulator Ofcom (Office of Communications). At the time the Bill was working its way through the House of Commons most of commercial broadcasting called for the BBC to come under the aegis of the new regulator. It is inevitable that pressure will increase during the current review of the BBC leading to charter renewal due in 2006 for independent regulation of the BBC. Questions about whether the BBC Governors are in the best position to act as executive and regulator will continue.[15] Ofcom (set to become a very powerful player in the new media landscape) is conducting its own review of public service broadcasting and various think tanks have suggested that there should be an independent regulator of the BBC.

Despite the publication of the Hutton Report, the controversy surrounding the issue of WMDs and the quality of intelligence which led to war is still being debated in the media. Following the announcement by President Bush of a bipartisan inquiry into the US' Iraqi intelligence, the British government announced (3 February 2004) to Parliament that it was setting up its own inquiry. Former cabinet secretary Lord Butler will chair a six-member committee looking at whether the pre-war intelligence was right or wrong.

## Notes

1   The following pages were added in the days following the publication of the Report, while the book was in production. We are grateful to Sage Publishers for allowing us this flexibility.
2   Opposition leaders were provided with copies at 6am on the day of publication.
3   At the time of writing, the leak is being investigated with a view to possible legal proceedings. See www.the-hutton-inquiry.org.uk/content/hi-pn290104.htm (press release dated 29.1.04).
4   http://news.bbc.co.uk/1/hi/uk_politics/3432105.stm, dated 27.1.04: 22.34 GMT.
5   See www.skypublicity.co.uk/skynews.asp
6   The full report is available on the Inquiry website: www.the-hutton-inquiry.org.uk.
7   Lord Hutton presents these as five issues: we have condensed his presentation at this point.
8   In a 'rallying round' of support for the BBC, and Greg Dyke in particular, a full-page paid advertisement, headed *'The independence of the BBC'*, was taken out in *The Daily Telegraph* (31.1.04: 9) by employees, presenters, reporters and contributors of the corporation.
9   This theme continued to be very prominent in reporting in subsequent days.
10  For a full text of Gilligan's statement see http://media.guardian.co.uk/huttoninquiry/story/0,13812,1135697,00.html.
11  It was the 'two-way' between the journalist Andrew Gilligan and presenter John Humphrys on the BBC's Today programme which began the whole row.
12  Gilligan had written an article for the *Mail on Sunday*, following his broadcast report, in which he claimed that Dr David Kelly had named Alistair Campbell, Prime Minister Blair's Director of Communication as the person who had 'sexed up' the September 2002 dossier.
13  Byford was appointed, by the Governors, as acting director general of the BBC following the resignation of Greg Dyke on 26 January 2004.
14  For details of the *Guardian*'s post-Hutton guidelines for journalists see http://media.guardian.co.uk/huttoninquiry/story/0,13812,1135126,00.html.
15  The Conservative Party has already called for an independent regulator for the BBC.

# REFERENCES

Adams, P. (2003) 'Reporters' log: final thoughts'. Available at http://www.bbc.co.uk/reporters. 19 April.

Allen, T. and Seaton, J. (1999) *The Media of Conflict*. London: Zed Books.

Amin, H. (2003) 'Watching the war in the Arab world', *Transnational Broadcasting Studies 10*. Available at http://www.tbsjournal.com/amin.html.

Arsenault, A. (2002) 'To embed or not to embed?'. Available at http://www.cbc.ca/news/features/iraq/correspondents/arsenault_adr. Parts 1, 2, 3. 31 December.

Associated Press (2003) 'War coverage spurs 'backpack' reporters'. Available at http://www.nytimes.com. 25 March.

Astor, D. (2003) 'Will journalists' equipment survive Iraq?'. Available at http://www.editorandpublisher.com. 28 March.

Aukofer, F. and Lawrence, W.P. (1995) *The Odd Couple*. Freedom Forum First Amendment Center, 5.

Axelrod, J. (2003a) 'Roughing it for front-row seat'. Available at http://www.tvweek.com. 17 March.

Axelrod, J. (2003b) 'Before bombs, a birth'. Available at http://www.tvweek.com. 24 March.

Bartholomew, R. (2003a) 'Embeds from smaller papers take different approach'. Available at http://editorandpublisher.com/edtiorpublisher/headlines/article_display.jsp?vnu_content_id=186026a. 9 April.

Bartholomew, R. (2003b) 'Military tells Harrisburg reporter to leave Iraq'. Available at http://www.editorandpublisher.com. 30 April.

Bauder, D. (2003a) 'Journalists embedded with military give thumbs up'. Available at http://cnews.canoe.ca/CNEWS/MediaNews/2003/03/21/48245-ap.html. 21 March.

Bauder, D. (2003b) 'ABC's Ted Koppel relishes the chance to go to war again'. Available at http://www.fgate.com/cgi-bin/article.cgi?file=/news/a . . . /entertainment1400EDT0516.DT. 6 April.

BBC News (2003a) 'Reporters' log: At war in Iraq'. Available at http://news.bbc.co.uk/2/hi/in_depth/2866547.stm. 20 March.

BBC News (2003b) 'POW footage breaks convention'. Available at http://news.bbc.co.uk/1/hi/world/middle_east/2881187.stm. 24 March.

BBC News (2003c) 'POWs and dead shown on TV'. Available at http://www.news.bbc.co.uk/1/hi/world/middle-east/2889255.stm. 26 March.

BBC News (2003d) 'Fighting the psy-ops war in Basra'. Available at http://news.bbc.co.uk/1/hi/world/middle_east/2903235.stm. 31 March.

Bennett, C. (2003) 'Is the BBC right to show our boys' bodies?'. Available at http://media.guardian.co.uk/iraqandthemedia/story/0,12823,966933 . . . 30 May.

Bennett, W. L. (1990) 'Toward a theory of press-state relations in the United States', *Journal of Communication*, 40, 103–105.

Bennett, W.L. (1994) 'The news about foreign policy', in W. Bennett and D. Paletz (eds), *Taken by Storm: The Media, Public Opinion and the Gulf War*. Chicago: University of Chicago Press. pp. 12–40.

Bennett, W.L. and Manheim, J. (1993) 'Taking the public by storm: information cueing and the democratic process in the Gulf conflict'. *Political Communication*, 10 (4): 331–51.

Bennett, W.L. and Paletz, D. (1994) *Taken by Storm: The Media, Public Opinion and the Gulf War*. Chicago: University of Chicago Press.

Berman, A. (2003) 'So far, editors pleased with embedded reporters'. Available at http://www.editorandpublisher.p . . . /cpt?action=cpt&expire=&url1ID= 5764107&fb=Y&partnerID=6. 20 March.

Bergman, C. (2003) 'Technology brings the battle home', *USC Annenberg Online Journalism Review*. Available at http://www.ojr.org/ojr/bergman/1048703210. php. 23 March.

Billiere, Sir P. de la (2003) 'If Blair did mislead us, he must go', *Daily Mail*, 2 June. p. 6.

Boorstin, D. (1961) *The Image*. London: Penguin Books.

Born, M. (2003) 'BBC dinner was a fine idea – but there's a hitch', *Daily Telegraph*, 30 May. p. 21.

Bourdieu, P. (1996) *On Television and Journalism*. London: Pluto.

Bovee, W.G. (1999) *Discovering Journalism*. Westport, CN and London: Greenwood.

Brown, C. and Elliott, F. (2003) 'Labour chairman says BBC is acting like "friend of Baghdad"', *Sunday Telegraph*, 30 March. p. 6.

Brown, J. (2003) '"They got it down": the toppling of the Saddam statue'. Available at http://www.counterpunch.org/brown04122003.html.12 April.

Burke, J. (2003) 'Hard hitting journalism'. Available at http://media.guardian.co.uk/ presspublishing/story/0,7495,916121,00.html. 17 March.

Byrne, C. (2003a) 'Thompson was "thorn in MoD's side"'. Available at http://www.media.guardian.co.uk/iraqandthemedia/story/0,12823,976229 . . . 13 June.

Byrne, C. (2003b) 'Iraq media operation guilty of "lack of context" admits MOD'. Available at http://media.guardian.co.uk/broadcast/story/0,7493,984759,00. html. 25 June.

Byrne, C. (2003c) 'US soldiers were main danger to journalists, says Simpson'. Available at http://media.guardian.co.uk/broadcast/story/0,7493,986599,00. html. 27 June.

Byrne, C. (2003d) 'Iraq – the most dangerous war for journalists'. Available at http://media.guardian.co.uk/iraqandthemedia/story/0,12823,932496,00.html. 9 April.

Byrne, C. (2003e) 'Editors blast Rumsfeld over "reckless" US strike'. Available at http://media.guardian.co.uk/iraqandthemedia/story/0,12823,933242,00.html. 10 April.

Campagna, J. and Roumani, R. (2003) 'Permission to fire', CPJ. Available at http://www.cpj.org/Briefings/2003/palestine_hotel/palestine_hotel.html. 27 May.

Campbell, A. (2003) *Diary*. Available at: www.the-hutton-inquiry.org.uk/ content/cab_39_0001to0002.pdf.

Cappella, J. and Jamieson, K. (1996) 'News frames, political reporting and media cynicism', *Annals of the American Academy of Political and Social Science*, 546, pp. 71–84.

Carruthers, S.L. (2000) *The Media At War*. Basingstoke: Macmillan.

Centre for Strategic Leadership (2003) 'Reporters on the ground: the military and the media's joint experience during Operation Iraqi Freedom'. http://www.au.at.mil/au/awc/awcgate/army-usawc/csl-media-iraq.pdf. October.

Cerre, M. (2003) 'His wake-up call: worst sandstorm of the year'. Available at http://www.tvweek.com. 17 March.

Champagne, P. (1988) 'Le cercle politique. Usages sociaux des sondages et nouvel espace politique', *Actes de la Recherche en Sciences Sociales*, 71/2.

Claiborne, R. (2003) 'Tightlips: embedded journalists learn about restricted access early on'. Available at http://www.abcnews.go.com. 14 March.

Clarke, V. (2001a) 'Seminar on the coverage of the war on terrorism'. Available at http://www.defenselink.mil/news/Nov2001/t11182001_t1108br.html. November.

Clarke, V. (2001b) 'Memo to bureau chiefs'. Available at http://www.defenselink.mil/news/Dec2001/d20011213media.pdf. 6 December.

Clarke, V. (2001c) 'ASD Clarke meeting with DOD National Media Pool bureau chiefs'. Available at http://www.defenselink.mil/news/Dec2001/t12132001_t1213asd. 13 December.

Clarke, V. (2003d) 'Assessing media coverage of the war in Iraq: press reports, Pentagon rules, and lessons for the future', *Brookings Institution*, 17 June.

Clarke, V. (2003e) 'ASD PA Clarke meeting with bureau chiefs'. Available at http://www.defenselink.mil/news/Feb2003/t02282003_t0227bc.html. 27 February.

Cook, J. (2003) 'Military, media, meet on battlefield to debate war coverage'. Available at http://www.cargotribune.com. 8 August.

Cowell, A. (2003) 'Preparing journalists for battle'. Available at http://www.nytimes.com/2003/03/25/business/worldbusiness/25BR . . . 25 March.

CPA (2003) Press Release, 12 October. Available at http://www.cpa-iraq.org. Accessed 14 October 2003.

CPJ (2003a) '27 journalists killed in 2003', Committee to Protect Journalists. Available at http://www.cpj.org/killed/killed03.html#unconfirmed. Accessed 30 October 2003.

CPJ (2003b) 'On assignment: covering conflicts safely', Committee to Protect Journalists. Available at http://www.cpj.org/Briefings/2003/safety/safety.html. Accessed 30 October 2003.

Daley, J. (2003) 'The BBC is playing at power games', *Daily Telegraph*, 2 September. p. 22.

Deans, J. (2003a) 'Al-Jazeera defiant over war dead footage'. Available at http://media.guardian.co.uk/broadcast/story/0,7493,922932,00.html. 27 March.

Deans, J. (2003b) 'Rivera gets army boot out of Iraq'. Available at http://media.guardian.co.uk/broadcast/story/0,7493,926683,00.html. 31 March.

Deans, J. (2003c) 'Sambrook admits "unfortunate" war comments'. Available at http://media.guardian.co.uk/broadcast/story/0,7493,928243,00.html. 2 April.

Deans, J. (2003d) 'BBC under fire after showing footage of dead soldiers'. Available at http://www.media.guardian.co.uk/iraqandthemediastory/0,12823,968713 . . . 2 June.

Deans, J. (2003e) 'Sky News reporter quits over bogus Iraq story'. Available at http://www.media.guardian.co.uk/iraqandthemedia/story/0,12823,100118. 18 July.

DeFoore, J. (2003) 'Photo-news access vs. independence: thoughts on media bootcamp'. Available at http://www.pdonline.com. 26 March.

Deggans, E. (2003) 'Embedded reporters' and insiders' view of conflict'. Available at http://www.sptimes.com/2003/03/21Columns/_Embedded_report . . . March 21.

Dodson, S. (2003) 'Brutal reality hits home', *Guardian G2*, 21 August. p. 21.

Dorman, W. and Livingston, S. (1994) 'News and historical context: the establishing phase of the Persian Gulf policy debate', in W. Bennett and D. Paletz (eds), *Taken by Storm: The Media, Public Opinion and the Gulf War*. Chicago: University of Chicago Press. pp. 63–81.

Downing, J. (1986) 'Government secrecy and the media in the USA and Britain', in P. Golding, G. Murdock and P. Schlesinger (eds), *Communicating Politics: Mass Communications and the Political Process*. Leicester: Leicester University Press. pp. 153–70.

Edwards, R. (2003) 'The propaganda war in Iraq'. Available at http://media.guardian.co.uk/iraqandthemedia/story/0,12823,921767... 26 March.

Engel, M. (1996) *Tickle the Public*. London: Gollancz.

Entman, R. and Page, B. (1994) 'The news before the storm. The Iraq war debate and the limits to media independence', in W. Bennett and D. Paletz (eds), *Taken by Storm: The Media, Public Opinion and the Gulf War*. Chicago: University of Chicago Press. pp. 82–101.

Ethiel, N. (ed.) (1998) 'The military and the media: facing the future', *Cantigny Conference Series*, Robert R. McCormick Foundation, 56.

Eudes, Y. (2003) 'Un jour dans la vie d'un 'embedded'', *Le Monde*, 17 April.

FAIR (2003) 'In Iraq crisis, networks are megaphones for official views', FAIR Study. Available at http://www.fair.org/reports/iraq-sources.html. 18 March.

Fairpress (2003) 'Fighting media bias'. Available at http://www.fairpress.org. 29 September.

Fisk, R. (2003) 'War journalists should not be cosying up to the military'. Available at http://www.zmag.org/content/showarticle.cfm?sectionID=15&Ite . . . 21 January.

Fleischer, A. (2003) 'Press briefing'. Available at http://www.whitehouse.gov/news/releases/2003/03/20030320-3.html. 20 March.

Fletcher, K. (2003) 'CNN's secret news agenda', *Daily Telegraph*, 18 April. p. 27.

Franken, B. (2003) 'Assessing media coverage of the war in Iraq: press reports, Pentagon rules, and lessons for the future', *Brookings Institution*, 17 June.

Franks, T. (2003) 'Transcript: Gen. Tommy Franks on *Fox News Sunday*'. Available at http://www.foxnews.com/printer_friendly_story/0,3566,84055,00.html. 13 April.

Freedland, J. (2003) 'Comment and analysis: the gaping hole in Iraq', *Guardian*, 30 April, p. 23.

Frost, C. (2000) *Media Ethics*. Harlow: Longman.

Getler, M. (2003). 'Close up and vivid reporting'. Available at http://www.washingtonpost.com. 9 April.

Goodman, T. (2003) 'TV isn't telling war's stories still pictures, words in newspapers, magazines all bring in the details'. Available at http://www.sfchronicle.com. 9 April.

Goot, M. and Tiffen, R. (eds) (1992) *Australia's Gulf War*. Carlton: Melbourne University Press.

Gow, J., Paterson, R. and Preston, A. (1996), *Bosnia by Television*. London: British Film Institute.

Gralnick, J. (2003) 'Lessons to survive by'. Available at http://www.tvweek.com. 21 March.

Greenslade, R. (2003a) 'Follow my leader?'. Available at http://media.guardian.co.uk/mediaguardian/story/0,7558,925902,00.html. 31 March.

Greenslade, R. (2003b) 'Fighting talk', *Media Guardian*. Avaliable at http://media.guardian.co.uk/mediaguardian/story/0,7558,987506,0h0.html. 30 June.

Greenslade, R. (2003c) 'So who really hates the BBC?'. Available at http://media.guardian.co.uk/mediaguardian/story/0,7558,1006965,00.html. 28 July.

Greenslade, R. (2003d) 'Off the fence'. Available at http://media.guardian.co.uk/mediaguardian/story/0,7558,1020592,00.html. 18 August.

Gunter, B., Nicholas, D., Russell, C. and Withey, R. (2003) *The Public and Media Coverage of the War on Iraq*. Available at http://www.edigitalResearch.com/edigitalresearch/newswatinIraq.htm.

Hafez, K. (2001) 'Mass media in the Middle East', in K. Hafez (ed.), *Mass Media, Politics and Society in the Middle East*. Cresskill, N.J.: Hampton. pp. 1–20.

Hallin, D.C. (1986) *The Uncensored War: The Media and Vietnam*. Berkeley: University of California Press.

Hallin, D. (1994) *We Keep America On Top Of The World*. London: Routledge

Harmon, A. (2003) 'Improved tools turns journalist into a quick strike force'. Available at http://www.nytimes.com//2003/03/24/business/media/24TECH.html. 24 March.

Harrison, K. (2003) 'War reporting: diary of a journalist with the Army'. Available at http://www.Timesonline.co.uk. 24 March.

Hastings, M. (2003) 'If heads must role at the BBC, Greg Dyke's should be the first'. *Sunday Telegraph*, 7 September. p. 23.

Hedges, C. (2003) 'The press and the myths of war', *The Nation Magazine*. Available at http://www.thirdworldtraveler.com/Chris%20_Hedges/Press_Myths_War.html. April 21.

Hennessy, P. and Walker, D. (1989) 'The Lobby', in J. Seaton and B. Pimlott (eds), *The Media in British Politics*. Aldershot: Dartmouth. pp. 110–29.

Hickey, N. (2002) 'Access denied', *Columbia Journalism Review*. Available at http://www.Cjr.org. January/February.

Hinsliff, G. (2003)' Downing Street in BBC bias row', *Observer*, 30 March.

HMSO (1982) House of Commons First Report from the Defence Committee, Session 1982-83. HMSO, December 1982, Volume 1.

Hodgson, J. (2001) 'Let reporters show emotion'. Available at http://www.media.*guardian*.co.uk/attack/story/0,1301,596093,00.html. 19 November.

Hoon, G. (2003a) 'No lens is wide enough to show the big picture'. Available at http://www.Times_online.co.uk. 28 March.

Hoon, G. (2003b) 'Hearing transcript'. Available at http://www.the-hutton-inquiry.org.uk/content/transcripts/hearing-trans39.htm. 22 September.

Huff, R. (2003) 'War is still a man's world'. Available at http://www.nydailynews.com. 24 March.

Hutton, Lord (2003) 'Investigation into the circumstances surrounding the death of Dr David Kelly'. Available at http://www.the-hutton-inquiry.org.uk.

IFJ (2000) 'International code of practice for the safe conduct of journalism'. IFJ report on media casualties in the field of journalism and newsgathering. Available at http://www.ifj.org.

IFJ (2003a) Press release, 12 February.

IFJ (2003b) 'Justice denied on the road to Baghdad'. Available at http://www.ifj.org. October.

IFJ (2003c) 'Press freedom and safety' Available at http://www.ifj.org/default.asp?Issue=PRESSFREEDOM&Language=EN. Accessed 28 October.

IPI (2003) 'Caught in the crossfire: the Iraq war and the media, a diary of claims and counterclaims'. Available at http://www.freemedia.at/IraqReport2003_p2.htm# IRAQ%20WAR%20AND%20MEDIA%20DIARY. 28 May.

Jenson, E. (2003) 'Veteran reporters go to war'. Available at http://www.latimes. com. 7 April.

Keeble, R. (1997) *Secret State, Silent Press*. London: John Libbey.

Kelley, M. (2003) 'Pentagon ponders embedded reporter policy'. Available at http://www.mercurynews.com/mld/mercurynews/news/special_packages/ iraq/6112625.htm. Posted 18 June.

Kellner, D. (1992) *The Persian Gulf TV War*. Boulder, CO: Westview.

Keniuk, R. (2003) 'Troops fire on students: 13 Iraqis killed in anti-US demo', *Daily Star*, 30 April, p. 2.

Kirkpatrick, D.D. (2003) 'War is test of high speed web'. Available at http://www.nytimes.com. 24 March.

Knightley, P. (2003) 'The battle for our hearts and minds', *Guardian*, 2 April, p. 22.

Konrad, R. (2003) 'New technology gives birth to 'backpack journalist''. Associated Press. Available at http://www.usatoday.com/tech/world/iraq/ 2003-03-25-backpack-journalists_x.htm. 25 March.

Koopman, J. (2003) 'Media learn to cover more than the story'. Available at http:// www.sfgate.com/cgi-bin/article.cgi?file=/chronicle/archive/2 . . . 10 February.

Kurtz, H. (2003a) 'Media's battlefield reporting outpaces Pentagon officials'. Available at http://www.washingtonpost.com. 24 March.

Kurtz, H. (2003b) 'Too painful to publish?'. Available at http:// washingtonpost.com. 25 March.

Lamloum, O. (2003) 'Une guerre annoncée par al-Jazira', in M. Lits (ed.), *Irak – Etats-Unis, Médiatiques*, 32: 18–20.

Lang, K. and Lang, G. (1994) 'Media coverage of Saddam's Iraq', in W. Bennett and D. Paletz (eds), *Taken by Storm: The Media, Public Opinion and the Gulf War*. Chicago: University of Chicago Press. pp. 43–62.

Lemieux, C. (2000) *Mauvaise Presse*. Paris: Editions Métailié.

Leonard, T. and Born, M. (2003) 'Should I go or should I stay now?', *Daily Telegraph*, 21 March. p. 21.

Lewis, J. (2003a) 'Biased broadcasting corporation. A survey of the main broadcasters' coverage of the invasion of Iraq shows the claim that the BBC was anti-war is the opposite of the truth', *Guardian*, 4 July, p. 27.

Lewis, J. (2003b) 'Changing their minds', *Guardian*, 30 September.

Like, M.L. (2003) 'Aboard the USS Abraham Lincoln'. Available at http:// www.seattlepi.com. 21 March.

Lits, M. (ed.) (2003a) *Irak – Etats-Unis, Médiatiques*, 32 (Summer).

Lits, M. (2003b) 'Une guerre de journalistes', *Médiatiques*, 32 (Summer), 38–42.

Littlejohn, R. (2003) 'Good evening ... here is the worst possible news'. Available at http://www.thesun.co.uk. Accessed 25 October 2003.

Lobe, J. (2003) 'The hazards of watching Fox News'. Available at http:// www.alternet.org/story/html?StoryID=16892.

Mangan, L. (2003) 'Them and us: the singular language of the embeds', *Media Guardian*, 7 April. p. 5.

Massing, M. (2003) 'The unseen war', *The New York Review*, 29 May, pp. 16–18.

Mazzetti, M. (2002) 'Dispatches From Media Boot Camp'. Available at http://slate.msn.com/id/2070993/entry/207412. 18 November.

McClintock, P. (2003) ''Embedded' journalists draw fire'. Available at http:// www.xtramsn.co.nz/entertainment/0,,3911-2224949,00.html. 20 March.

McCreary, T. (2003) 'ASD PA Clarke meeting with bureau chiefs'. Available at http://www.defenselink.mil/news/Feb2003/t02282003_t0227bc.html. 27 February.

McGregor, R. (2003) 'Of all things – the preacher, Brigadier-General Vincent Brooks', *Financial Times Magazine*, 26 April.

McLaughlin, G. (2002) *The War Correspondent*. London: Pluto.

Meade, J.T. (2003) 'Media exile in Qatar'. Available at http://www.sky.com. 25 March.

*Media Guardian* (2003) 'Rageh to riches'. Available at http://media.guardian.co.uk/iraqandthemedia/story/0,12823,695142,00.html. 28 May.

Media Tenor (2003) Media Tenor *Quarterly Journal*, 2. Available via http://www.innovatio.de.

Mermin, J. (1996) 'Conflict in the sphere of consensus? Critical reporting on the Panama Invasion and the Gulf War', *Political Communication*, 13 (2): 181–94.

Miller, D. (2003) 'Taking sides. The anti-war movement accuses the BBC of having had a pro-war bias; the government says it was too Baghdad-friendly. So who is right?', *Guardian*, 22 April.

Mitchell, G. (2003a) 'America's journalists debate pending war'. Available at http://www.editorandpublisher.com. 29 January.

Mitchell, G. (2003b) 'Unembedded reporters face grave dangers'. Available at http://www.editorandpublisher.com. 26 March.

Mitchell, G. (2003c) 'Fifteen stories they've already bungled'. Available at http://www.editorandpublisher.com. 27 March.

Morgan, J. (2001) 'Rivals backlash against "foolhardy" Ridley', *Press Gazette*. Available at http://www.pressgazette.co.uk. 11 October.

Morrison, D. and Tumber, H. (1985) 'The foreign correspondent: dateline London', *Media, Culture and Society*, 7: 445–70.

Morrison, D.E. and Tumber, H. (1988) *Journalists at War*. London: Sage.

Mowlana, H., Gerbner, G. and Schuller, H.I. (eds) (1992) *Triumph of the Image*. Boulder, CO: Westview.

Murphy, D. (1991) *The Stalker Affair*. London: Constable.

Naim, M. (2003) 'Sabotages et attaques antiaméricaines maImènent les éspoirs de reconstruction en Irak', *Le Monde*, 19 August, p. 4.

Nasser, S. (2003) 'Al-Hayat'. Available at http://english.daralhayat.com/opinion/08-2003/Article.20030802.c2d7526.c0a8.0/ed.c054d9efa1e3/story.html. Accessed 2 August.

News Safety Institute (2003) *'Dying to Tell the Story'*. Belgium News Safety Institute.

Norton-Taylor, R. (2003) 'Tony Blair must be held to account. We now know that he was not honest about the outing of Kelly', *Guardian*, 17 October.

O'Farrell, J. (2003) 'Subplots abound'. Available at http://www.media.guardian.co.uk/iraqandthemedia/story/0,12823,100062. 18 July.

O'Heffernan, P. (1994) 'A mutual exploitation model of media influence in US foreign policy', in W. Bennett and D. Paletz (eds), *Taken by Storm: The Media, Public Opinion and the Gulf War*. Chicago: University of Chicago Press. pp. 231–49.

Online Newshour (2003) 'Perspectives'. Available at http://www.pbs.org/newshour/bb/military/jan-june03/perspective_3 . . . 22 March.

Outing, S. (2003) 'War: a defining moment for net news'. Available at http://www.editorandpublisher.com/editorandpubl . . ./article_display.jsp?vnu_content_content_id=184857. 9 April.

Owen, J. (2001) 'Training journalists to report safely in hostile environments', *Nieman*

*Reports,* 55 (4): 25–7, Winter. The Nieman Foundation for Journalism At Harvard University.

Page, C. (2003) "Embedded' … but not "in bed with"'. Available at http://www.washingtontimes.com/commentary/20030311-4538396.htm. 11 March.

Paine, K.D. (2003) 'Army intelligence: army public affairs gets it right this time'. http://www.themeasurementstandard.com/issues/303/eng/painemilitary303.asp. 28 March.

Palmer, J. (2000) *Spinning into Control: News values and Source Strategies.* London: Continuum Books/Leicester University Press.

PEJ (Project for Excellence in Journalism) (2003) 'Embedded reporters: what are Americans getting?' Available at http://www.journalism.org/resources/research/reports/war/postwar/lynch.asp.

Perdum, T.S. and Rutenberg, J. (2003) 'Reporters respond eagerly to Pentagon welcome mat'. Available at http://www.nytimes.com. 25 March.

Phares, W. (2003) 'Jeehad TV'. Available at http://www.nationalreview.com. 26 March.

Pietropaoli, S. (2003) 'ASD PA Clarke meeting with bureau chiefs'. Available at http://www.defenselink.mil/news/Feb2003/t02282003_t0227bc.html. 27 February.

Plunkett, J. (2003) 'CNN star reporter attacks war coverage', *Guardian,* 16 September.

Poniewozik, J. (2003) 'Real battles in real time'. Available at http://www.time.com. 31 March.

Porch, D. (2002) 'No bad stories'. Available at http://www.Nwc.navt.mil/press/review/2002/winter/art5-w02.

Quenqua, D. (2003) 'White House prepares to feed 24-hour news cycle'. Available at http://www.prweek.com/news/news_story.cfm?ID=174751&site=3. 24 March.

Reuters (2003) 'Pentagon keeps return of Iraqi war dead from media'. Available at http://www.digitalmass.com/news/wire_story.html?uri=/~. 29 March.

Rutenberg, J. (2003) 'Reporting war under eyes of Iraqi "minders"'. Available at http://www.nytimes.com. 4 April.

Sabato, L. (1993) *Feeding Frenzy: How Attack Journalism has Transformed American Politics* (2nd edn). New York, NY: Free Press/MacMillan.

Sadkovitch, J.J. (1998) *The US Media and Yugoslavia, 1991–1995.* Westport, VA: Praeger.

Sancho, J. (2003) *Conflict Around the Clock.* London: Independent Television Commission.

Schlesinger, P. and Tumber, H. (1994) *Reporting Crime.* Oxford: Clarendon.

Schlesinger, R. (2003) 'Pressed into service'. Available at http://www.boston.com/globe/magazine/2003/0126/war_entire.htm. 26 January.

Schudson, M. (1978) *Discovering the News: A Social History of American Newspapers.* New York, NY: Basic Books.

Seib, P.M. (2002) *The Global Journalist: News and Consciousness in a World of Conflict.* Lanham, MD and Oxford: Rowman and Littlefield.

Shafer, J. (2003a) 'Sacking Arnett for the wrong reason'. Available at http://slate.msn.com/id/2080947/. 31 March.

Shafer, J. (2003b) 'Embeds and unilaterals'. Available at http://slate.msn.com/id/2082412/. 1 May.

Shaw, D. (2003) 'Embedded reporters make for good journalism'. Available at http://www.calendarlive.com. 6 April.

Sidle Report (1984) News Release No. 450/84, Office of the Assistant Secretary of Defence (Public Affairs), 23 August.

Sievers, L. (2002) Nightline: dangerous business. Online posting. Available email: nightline mailing list (l@alist0.starwave.com), accessed 12 March 2002.

Sigal, L. (1973) *Reporters and Officials*. Lexington, MA: D.C. Heath.

Smith, T. (2003) 'Assessing media coverage of the war in Iraq: press reports, Pentagon rules, and lessons for the future', *Brookings Institution*, 17 June.

Smolkin, R. (2003) 'Media mood swings', *American Journalism Review*. Available at http://www.ajr.org/Article.asp?id=3040. June.

Steinreich, D. (2003) 'Fibbing it up at Fox'. Available at http://www.lewrockwell.com/orig/steinreich8.html. 22 May.

Stewart, I. and Carruthers, S.L. (1996) *War, Culture and the Media*. Trowbridge: Flicks Books.

Strupp, J. (2003a). 'Christian Science Monitor reporter kicked out of unit'. Available at http://www.editorandpublisher.com. 27 March.

Strupp, J. (2003b) 'How papers are covering Iraqi civilian casualties'. Available at http://www.editorandpublisher.com. 8 April.

Swanson, D.J. (2003) 'Critics question embedding of journalists in Iraq war'. Available at http://www.montereyherald.com/mld/montereyherald/news/politics . . . 26 March.

Sylvester, R. (2003) 'The UK media has lost the plot ... it's the equivalent of reality TV', *Daily Telegraph*, 7 April. p. 8.

Synovitz, R. (2003) 'Iraq: Pentagon starts embedding reporters with troops in an effort to tell 'army story''. Available at http://www.rferl.org/nca/features/2003/03/11032003184830.asp. 26 March.

Taylor, P.M. (1992) *War and the Media*. Manchester: Manchester University Press.

Taylor, P.M. (1997) *Global Communication, International Affairs and the Media Since 1994*. London: Routledge.

Taylor, P.M. (1999) *British Propaganda in the Twentieth Century: Settling Democracy*. Edinburgh: Edinburgh University Press.

Taylor, P.M. (2003) '"We know where you are": Psychological operations media during Enduring Freedom', in D. K. Thussu and D. Friedman (eds), *War and the Media*. London: Sage.

Thompson, M. (2003) *Media Guardian*, 29 September. p. 3.

Thorpe, V. (2003) 'BBC stands by its man on eve of judgment day', *Observer*, 6 July.

Thrall, A.T. (2000) *War in the Media Age*. Cresskill: Hampton.

Timms, D. (2003a) 'News websites see traffic soar'. Available at http://www.media.guardian.co.uk. 20 March.

Timms, D. (2003b) 'Dyke attacks "unquestioning" US media', *Guardian*, 24 April.

Transnational Broadcasting Studies (2003) *Media on Media*, no. 10. Available at http://www.tbsjournal.com.

Tuchman, G. (1972) 'Objectivity as a strategic ritual: an examination of newsmen's notions of objectivity', *American Journal of Sociology*, 77: 660–79.

Tumber, H. (2002a) 'Reporting under fire' in B. Zelizer and S. Allan (eds), *Journalism After September 11*. London and New York: Routledge.

Tumber, H. (2002b) 'Sources, the media and the reporting of conflict', in E. Gilboa (ed.), *The Media and International Conflict*. Ardsley: Transnational. pp. 135–52.

Tumber, H. and Prentoulis, M. (2003) 'Journalists under fire: subcultures, objectivity and emotional literacy', in D.K. Thussu and D. Friedman (eds), *War and the Media*. London: Sage.

US Department of Defense (2003) 'Public affairs guidance on embedding media during possible future operations'. Available at http://www.defenselink.mil/news/Feb2003/d20030228pag.pdf. February.

Valo, M. (2003) 'Les dérapages médiatiques de la première guerre du Golfe', *Le Monde*, 26 March.

Waisbord, S. (2002) 'Journalism, risk and patriotism', in B. Zelizer and S. Allan (eds), *Journalism after September 11*. London: Routledge. pp. 201–14.

Walcott, J. (2003) 'Assessing media coverage of the war in Iraq: press reports, Pentagon rules, and lessons for the future', *Brookings Institution*, 17 June.

Wells, M. (2003a) 'Sky suspends journalist over bogus story'. Available at http://www.media.*guardian*.co.uk/iraqandthemedia/story/0,12823,999744. 17 July.

Wells, M. (2003b) 'Pie in the Sky?', *Media Guardian*, 25 August. p. 2.

Wells, M. (2003c) 'TV watchdog checks claims of bias on Murdoch channel', *Guardian*, 8 May.

Wells, M. and Campbell, D. (2003) 'CNN defies Pentagon pictures plea'. Available at http://www.media.*guardian*.co.uk. 25 March.

Wells, M. and O'Carroll, L. (2003) 'Sky head of news ordered back to investigate fake war story'. Available at http://www.media.*guardian*.co.uk/iraqandthemedia/story/0,12823,100058. 18 July.

White, M. and Hall, S. (2003) 'BBC under fire over chaos reports'. Available at http://media.*guardian*/broadcast/story/0,7493,935297,00.html. 12 April.

Whitman, B. (2003a) 'Department of Defence media support plan'. Available at http://www.fpc.state.gov/17209.htm. 30 January.

Whitman, B. (2003b) 'ASD PA Clarke meeting with bureau chiefs'. Available at http://www.defenselink.mil/new/Feb2003/t02282003_t0227bc.html. 27 February.

Will, G. (2003) 'The arrogance of liberals'. Available at http://www.townhall.com/columnists/georgewill/gw20030123.shtml. 23 January.

Williams, M.H. (2003) 'Analysis: MoD is ready for Iraq war of words'. Available at http://www.prweek.com. 21 March.

Willis, J. (1991) *The Shadow World. Life Between the News Media and Reality*. New York: Praeger.

Wolff, M. (2003a) 'Live from Doha'. Available at http://www.newyorkmetro.com/nymetro/news/media/columns/medialife/n_8545/. 11 April.

Willis, J. (1991) *The Shadow World. Life Between the News Media and Reality*. New York: Praeger.

Wolff, M. (2003b) 'I was only asking'. Available at http://media.*guardian*.co.uk/media*guardian*/story/0,7558,036087,00... 14 April.

Yago, G. (2003) 'War reporter boot camp'. Available at http://www.mtv.com/news/articles/1469817/02062003/id_0.jhtml. 7 February.

York, G. (2003) 'Destination Baghdad'. Available at http://www.workpolis.com/servLet/Content/qprinter/20030322/... 22 March, accessed 26 March.

Younge, G. (2003) 'Don't mention the dead', *Guardian* G2, 7 November. p. 2–3.

Young, P. and Jesser, P. (1997) *The Media and the Military*. Basingstoke: Macmillan.

# INDEX